westermann

W0387992

FiNALE Prüfungstraining

Nordrhein-Westfalen

Zentralabitur 2022

Englisch

Thomas Lehnen
Miriam Schulz
Claudia Schwarz-Brownbill

FiNALEonline.de

Liebe Abiturientin, lieber Abiturient,

sobald die Original-Prüfungsaufgaben zur Veröffentlichung freigegeben sind, können sie unter www.finaleonline.de zusammen mit ausführlichen Lösungen kostenlos heruntergeladen werden.
Gib dazu einfach diesen Code ein:

EN9P7T7

Einfach mal reinschauen: www.finaleonline.de

westermann GRUPPE

Bildnachweis:
|Peter Wirtz Fotografie, Dormagen: Titel, 2.1. |Singer, Andy, Saint Paul, MN: 134.1.

Druck 1 / Jahr 2021

Redaktion: lüra – Klemt & Mues GbR
Kontakt: finale@westermanngruppe.de
Layout: Druckreif! Sandra Grünberg, Braunschweig
Umschlaggestaltung: Gingco.Net, Braunschweig
Umschlagfoto: Peter Wirtz, Dormagen
Druck und Bindung: westermann druck GmbH, Braunschweig

ISBN 978-3-7426-**2217**-4

FiNALEonline.de

FiNALEonline ist die digitale Ergänzung zu deinem Abiturband. Hier findest du eine Vielzahl an Angeboten, die dich bei deiner Prüfungsvorbereitung zusätzlich unterstützen.

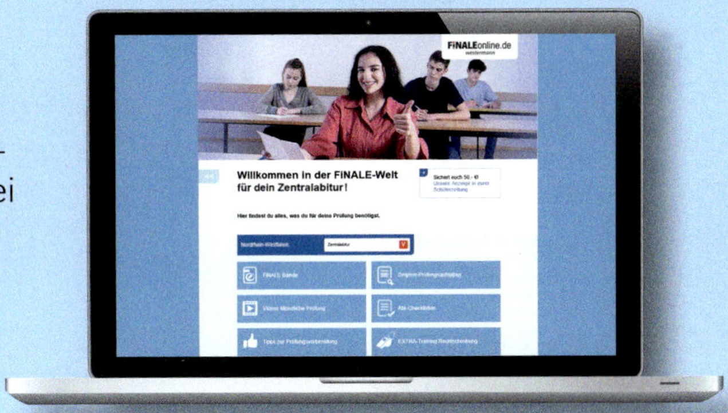

Das Plus für deine Vorbereitung:

- Original-Prüfungsaufgaben mit Lösungen (bitte Code von Seite 2 eingeben!)
- EXTRA-Training Rechtschreibung
  So kannst du einem möglichen Punktabzug bei deinen Abi-Klausuren vorbeugen.
- Videos zur mündlichen Prüfung
- Tipps zur stressfreien Prüfungsvorbereitung
- Abi-Checklisten mit allen prüfungsrelevanten Themen

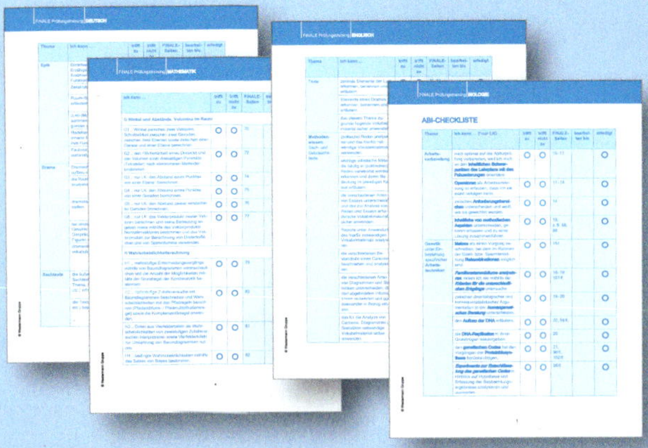

Abi-Checklisten

Sie helfen dir, den Überblick über den Prüfungsstoff zu behalten.

FiNALEonline.de

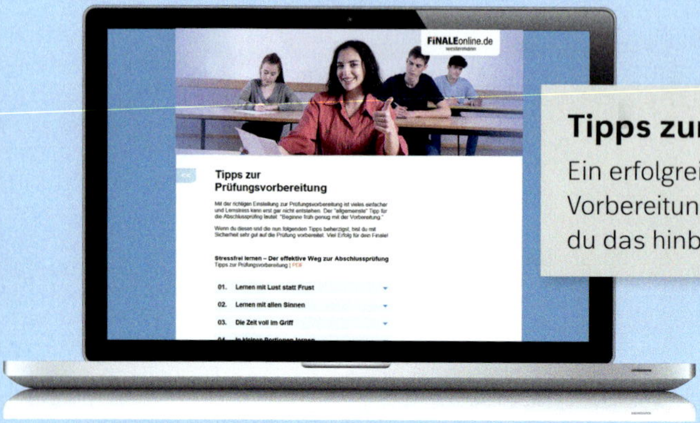

Tipps zur Prüfungsvorbereitung

Ein erfolgreiches Abitur erfordert eine gezielte Vorbereitung ohne unnötigen Lernstress. Wie du das hinbekommst, erfährst du hier!

Videos zur mündlichen Prüfung

Nur wenige Abiturienten wissen genau, wie sie abläuft, die „Mündliche". Die Videos geben dir Einblick in den Ablauf der Prüfung und Tipps für die richtige Vorbereitung.

Die Kombination aus FiNALE-Buch und FiNALEonline bietet dir die optimale Vorbereitung für deine Prüfung und begleitet dich sicher zu einem erfolgreichen Abitur 2022!

www.finaleonline.de

Inhaltsverzeichnis

Newspaper Article/Internet Article

Literarische Texte

Beispiele für Prüfungsaufgaben zu den Fokusthemen

Aufgaben mit Bearbeitungsschritten und Beispiellösungen

Aufgaben mit Bewertungskriterien

Original-Prüfungsaufgaben 2020 und 2021

Die sprachliche Leistung im Abitur

Arbeiten mit *Finale*

Finale Prüfungstraining Englisch möchte Ihnen eine praxisnahe Hilfe zur Vorbereitung auf die Abiturprüfung sein. Im Praxis-Teil finden sich zu allen geforderten Themenbereichen authentische Aufgaben, die dem aktuell geltenden neuen Format entsprechen. Daneben finden Sie die Original-Prüfungsaufgaben 2020. Unter unseren Beispielaufgaben sind sowohl Beispiele für Grundkurse als auch für Leistungskurse. Im Abitur unterscheidet sich die Aufgabe für Leistungskurse von denen für Grundkurse einerseits durch den Textumfang, andererseits durch den Schwierigkeitsgrad der Texte, der sich in der Regel aus der Komplexität der Syntax und des Wortschatzes ergibt. Beide Kriterien spielen für Übungstexte keine große Rolle. Auch als Grundkursschülerin oder -schüler sind Sie durch den Englischunterricht mit längeren und komplexeren Texten vertraut. Als Leistungskursschülerin oder -schüler können Sie eine Textanalyse auch an kürzeren, einfacheren Texten üben. Die inhaltlichen Vorgaben sind für beide Kursarten weitgehend gleich.

Je eine Aufgabe zu einem literarischen Text und einem Sach- und Gebrauchstext ergänzt um eine Sprachmittlungs-Aufgabe zu einem deutschen Text wird kleinschrittig erarbeitet und schließt mit einer Musterlösung. Dies soll für Sie eine exemplarische Hilfe sein auf dem Weg von den Ausgangstexten über das Textverständnis, die Methodik der Textanalyse, die Evaluation und die Sprachmittlung hin zur Gliederung und sprachlichen Darstellung der Zieltexte. Den weiteren Aufgabenbeispielen folgen Bewertungskriterien ganz in der Form, wie Ihre Lehrerinnen und Lehrer sie zur Korrektur der Abiturarbeiten an die Hand bekommen. Sie dienen Ihnen zur Selbstkontrolle in Ihrem fortschreitenden Prüfungstraining. Zu Ihrer Orientierung haben wir auch entsprechende Punkte vergeben. „Gummipunkte", Punkte für ein „weiteres aufgabenbezogenes Kriterium", wie es sie im Abitur gibt, erschienen uns für die Beispielaufgaben jedoch wenig sinnvoll.

Geschrieben wurde dieses Buch im Jahr 2021, damit es frühzeitig zur Vorbereitung auf das Abitur 2022 beitragen kann. Die zu diesem Zeitpunkt aktuellen Abituraufgaben 2020 werden jeweils mit einer Musterlösung angeboten. Original-Schülerlösungen unterliegen weiterhin der Geheimhaltung und können nicht veröffentlicht werden. Dennoch versuchen wir, unsere Musterlösung auf der Grundlage unserer Korrekturarbeit der Abiturarbeiten 2020 zu erstellen. Sie greifen die tatsächlich gegebenen Probleme und Fehlerschwerpunkte der Abiturientinnen und Abiturienten auf.

Der eindringliche Wunsch unserer Abiturienten nach einer kompakten inhaltlichen Übersicht über die verbindlich vorgegebenen Themen des Zentralabiturs hat uns bewogen, diese relevanten Inhalte im Kapitel „Basiswissen" zusammenzustellen. Natürlich kann dieses weder den Englischunterricht der Qualifikationsphase noch dessen Vor- und Nachbereitung ersetzen. Es hilft Ihnen jedoch, das im Unterricht erworbene Wissen zu strukturieren und in seinen Grundzügen abzurufen. Um den Umgang mit dem thematischen Vokabular zu vertiefen, ist dieser Teil in englischer

Sprache geschrieben und wird durch Glossare zum thematischen Vokabular ergänzt. Bei den amerikanischen Texten wird auch in den Erläuterungen dazu amerikanisches Englisch verwendet, ansonsten wird die britische Schreibweise benutzt.

Die sprachliche Leistung spielt in der Fremdsprache trotz aller inhaltlich-thematischer Kompetenz immer noch die herausragende Rolle. Während man in der Abiturklausur für den Inhalt maximal 60 Punkte erreichen kann, erhält man für eine perfekte sprachliche Leistung 90 Punkte. Ein sicherer Umgang mit den Strukturen und Wörtern der englischen Sprache ist also unabdingbar. Deshalb haben wir in *Finale* ein Kapitel zur sprachlichen Leistung aufgenommen, in dem es vor allem um kommunikative Textgestaltung und Ausdrucksvermögen geht, die im Zentralabitur – wie die sprachliche Richtigkeit – mit jeweils 30 Punkten bewertet werden.

Wir wünschen Ihnen viel Erfolg!

Informationen und Tipps zur Prüfung

Inhalte des Faches Englisch in der gymnasialen Oberstufe

Gelegentlich beklagen sich Schülerinnen und Schüler und auch Eltern über die Anforderungen und Inhalte des Englischunterrichts, insbesondere der Klausuren und der schriftlichen Abiturprüfung. Textanalyse und kreative Textproduktion erscheinen ihnen nicht als Fertigkeiten, die man im Leben braucht. Auf Unverständnis trifft gelegentlich auch die Bewertung – hat man doch gerade mit einem Australier gechattet, der sich anerkennend zu den Englischkenntnissen äußerte, oder im Urlaub einen Engländer getroffen, mit dem man sich prima bei einer Cola unterhalten konnte. Die Fähigkeit, sich mit anderen unterhalten zu können, ist also offensichtlich nicht der alleinige Aspekt, der in der Oberstufe und im Abitur bewertet wird.
Natürlich ist es primäres Ziel des Englischunterrichts, **kommunikative Kompetenz** zu vermitteln, also Schülerinnen und Schüler in die Lage zu versetzen, im englischsprachigen Ausland oder auch mit dem Englischen als *lingua franca* angemessen zu kommunizieren. Sieht man sich den Kernlehrplan für die Sekundarstufe I an, so wird man schnell erkennen, dass selbst die geforderten Kompetenzen für das Ende der Sekundarstufe I weit über die Kommunikation in Alltagssituationen hinausgehen. Zur Vorbereitung der Schülerinnen und Schüler auf ein Studium an der Hochschule, auf einen beruflichen Weg in Großunternehmen oder international tätigen mittelständischen Unternehmen orientiert sich der Kernlehrplan Englisch am Leitziel der interkulturellen Handlungsfähigkeit. Deshalb behandelt der Englischunterricht soziokulturell und global bedeutsame Themen, die in Texten und Medien dargestellt werden.

In diesem Zusammenhang spricht der Kernlehrplan von verschiedenen **Kompetenzbereichen:**
- funktionale kommunikative Kompetenz
- interkulturelle kommunikative Kompetenz
- Text- und Medienkompetenz
- Sprachlernkompetenz
- Sprachbewusstheit

Funktional kommunikative Kompetenzen sind Leseverstehen, Schreiben, Hör-/Hörsehverstehen, Sprechen und Sprachmittlung. Außerdem zählt man die Verfügbarkeit sprachlicher Mittel dazu, d. h. Wortschatz, Grammatik, Rechtschreibung und Aussprache.
Interkulturelle kommunikative Kompetenz ist das Zusammenspiel von Wissen, Einstellung und Bewusstheit. Vor dem Hintergrund ihrer eigenen Kultur sollen Schülerinnen und Schüler in der Lage sein, sowohl Empathie als auch kritische Distanz gegenüber kulturellen Besonderheiten zu entwickeln.
Für den Erwerb von **Text- und Medienkompetenz** vermittelt der Englischunterricht eine Fülle von Teilkompetenzen. Der Begriff Text umfasst hier – wie immer –

Sachtexte sowie literarische Texte, Filme, Bilder, Diagramme, Statistiken, Grafiken etc. Das Kapitel „Methoden der Textarbeit" wird sich eingehend damit befassen.

Für den **Umgang mit Texten** in der Q1 und der Q2 gibt der Kernlehrplan folgendes vor:

Sach- und Gebrauchstexte

Texte der privaten und öffentlichen Kommunikation
- Brief, Kommentar, Leitartikel, politische Rede, Leserbrief, Werbeanzeige

Texte in wissenschaftsorientierter Dimension
- Lexikonauszüge, ein längerer Sachbuchauszug

Texte in berufsorientierter Dimension
- Stellenanzeigen, PR-Materialien, Exposé, Protokoll

literarische Texte

lyrische Texte
- zeitgenössische Gedichte, Gedichte in historischer Dimension

narrative Texte
- ein zeitgenössischer Roman, *short stories*

dramatische Texte
- Auszüge aus einem oder aus verschiedenen Shakespeare-Dramen, ein zeitgenössisches Drama, Auszüge aus einem Drehbuch

diskontinuierlicher Texte

Text-Bild-Kombinationen
- Bilder, Cartoons

Grafiken
- Tabellen, Karten, Diagramme

medial vermittelte Texte

auditive Formate
- *radio features/podcasts,* Auszüge aus einem Hörbuch

audiovisuelle Formate
- ein Spielfilm, *documentary/feature, news*

digitale Texte
- *blogs/video blogs,* Beiträge in Internetforen

Sprachlernkompetenz beinhaltet das selbstständige Gestalten des Lernens durch das Entwickeln von Strategien aber auch durch den sicheren Umgang mit Hilfsmitteln, z. B. mit dem Wörterbuch.

Sprachbewusstheit beinhaltet Einsichten zum Beispiel in Varianten des Sprachgebrauchs, in verschiedene Register und Stilebenen, in Beziehungen zwischen Sprache und Kultur, aber auch die Bewusstheit von sprachlicher Manipulation.

Obligatorische Themen und Inhalte für das Zentralabitur

Das Ministerium gibt auf der Grundlage der Kernlehrpläne Vorgaben für eine Schwerpunktsetzung im Hinblick auf das Zentralabitur. Konkret gelten für das Abitur 2022 die folgenden Fokussierungen zu der im Kernlehrplan festgelegten Obligatorik. (Die vollständige Übersicht ist zu finden auf der Website des Ministeriums: https://www.standardsicherung.schulministerium.nrw.de/cms/zentralabitur-gost/faecher/getfile.php?file=4989)

Inhaltliche Schwerpunkte

Amerikanischer Traum – Visionen und Lebenswirklichkeiten in den USA

- America myths and realities:
  - freedom and success (Grundkurs)
  - freedom and equality (Leistungskurs)

Das Vereinigte Königreich im 21. Jahrhundert – Selbstverständnis zwischen Tradition und Moderne

- Tradition and change in politics and society
  - multicultural society
  - monarchy and modern democracy (Leistungskurs)

Postkolonialismus – Lebenswirklichkeiten in einem weiteren anglophonen Kulturraum

- Voices from the African Continent: Focus on Nigeria

Chancen und Risiken der Globalsierung

- Studying and working in a globalized world
- Voices from the African Continent: Focus on Nigeria
- The impact of globalization on culture and communication (Grundkurs)

Literatur und Medien in ihrer Bedeutung für den Einzelnen und die Gesellschaft

- The impact of Shakespearean drama on young audiences today:
  - study of extracts and film scenes (tragedy or comedy) (Leistungskurs)
  - Study of film scenes (Grundkurs)
- Visions of the future
  - utopia and dystopia
  - ethical issues of scientific and technological progress

Fortschritt und Ethik in der modernen Gesellschaft (Leistungskurs)

- Visions of the future
  - ethical issues of scientific and technological progress
  - utopia and dystopia

Lebensentwürfe, Studium, Ausbildung, Beruf international – Englisch als *lingua franca*
- Studying and working in a globalized world

Zieltextformate

In der dritten Teilaufgabe des Klausurteils A haben die Schülerinnen und Schüler die Wahl zwischen einer Stellungnahme und einer kreativen Aufgabe. Dazu wird Vertrautheit mit folgenden Textformaten vorausgesetzt:
- letter/email (formal letter, letter to the editor, personal letter)
- speech script (talk, public/formal speech, debate statement)
- newspaper article/internet article (report, comment)
- *im Leistungskurs zusätzlich:* (written) interview
- Ausgestaltung, Fortführung oder Ergänzung eines literarischen Ausgangstextes (narrative Texte, zusätzlich im Leistungskurs: dramatische Texte, film scripts)

Die Fachkonferenzen jeder einzelnen Schule gestalten ihre Unterrichtssequenzen auf der Grundlage der geforderten Inhalte und der vom Lehrplan geforderten Obligatorik.

Grundsätze der Abiturprüfung

Aufgabenarten

Aus der Oberstufe sind Ihnen verschiedene Klausurvarianten bekannt. Von den fünf Kompetenzen Leseverstehen, Schreiben, Sprechen, Hör-/Hörsehverstehen und Sprachmittlung werden immer drei geprüft. So kennen Sie etwa die Textanalyse mit zusätzlicher Sprachmittlungsaufgabe oder die Filmanalyse mit zusätzlichem Multiple-Choice-Test zum Leseverstehen oder gar drei verschiedene Einzelaufgaben zu Leseverstehen, Schreiben und Sprachmittlung.

Für das Abitur 2022 ist vom Ministerium nur eine Aufgabenart vorgesehen, nämlich Schreiben und Leseverstehen in Klausurteil A, Sprachmittlung in Klausurteil B. Sie haben die Wahl zwischen zwei Aufgaben, die Ihnen im Klausurteil A entweder einen literarischen Text oder einen Sach- und Gebrauchstext vorlegen. Der Text kann in beiden Fällen durch eine Grafik, einen Cartoon o. Ä. ergänzt werden. Klausurteil B ist in beiden Fällen ein deutschsprachiger Sachtext.

Die Aufgabe des **Klausurteils A** besteht aus einem Text mit den Ihnen bekannten drei Teilaufgaben *(comprehension – analysis – evaluation/re-creation of text)*. In der dritten Teilaufgabe *(evaluation/re-creation of text)* wird Ihnen eine Wahlmöglichkeit zwischen einer kreativen Aufgabe und einer Stellungnahme gegeben. Die Übungsklausuren im Kapitel „Beispiele für Prüfungsaufgaben“ bieten beide Aufgabentypen, meist geben sie eine Wahlmöglichkeit.

Die Sprachmittlung, **Klausurteil B,** kann auch die erste Teilaufgabe der Klausur sein. Dann kann sich die Stellungnahme in Klausurteil A zusätzlich auf die deutsche Textvorlage beziehen.

Der englische Text hat im Leistungskurs einen Umfang von maximal 1000 Wörtern, im Grundkurs maximal 800 Wörtern. Der deutsche Text umfasst in beiden Kursarten zwischen 450 und 600 Wörter. Als Ausgangstexte eignen sich nur authentische Texte, d. h. sie dürfen nicht adaptiert oder stark gekürzt sein.

TIPP

Die Bearbeitungszeit und auch die Texte sind in der Q2 und im Abitur deutlich länger als in der Q1 und der EF und auch länger als in den Jahrgängen zuvor. Dies bedeutet nicht, dass Sie mehr schreiben sollen. Das Ministerium schreibt auf seiner Website:
„Der zentrale Leitgedanke der Umsetzung in Nordrhein-Westfalen besteht darin, dass die zusätzliche Bearbeitungszeit in den Abiturklausuren nicht in erster Linie eine Erhöhung der quantitativen Anforderungen nach sich zieht, sondern primär eine vertiefte Auseinandersetzung der Schülerinnen und Schüler mit dem Thema bzw. Gegenstand der Prüfung ermöglicht.“[1]
Tun Sie also, was die Aufgabenstellung von Ihnen verlangt, nicht mehr! Halten Sie sich nicht mit der Textkomposition auf, wenn keiner Sie danach fragt! Paraphrasieren oder zitieren Sie nicht komplette Textpassagen! Das wäre eine rein inhaltliche Widergabe. Zitieren Sie keinen Satz, wenn es um ein Wort geht! Vergessen Sie Ihre Deutschklausuren! Deutsch ist anders!

1 https://www.standardsicherung.schulministerium.nrw.de/cms/zentralabitur-gost/uebersicht/dauer-2021.php

Anforderungsbereiche

Die Teilaufgaben der Prüfungsklausuren entsprechen den folgenden Anforderungsbereichen, die Sie bereits aus der Qualifikationsphase kennen.

Anforderungsbereich I: *comprehension/orientation/context*
- Wiedergabe der zentralen Aussagen eines Textes (meist Inhaltsangabe),
- Einordnung des Textes in einen Kontext unter Verwendung von Hintergrundwissen,
- Einleitung eines komplexen Textes.

Anforderungsbereich II: *analysis*
- Anwendung von Fachmethoden: textanalytische Verfahren, Einsatz von Lesetechniken,
- gezielte Anwendung von Kenntnissen und Wissen – z. B. soziokulturelles oder metasprachliches Wissen (= Wissen über Sprache),
- exakte Arbeit am sprachlichen Detail, Belegen und Zitieren, problemlösende Argumentation.

Anforderungsbereich III: *evaluation*
für die analytisch-interpretierende Aufgabenstellung:
- Bewertung der Problemlösung, Einordnen der Ergebnisse in einen größeren Zusammenhang,
- persönliche Stellungnahme, eigene Meinung (erst hier und nicht etwa in AFB II oder I).

Anforderungsbereich III: *evaluation/re-creation of text*
für die anwendungs-/produktionsorientierte Aufgabenstellung:
- Umsetzung, Bewertung, Reflexion der Problematik des Ausgangstextes bzw. der Analyse im Aufgabenbereich II in Form einer kreativen Aufgabe: Perspektivwechsel (Sicht einer anderen Figur),
- Füllen von Leerstellen (Weitererzählen, neues Ende),
- Textsortenwechsel (Brief an Protagonisten, Leserbrief, Brief an *agony aunt*, Tagebucheintrag, Dialog, etc.).

Die einzelnen Anforderungsbereiche sollen nicht in drei voneinander unabhängigen Texten behandelt werden. Der Zieltext ist ein geschlossener, kohärenter Text, der sich als Essay in seinen drei Teilen etwa in eine Hinführung zum Thema, einen Hauptteil und eine Schlussbetrachtung gliedert. Eine kreative Teilaufgabe wird sich naheliegenderweise nicht in den geschlossenen Zieltext eingliedern, da sie in der Regel ein völlig anderes Textformat hat.

Operatoren

Für die Formulierung der Aufgaben gibt es klare Vorgaben. Verben für die Arbeitsanweisungen (= Operatoren) müssen in ihrer exakten Bedeutung verstanden werden. Eine ungefähre Ahnung, was gefordert ist, reicht keinesfalls aus!
Die folgende Operatorenübersicht ist der Website des Ministeriums entnommen. Die mittlere Spalte definiert die genaue Wortbedeutung des Verbs, die dritte Spalte gibt jeweils ein Beispiel für eine Aufgabenstellung.
Beachten Sie, dass die Operatoren im Anforderungsbereich I vor allem deutlich machen, welcher Umfang der inhaltlichen Wiedergabe von Ihnen verlangt wird. „Outline", „summarize" oder „write a summary" verlangen eine knappe Wiedergabe des Textes oder auch nur einer relevanten Textpassage. „Describe" oder „point out" hingegen erwarten eine ausführliche Beschreibung bzw. Erläuterung des im Text dargestellten Sachverhalts. Letzteres kommt vor allem infrage, wenn der Ausgangstext sehr komplex ist, wie z. B. eine Erörterung, oder sehr dicht, wie beispielsweise ein Gedicht. Ihr Textverständnis weisen Sie dann nicht durch eine knappe Zusammenfassung, sondern durch eine Beschreibung oder Erläuterung in Ihren eigenen Worten nach.

TIPP

Achten Sie darauf, dass Sie, auch wenn Sie zu einer Skizzierung *(outline)* oder Zusammenfassung *(summary)* des Inhalts aufgefordert werden, stets die wesentlichen Inhaltspunkte benennen. Eine abstraktere, allgemeiner gehaltene Zusammenfassung kann durchaus eleganter sein, wird aber durch den Punktekatalog der Bewertungskriterien möglicherweise nicht erfasst.

Die Übersicht enthält Operatoren, die für das im Abitur vorgesehene Klausurformat Schreiben mit integriertem Leseverstehen in Klausurteil A und Sprachmittlung in Klausurteil B infrage kommen.
Weitere Operatoren für weitere Kompetenzbereiche sind auf der Website des Ministeriums zu finden (https://www.standardsicherung.schulministerium.nrw.de/cms/zentralabitur-wbk/faecher/getfile.php?file=2210).
Die Operatoren können unterschiedlichen Anforderungsbereichen zugeordnet werden.

Klausurteil A (Schreiben, Leseverstehen integriert)

Operator	Erläuterung	Illustrierendes Aufgabenbeispiel	AFB
analyse	describe and explain in detail	Analyze the opposing views on class held by the two protagonists. Examine the author's use of language.	II
assess	express a well-founded opinion on the nature or quality of sb./sth.	Assess the importance of standards in education.	III
evaluate	express a well-founded opinion on the nature or quality of sb./sth.	Evaluate the author's view of the present impact of the American Dream …	III
examine	describe and explain in detail	Examine the opposing views on social class held by the two protagonists.	II
give/write a characterization of	provide a thorough analysis of a character	Characterize/Write a characterization of the principal figures in the play.	II
comment (on)	state one's opinion clearly and support one's view with evidence or reasons	Comment on the writer's view of gender roles.	III
compare	show similarities and differences	Compare the attitude of the two characters towards war.	II
describe	give a detailed account of what sb./sth. is like	Describe the way the playwright creates an atmosphere of suspense.	I II
discuss	give arguments or reasons for and against, especially to come to a well-founded conclusion	Discuss the message of the cartoon, referring to work done on the British monarchy.	III
explain	make sth. clear by giving reasons for and details, aspects of sth.	Explain the protagonist's obsession with money.	II
illustrate	use examples to explain or make clear	Illustrate the way in which according to the author school life in Britain differs from that in Germany.	II

interpret	explain the meaning, purpose or message of sth.	Interpret the sonnet, focusing on the way structure and imagery are used to express the speaker's insight into the nature of time.	II
outline	give the main features, structure or general principles of sth.	Outline the author's views on love, marriage and divorce.	I
point out	find and explain certain aspects	Point out the author's main ideas on ...	I
state	present the main aspects of sth. briefly and clearly	State the author's key reasons for taking a gap year.	I
summarize, sum up	give a concise account of the main points or ideas of a text, issue or topic	Summarize/Sum up the information about green energy given in the text.	I
write (+ text type)	produce a text with specific features	Write the ending of the story/a letter to the editor/a dialogue, etc. Write an interior monologue that reflects the character's view of the situation and her/his feelings.	III

Klausurteil B Sprachmittlung isoliert

Die Aufgabenstellung für die Sprachmittlung enthält einen situativen Kontext mit Hinweisen zu Adressat und Zieltextformat.

Operator	**Erläuterung**	**Illustrierendes Aufgabenbeispiel**
explain	make sth. clear taking into account culture-related differences if necessary	Based on the text on environmental policy explain the principle of waste separation in Germany in an email to your British friend.
outline	give a concise account of the main points or ideas of a text, clarifying culture-related aspects if necessary	Outline Mr. Liu's career in Germany in an article for your international school project's website on Successful Immigrants.
present	give a concise account of the main points or ideas of a text, clarifying culture-related aspects if necessary	For an international school project in the EU, present the relevant information on the image of migrants in German media in a formal email to your partner school in Spain.

summarize, sum up	give a concise account of the main points or ideas of a text, clarifying culture-related aspects if necessary	Sum up Manuel's views on working and living as a gap year student in India for your blog. Where necessary add information which might help to avoid possible misunderstandings.
write (+ text type)	produce a text with specific features	Using the information in the German text write an article in English for your project website in which you inform your Polish partners how to get a sports scholarship at a German university.

Bewertung

Für die Bewertung wird den Lehrerinnen und Lehrern ein Raster mit Bewertungskriterien an die Hand gegeben, sowohl für die sprachliche als auch für die inhaltliche Leistung. Es können bei einer Abiturklausur insgesamt 150 Punkte erreicht werden, davon 90 für die Darstellungsleistung (Sprache) und 60 für den Inhalt. Dabei ist die Verteilung der Punkte auf die verschiedenen Anforderungsbereiche immer gleich.

Klausurteil A (Schreiben/Leseverstehen)

Anforderungsbereich I :	12 Punkte
Anforderungsbereich II:	16 Punkte
Anforderungsbereich III:	14 Punkte
Klausurteil B (Sprachmittlung):	18 Punkte
Für die Gesamtbewertung der Abiturklausur gibt das Ministerium die folgende Tabelle vor.	
Gesamtpunkte Inhalt:	**60 Punkte**

Grundsätze für die Bewertung (Notenfindung)

Für die Zuordnung der Notenstufen zu den Punktzahlen ist folgende Tabelle zu verwenden:

Note	Punkte	Erreichte Punktzahl
sehr gut plus	15	150 – 143
sehr gut	14	142 – 135
sehr gut minus	13	134 – 128
gut plus	12	127 – 120
gut	11	119 – 113
gut minus	10	112 – 105
befriedigend plus	9	104 – 98
befriedigend	8	97 – 90
befriedigend minus	7	89 – 83
ausreichend plus	6	82 – 75
ausreichend	5	74 – 68
ausreichend minus	4	67 – 58
mangelhaft plus	3	57 – 49
mangelhaft	2	48 – 40
mangelhaft minus	1	39 – 30
ungenügend	0	29 – 0

TIPP zum Punktesammeln

Die Wertigkeit des Anforderungsbereiches III darf man nicht unterschätzen. Mit 14 Punkten ist er fast so gewichtig wie Anforderungsbereich II. Halten Sie sich mit der Analyse nicht so lange auf, dass Ihnen für eine Stellungnahme nur noch wenige Minuten bleiben. Das würde Sie viele Punkte kosten.
Überdies: Wenn Ihre Stärken nicht in der Textanalyse liegen, Sie aber aus anderen Fächern wie Erdkunde oder Biologie so viel Sachkenntnis haben, dass Sie qualitativ hochwertig zu Sachthemen Position beziehen können, dann setzen Sie dort Ihren persönlichen Schwerpunkt!

Die mündliche Abiturprüfung im Fach Englisch

Während einige von Ihnen Englisch als schriftliches Abiturfach gewählt haben, werden andere sich für Englisch als 4. Abiturfach entschieden haben und damit eine mündliche Abiturprüfung ablegen müssen.
Auch für den Fall, dass Sie Englisch als schriftliches Abiturfach gewählt haben, könnte es trotzdem sein, dass Sie an einer mündlichen Nachprüfung teilnehmen müssen, nämlich wenn Sie Ihre Prüfungen nicht bestanden haben. In bestimmten Fällen besteht auch die Möglichkeit, die Abiturnote durch die Teilnahme an einer freiwilligen mündlichen Nachprüfung zu verbessern.
Ganz egal, welcher Fall für Sie von Bedeutung ist: Die Vorbereitung und der Ablauf der mündlichen Prüfung im Fach Englisch ist immer gleich.

Die mündliche Prüfung im Fach Englisch dauert insgesamt **mindestens 20,** aber **höchstens 30 Minuten** und ist in zwei Prüfungsteile aufgeteilt, deren Dauer ungefähr gleich lang ist.
Vor Beginn der Prüfung haben Sie **30 Minuten Zeit,** das Ihnen von Ihrem Fachlehrer oder Ihrer –lehrerin für den ersten Prüfungsteil vorgelegte **Material vorzubereiten.** Als Hilfsmittel stehen Ihnen hier ein **ein- und zweisprachiges Wörterbuch** und **gegebenenfalls ein herkunftssprachliches Wörterbuch** zur Verfügung. Die Notizen, die Sie hier anfertigen, dürfen Sie mit in die Prüfung nehmen und als Grundlage für Ihren Vortrag nutzen.

Anders als im schriftlichen Abitur können Sie hier **nicht** zwischen verschiedenen Materialien auswählen.
Das Material, dass Ihnen von Ihrem Fachlehrer oder Ihrer –lehrerin vorgelegt wird, stellt einen **Bezug zu den Themenfeldern der Qualifikationsphase** her. Zur häuslichen Vorbereitung verweisen wir hier auf die Kapitel zum Basiswissen auf den Seiten 20 bis 79.

Im **ersten Prüfungsteil** sollen Sie – auf Basis des Ihnen zur Vorbereitung vorgelegten Materials – **einen zusammenhängenden und weitgehend freien Vortrag halten, selbstständig** eine **nachvollziehbare Argumentation** entwickeln und **eine Einordnung in den entsprechenden Themenkomplex** vornehmen.
Grundsätzlich ist der erste Prüfungsteil nichts anderes als eine „mündliche Version" einer Klausur. Daher empfehlen wir Ihnen, die in diesem Buch enthaltenen Klausuren zur Vorbereitung auf die mündliche Prüfung durchzuarbeiten.

Im Grunde bestehen **zwei Möglichkeiten, wie das** von Ihnen vorzubereitende **Material aussehen kann.**
Es können Ihnen **ein oder mehrere Texte beziehungsweise ein längeres Zitat** mit einem Wortumfang von **ca. 200 bis 300 Wörtern** vorgelegt werden. Bei den Texten kann es sich um **literarische Texte oder** um **Sach- und Gebrauchstexte** handeln.
Ihr Fachlehrer oder Ihre -lehrerin kann Ihnen aber auch **eine oder mehrere visuelle**

Darstellungen (Diagramm, Grafik, Cartoon, Statistik, Bild) vorlegen, die er/sie **gegebenenfalls um** einen **Text ergänzt.**

Im **zweiten Prüfungsteil** wird Ihnen **kein weiteres Material** vorgelegt. Gegenstand dieses Prüfungsteils sind **ein weiterer bzw. mehrere weitere Themenkomplexe zu den Themenfeldern der Qualifikationsphase.**
Hier sollen Sie zeigen, dass Sie **größere Zusammenhänge erkennen und herstellen** können.

Da neben Ihrer inhaltlichen Leistung auch Ihre sprachliche Leistung bewertet wird, sei an dieser Stelle nochmals auf die Listen mit nützlichen Wörtern und Wendungen im Buch (ab S. 210) verwiesen.
Beachten Sie auch die Strategien zur Wortschatzarbeit und Vermeidung „gängiger" Fehler.
Achten Sie in beiden Prüfungsteilen darauf, dass Ihre Ausführungen für die Prüfungskommission verständlich und nachvollziehbar sind.
Bemühen Sie sich darum, im ersten Prüfungsteil Ihre Gedanken und Anmerkungen möglichst strukturiert und frei vorzutragen.
Nutzen Sie die Vorbereitungszeit dazu, Ihre Notizen zu strukturieren. Selbstverständlich dürfen und sollen Sie auf diese zurückgreifen, aber lesen Sie bitte nicht einfach nur alles von Ihrem Notizzettel ab.

Basiswissen

Freedom and Justice – Myths and Realities

Concepts of the American Dream

The USA

The USA was – and still is – a country of unlimited opportunities, where people can work their way "from rags to riches". It has attracted millions of both legal and illegal immigrants over the centuries, who hoped to find a better life there without the kind of persecution or obstacles they had to face in their home countries.

Keyword:

The American Dream: There is no single definition of what the American Dream actually is, as it varies for each and every American.
The term was first used by James Truslow Adams, an American historian, in his book *The Epic of America*, in 1931: "[The] American Dream [is] the dream of a land in which life should be better and richer and fuller for every man with opportunity for each according to his ability or achievement."

In the following pages we are going to take a look at some of the key concepts generally associated with the American Dream, many of which are often touched upon in political speeches.
Please note that these key concepts often overlap and are closely related.

Freedom

The first thing many immigrants saw when they came by ship to New York City during the 19th and the first half of the 20th century, was the Statue of Liberty, which is located on Liberty Island.

The Statue of Liberty

- given to the USA as a gift from France in 1886, to celebrate the first 100 years of American independence from Britain (the centennial)
- a robed woman, holding a lit torch in her right and a tablet in her left hand, showing the date of the Declaration of Independence (July 4, 1776)
- underneath her right foot the remains of broken shackles can be seen
- one of the most famous American icons, symbolizing enlightenment, independence, liberty and freedom
- the theme of Emma Lazarus' famous poem "The New Colossus" (1883), which can be seen on a bronze plaque inside the statue
- located in Upper New York Bay, just like Ellis Island

Ellis Island

- the place where most immigrants first set foot on American soil
- an island of hopes but also an island of tears for a number of immigrants, as some of them were detained there for legal or medical reasons or even sent back
- the gateway to a new – better – life for the majority of immigrants
- a federal immigration station from 1892 to 1954

The Puritans

The Puritans' beliefs and values had a lasting impact on New England society:

- towards the end of the 16th century some English Protestants felt that Protestantism in England was not much different from Catholicism
- decided to leave England, seeking their luck elsewhere
- first settled in Holland (1608), but moved back to England
- wished to remain English subjects but free to worship God the way they wanted to
- intention: to purify the Church of England, not to leave it
- September 1620: a group of 102 people left England, sailed on a ship called the Mayflower, arrived in America 65 days later, in a bay they called Plymouth Bay.

The New Canaan

In the Bible Canaan was the land God promised to the Israelites. God ordered Moses to lead the people from captivity in Egypt to Canaan – "a land of milk and honey". America sees itself in this tradition. The idea of America as the "New Canaan", the land of milk and honey, is closely linked to the idea of "manifest destiny".

Manifest Destiny/The Frontier

Manifest Destiny

The term "Manifest Destiny" was coined by the American journalist John L. O'Sullivan in 1839:

- stands for the belief that America is the one nation ordered by God to expand across the North American continent
- *The Great Nation of Futurity* by John L. O'Sullivan: "[America is] the nation of progress, of individual freedom, of universal enfranchisement." According to him the American people have been chosen "... to establish on earth the moral dignity and salvation of man – the immutable truth and beneficence of God."[1]
- America = a country that is superior to all other countries
- stresses virtue of the American people, as they are the ones to establish moral rules and values across the globe.

American patriotism is deeply rooted in the concept of "Manifest Destiny".
The concept of "Manifest Destiny" is closely linked to the concept of the frontier.

1 aus: "The Great Nation of Futurity," *The United States Democratic Review*, Volume 6, Issue 23, pp. 426 – 430.

The frontier

- the expansion of the American nation from coast to coast, pushing the borderline between civilization and wilderness further and further back
- Pacific coast was reached in the 2nd half of the 19th century
- after this mission new challenges – new frontiers – were needed, e.g. space exploration (like the moon landing in 1969), scientific and technological progress

Life, liberty and the pursuit of happiness

Declaration of Independence

- written in 1776 by Thomas Jefferson
- all American citizens are created equal: "We hold these truths to be self-evident, that all men are created equal, that they are endowed by their Creator with certain unalienable rights, that among these are life, liberty and the pursuit of happiness."
- possibility for every American (at first, women were excluded from this definition) to lead his/her life the way he/she wants to, making his/her own personal dreams come true
- stresses the rights of the individual, while at the same time taking the rights of others into consideration
- 1776: the thirteen colonies declared their independence from England, and were, therefore, at war with England
- Declaration of Independence questioned the rights of the British king, George III, in that it stated that everyone was created equal (quite revolutionary at the time)
- The fact that the new American government was to be radically different from that of the British king was pointed out in the preamble to the American constitution.

American Constitution

- written in 1787
- new ideas of a democratic state stated in the **preamble** of the constitution: "We the People of the United States, in Order to form a more perfect Union[2], establish Justice, ensure domestic Tranquility, provide for the common defense, promote the general Welfare, and secure the Blessings of Liberty to ourselves and our Posterity, do ordain and establish this Constitution for the United States of America."

Bill of Rights

- first ten amendments to the American Constitution
- written because some delegates feared that the new American government would threaten everyone's ability to achieve personal freedom and the pursuit of happiness
- First Congress of the United States originally proposed twelve amendments in 1789, ten of which were added to the constitution as a preamble
- amendments known as the Bill of Rights

2 Barack Obama took up the idea of "a more perfect union" in a speech he delivered on May 28, 2008, in which he elaborated on the issues of race and inequality in the USA.

- guarantee America's citizens certain inalienable rights, e.g. freedom of religion, freedom of speech and the press as well as the right to bear arms

The American Dream today

Keywords:

Multicultural society: a society where various ethnic groups and their cultural heritage are accepted in their own right

Salad bowl: the various ethnicities living in the United States adding their own traditions, cultural values, etc. to the American people; the various heritages do not merge into one, but stay distinct ("unity in diversity")

Melting pot: the various ethnic groups do not retain their cultural heritage but amalgamate into one new nation

The term first appeared in an essay by Jean de Crèvecoeur entitled "Letters from an American farmer" in 1782.

The term "salad bowl" is now considered to be more politically correct.

- The American Dream itself has come to be seen more critically.
- A considerable number of critics regard the American Dream as an illusion, as not everyone has access to the possibilities usually associated with it.
- Examples of American nightmares are the Vietnam War, September 11, 2001, and the financial crisis starting in 2008.

During his election campaign, current US president Joe Biden declared that he would reform the US immigration system and reverse the restrictions implemented by former US president Donald Trump. The number of prospective new immigrants would be increased and those immigrants living in the United States illegally should be pardoned and thereby been given the chance to become legal US citizens. In addition to that, restrictions would be lifted so that more refugees could be admitted to the USA. The number of green cards issued would be raised to match the increasing demand. Instead of pursuing Trump's vision of building a wall on the border to Mexico to stop illegal immigration from South American countries, Biden plans to make border screening more effective.

On his first day in office President Biden sent a bill to Congress to put his plans for a fair, human and reformed immigration system into action.

Unaccompanied minors are allowed to enter the USA while it is decided whether they are allowed to stay or will be sent back to their home country. This has led to false rumours that the US borders are open to migrants and an increased rise in the numbers of unaccompanied migrant children. Sadly, the number of these underage immigrants is still fairly high. Biden has urged families not to send their children unaccompanied on this dangerous journey to the USA.

The Present Economic Situation in the US

The question whether the American Dream is still alive today is one which cannot be answered with either "yes" or "no", as the concept of the American Dream is not static. It depends on several aspects, e.g. a person's individual definition of and belief in the concept of the American Dream and the point of view one takes.
With regard to the present economic situation in the US, it is often said that the American Dream has been shattered for many people. The financial crisis that began in 2008 made the aim of achieving financial security a distant prospect.
In the following you will find a very short and simplified version of why for many Americans the quest for financial security has become difficult over the last few years. For many people, owning a house is the goal of a lifetime. This is also true for US citizens, and for many years getting a loan necessary to build or buy a house was not difficult, even for people without a steady or with a low income. This resulted in people taking bigger loans than they could actually afford. They hoped that in the worst case of not being able to pay back the loan, they could still sell their houses, thereby making a profit. In most cases paying back the loan was not a problem as long as the mortgage rates were low.
When the base rate *(Leitzinsen)* increased, many house owners had difficulties paying back their loans. A huge number of houses suddenly had to be sold, which lowered the price, as there was also a decline in demand. In some cases that actually meant that the price for which a house could be sold was lower than the house owner's loan. So instead of making a profit, selling a house in many cases meant incurring a loss. In the meantime, the banks had started to speculate with their customers' loans. Loans of good, average and bad credit rating were combined into so-called "Mortgage Backed Securities" (MBS). By combining loans of different credit ranking, banks hoped to limit the risk if someone failed to pay back a loan. These "Mortgage Backed Securities" were then sold to other banks worldwide, which meant profit for the seller. This practice went well for several years, but when more and more house owners could not pay back their loans, their banks started to lose large sums of money.
On 15th September 2008, one of America's biggest banks, Lehman Brothers, crashed. This marked the beginning of a series of bank crashes. Unemployment increased and as many Americans had less money to spend, this led to a drop in consumption as well. The burst of the housing bubble did not remain an American problem for long. It soon affected the economy of other countries, among them Germany, the Benelux countries and Iceland. Government bailouts for banks and economic stimulus plans were decided and put into action. Nevertheless, many countries were hit by recession.

In 2019, the US economy was in parts still recovering from the economic crisis of 2008, but unemployment dropped from its highest level of 10% in October 2009 to just under 3.0 % in January 2020.[3] Due to the Corona crisis, this figure is now rising again. It is impossible to foresee the future economic development. In April 2020 the unemployment rate was up to 4.8 %, in February 2021 it was 6.2 %.

3 http://data.bls.gov/timeseries/LNS14000000

For both major parties in the US, economic growth and an increase in the number of jobs are top issues, although their approaches are quite different.
On November 3, 2020 Joseph "Joe" Robinette Biden Jr., the Democratic Party candidate, won the U.S. presidential elections against Donald Trump. During both of Barack Obama's terms in office as US president, Joe Biden served as Vice-President of the USA. Prior to his finally successful run for the presidency, Biden had announced his candidacy in 1988 and 2009, but on both occasions he withdrew from the race for presidency.
Born on November 20, 1942, Biden grew up in Pennsylvania and Delaware. He worked as a lawyer until he was sworn in as a senator for the state of Delaware at the age of 29. He kept this position until his election as Vice-President to Barack Obama in 2009. Kamala Harris was elected with Biden as the first female Vice-President of the USA. She is also the first African American and first Asian American to hold this office.
Among Biden's election pledges were fighting COVID-19, dealing with the climate crisis, making health care affordable for everyone, and renewing the country's immigration system. Rejoining the Paris climate agreement, which the USA had left under Donald Trump, was a first step to acknowledging the urgent global challenge of the climate crisis.
Given the relatively narrow margin of Biden's victory in the presidential election, Donald Trump, together with his supporters and many members of the Republican Party, did not readily accept the outcome. Trump continued to use the social microblogging platform Twitter to spread his theory of fraudulent elections and a "stolen" victory. Several of his tweets questioned the legitimacy of the election. Many were also regarded as a glorification of violence. As a consequence, Twitter permanently suspended Donald Trump's Twitter account earlier this year.
The tension in the USA that erupted in the wake of Trump's constant accusations of electoral fraud, led to a large number Trump's supporters violently storming the Capitol in Washington DC on January 6, 2021 – a mere two weeks before Biden's inauguration. Trump had summoned his supporters to march to Washington to protest against the "stolen" election and Joe Biden's congressional certification. The angry mob that stormed the Capitol wreaked havoc. Photographs and videos taken during the raid showed that some of the protesters were heavily armed and aggressive.
Media coverage of this incident went around the globe and caused horror, shock, disgust and disbelief in governments and citizens worldwide. American and international politicians alike criticized Trump for not condemning, but rather inciting, the violence. In the aftermath of the riots, there have been attempts to press legal charges against Trump for the role he played in this incident. On January 7, 2021, Donald Trump – again on Twitter – promised a smooth transition of power.
Trump himself did not attend Joe Biden's inauguration ceremony, thereby breaking with a 152-year-long tradition. Instead, outgoing Vice-President Mike Pence paid his respects to Joe Biden and new Vice-President Kamala Harris.

During his election campaign President Joe Biden frequently declared the dangers of climate change to be one of the most pressing current global challenges. He kept his promise to rejoin the Paris Climate Agreement by releasing the following statement on the January 20, 2021, only a few hours after being sworn in as President: "I, Joseph R. Biden Jr., President of the United States of America, having seen and considered the Paris Agreement, done at Paris on December 12, 2015, do hereby accept the said Agreement and every article and clause thereof on behalf of the United States of America."[4]

Glossary – Freedom and Justice

assimilation	Assimilation; Angleichung an Bestehendes
base rate	Leitzinsen
civil disobedience	bürgerlicher Ungehorsam
Civil Rights Movement	die Bürgerrechtsbewegung
credit rating	Beurteilung der Kreditwürdigkeit, Bonitätsbeurteilung
cultural heritage	Kulturerbe; kulturelles Erbe
Declaration of Independence	Unabhängigkeitserklärung
discrimination; deprivation	Benachteiligung; Diskriminierung
drop in consumption	Konsumrückgang
E pluribus unum	lat.: aus vielen Eines; ursprünglich bezogen auf die verschiedenen Staaten, aus denen die USA bestehen; heute vielmehr bezogen auf die vielen ethnischen Gruppen und Volksgruppen, aus denen sich die Bevölkerung der USA zusammensetzt
economic stimulus plan	Konjunkturprogramm
entrepreneur	Unternehmer
equality; equal opportunities	Gleichheit; gleiche Chancen
fame	Ruhm
freedom; ~ of speech; ~ of the press; religious ~	Freiheit; Redefreiheit; Pressefreiheit; Religionsfreiheit
frontier	Grenze (zwischen Zivilisation und Wildnis)
gold rush	Goldrausch
government bailouts	Rettungsaktion durch die Regierung

4 Source: White House Briefing Room, https://www.whitehouse.gov/briefing-room/statements-releases/2021/01/20/paris-climate-agreement/)) Biden's act of rejoining the Paris climate agreement was internationally received with praise and relief.

identity	Identität
Immigration Act	Einwanderungsgesetz
"In God we trust"	Wir vertrauen auf Gott; offizieller Wahlspruch der USA
inauguration; inaugural speech	Amtseinführung; Amtsantrittsrede
liberation	Befreiung
loan	Darlehen
melting pot vs. salad bowl	„Schmelztiegel" vs. „Salatschüssel" (unterschiedliche Konzepte, die die Vielfalt unterschiedlicher Kulturen in den USA charakterisieren)
mortgage	Hypothek
multiculturalism	Multikulturalität
naturalisation	Einbürgerung
pioneer; pioneer spirit	Pionier; Pioniergeist
Promised Land; the land of milk and honey; God's own country; the New Canaan	das gelobte Land
recession	Rezession
refugee; refugee camp	Flüchtling; Flüchtlingslager
segregation; desegregation	Rassentrennung; Aufhebung der Rassentrennung
success	Erfolg
supply and demand	Angebot und Nachfrage
the housing bubble	die Immobilienblase
the pursuit of happiness	das Streben nach Glück
to achieve financial security	finanzielle Sicherheit erlangen
to attain self-fulfillment	sich selbst verwirklichen
to be persecuted; religious/political persecution	verfolgt werden; religiöse/politische Verfolgung
to go from rags to riches; from dishwasher to millionaire	vom Tellerwäscher zum Millionär
to immigrate; immigrant; immigration; an influx of immigrants	einwandern; Einwanderer; Einwanderung; Zustrom von Einwanderern
to incur a loss	(einen) Verlust machen
to pledge allegiance to the flag	den Fahneneid leisten
to prosper	Erfolg haben; in Wohlstand leben
to settle; settler; settlement	besiedeln; Siedler; Siedlung
unalienable/inalienable rights	unveräußerliche Rechte

Tradition and Change in Politics and Society

Monarchy and Modern Democracy (in Britain)

Keyword:

British constitution: is not set out in a single document.
It is founded on conventions that are universally accepted, but which have never been formally defined. It is also founded on numerous acts and resolutions of Parliament, as each individual act of Parliament contributes to the constitution. Thus it is adaptable to changing political conditions.

Separation of Powers

The following three branches represent the powers and areas of responsibility:
Legislature: Parliament
Executive:
- government
- government departments responsible for national administration
- local authorities
- public corporations responsible for particular nationalized industries (controlled by Government; most of these have now been privatized)

Judiciary: the Courts
There are **two kinds of law:**
- common law: historic body of conventions ("it has always been like that")
- statute law: parliamentary and EU legislation

Parliament

Elements of Parliament

Queen – House of Lords – House of Commons
- Agreement of all three elements is required to pass legislation.
- Parliament is directly responsible to the electorate – no written constitution.
- An Act of Parliament cannot be disputed by the law courts.

Functions of Parliament

- pass laws
- scrutinize government policy and administration
- debate the major issues of the day

The House of Lords (House of Peers, Upper House, Second Chamber)

The House of Lords consists of hereditary peers, who inherit their peerage, and life peers, whose peerages are granted to them personally for their lifetime.

The political power of the Peers has been gradually reduced over the years, and they have recognized the supremacy of the elected chamber, the House of Commons.

Functions of the House of Lords are

- to discuss, examine or delay Bills
- to introduce Bills.

It used to be the highest court of appeal (since October 2009 this function has been served by the Supreme Court of the United Kingdom).

The House of Commons (Lower House)

646 members are directly elected by voters in the constituencies.
The House of Commons is the actual legislative body of the United Kingdom.

The Queen

The Queen has no overt power but is formally part of the government system.
The Queen is the

- head of State
- symbol of national unity
- head of the executive
- head of the judiciary
- commander-in-chief of the armed forces
- "supreme governor" of the Church of England.

Important functions

The Queen

- appoints the Prime Minister – by inviting the leader of the majority in the House of Commons to form a Government
- summons and dissolves Parliament
- gives Royal Assent to legislation (given as a matter of course)
- formally appoints ministers, judges, officers, diplomats, bishops
- can pardon people
- confers peerages (see below) and knighthoods
- represents the country at home and abroad.

General elections

The election period extends over a maximum of 5 years. Elections are ordered by the Queen on the advice of the Prime Minister.
The Prime Minister calls a new election at any time before the end of the 5-year election period. The United Kingdom is divided into 646 constituencies. Voters from each constituency elect their Member of Parliament (MP) by simple majority vote. The system is also called "first-past-the-post system". The candidate who gains the most votes in each

constituency gets a seat in Parliament. The political party that gains most seats forms the government. This system is preferred by the big parties, because it secures clear majorities. Smaller parties, which may have the support of a considerable proportion of the population, are never represented according to the proportion of the votes cast for them.
By-elections: elections in a single constituency when an MP has to be replaced during the legislative period.

Political parties

The Conservative Party (Tories)

Right-wing party, associated with
- nationalism
- law and order
- private enterprise
- minimal interference of the state in the economy.

The Labour Party

Traditional party of the "working class", formerly associated with
- state control and planning
- nationalization of key industries
- welfare
- affiliation to the trade unions.

However, with Tony Blair the party now known as New Labour changed direction away from socialist ideals towards an acceptance of the free market economy, opening itself to voters from the middle classes.

Governments since 1979

1979	Margaret Thatcher	Conservative	"Thatcherism": ruthless application of free market principles ("Iron Lady")
1983	Margaret Thatcher		
1987	Margaret Thatcher		
1991	John Major	Conservative	
1997	Tony Blair	Labour	"New Labour": more social democratic than socialist
2005	Tony Blair		
2007	Gordon Brown	Labour	
2010	David Cameron	Conservative	
2015	David Cameron	Conservative	
2016	Theresa May	Conservative	
2019	Boris Johnson	Conservative	

Her Majesty's Government

The Prime Minister is appointed by the Queen and the ministers are appointed by the Queen on the recommendation of the Prime Minister.
The Prime Minister is always a member of the House of Commons. He or she presides over the cabinet, allocates functions to the ministers, and informs the Queen regularly at private meetings. He or she lives at Number 10 Downing Street.

Important members of the present cabinet (April 2021)

Prime Minister	Boris Johnson
Chancellor of the Exchequer	Rishi Sunat
Secretary of State for the Home Department	Priti Patel
Secretary of State for Foreign and Commonwealth Affairs	Dominic Raab
Secretary of State for Defence	Ben Wallace

Ministers are traditionally referred to as "The Right Honourable" (The Rt. Hon.), e.g. "The Rt. Hon. Boris Johnson MP"

Her Majesty's Opposition

The leader of the opposition forms a "shadow cabinet", which can take over at any time if the government loses the support of the majority in parliament.

The Privy Council

The main function of Her Majesty's Most Honourable Privy Council is to advise the Queen on the approval of legislation. Its members are senior politicians who were or are members of either the House of Commons or the House of Lords.

Local government

The system of local government differs in the four countries of the UK. The systems are much too complex to be presented here. You should keep in mind though, that political decisions have to be taken at different levels. There are county councils, district councils and parish councils, which are responsible for all kinds of local affairs, e.g. waste management, transport, traffic, housing, education, licensing, cemeteries, etc.

Devolution

Devolution is the granting of powers to the parliaments of Scotland, Wales and Northern Ireland. At the end of the 1990s the National Assembly of Wales and the Scottish Parliament were inaugurated, with competence to rule on issues like agriculture, fisheries and forestry, education, health, and tourism, whereas Westminster (the UK government) retained power in fields such as foreign affairs, defence, taxation, fiscal policy, and labour market policy. Because of the Troubles, devolution in Northern

Ireland was only implemented in 2007. In the 2014 referendum on full independence held in Scotland there was a narrow majority for the country to remain in the UK. After the Brexit decision the Scottish Parliament has decided to ask the British Government to be allowed to hold a second referendum on independence in order to give Scotland the chance to stay in the EU.

Society

Class

The British are very class-conscious. Class distinctions are recognizable in speech, habits, style, tastes, and values. The Office of National Statistics produced a detailed socio-economic classification in 2020[1]. Although many top-ranking people may earn a lot of money, the classification is not based on income alone but on the distinctions mentioned above. In the last three decades class distinctions have become less obvious. The country has become more of a meritocracy, i. e. a society where achievement counts most. But traditional everyday terms are still used to refer to social classes: *upper class, upper-middle class, lower-middle class, working class.*

Ethnicity

Britain has become a multinational society in the last half century (see chapter "Multicultural society", p. 35)

Britain and the EU

Traditionally Britain has preferred to stay out of Europe. The terms "Europe" and "the Continent" have always referred to the European mainland.
Britain had been a member of the EU since 1973 (then the EC). Britain never joined the monetary union (i. e. they do not have the euro) and never signed the Schengen Agreement, which permits travelling without border controls between 25 European countries.
On June 23, 2016 a referendum about Britain's membership in the EU was held (cf. p. 33). There is a continuing debate on Brexit in Britain between those in favour of the EU and the "Eurosceptics". Eurosceptics are to be found among the supporters of the nationalist right and the Conservative party, but also among Labour Party members. Anti-European propaganda is to be found particularly in the tabloid papers like the *Sun* or the *Daily Mail.*

Main arguments of the Eurosceptics

The EU is
- expensive to run
- dominated by big countries at the expense of the smaller members

1 https://www.ons.gov.uk/methodology/classificationsandstandards/standardoccupationalclassificationsoc/soc2020/soc2020volume3thenationalstatisticssocioeconomicclassificationnssecrebasedonthesoc2020#classes-and-collapses

- too powerful
- trying to impose regulation in policy areas that should be the responsibility of national governments (e.g. health, education, law, tax)
- corrupt and money-wasting
- a security risk with its open borders
- host to millions of immigrants, some of them hostile and violent
- undemocratic.

Arguments in favour of the European Union

- The EU has created the world's largest international trade market.
- People have the choice to live and work anywhere in the EU.
- Many formerly poor countries have prospered in the EU, and poor regions receive special grants.
- Consumers have more rights.
- Europol provides cooperation on crime.
- The EU has passed many laws to ensure better environmental, consumer and health standards.
- Tourists receive free medical aid.
- Travel in the EU has become easier and cheaper.
- Human rights legislation has helped individuals in all EU countries.

Brexit

Keyword:

Brexit: shorthand way of saying the UK is leaving the EU – merging the words **Br**itain and **exit**

Cause: A referendum on 23 June 2016 → Leave won by 52% to 48%.
The referendum turnout was 71.8%, with more than 30 million people voting.

UK Breakdown

England voted for Brexit by 53.4% to 46.6%
Wales voted for Brexit by 52.5% to 47.5%.
Scotland and Northern Ireland both backed staying in the EU.
Scotland backed Remain by 62% to 38%,
Northern Ireland voted Remain by 55.8% to 44.2%

After the referendum

Prime Minister David Cameron, who was against Brexit, resigned.
Britain was supposed to leave the EU on 29 March 2019 but the departure date had to be postponed. There were lengthy negotiations after the referendum. Basically, they had been about the 'deal', the conditions under which the UK would leave the EU. The outcome of these negotiations was the "Withdrawal Agreement" which covered several key points, the most controversial of which deals with the border between

the Republic of Ireland and Northern Ireland. This border, which is invisible today, would become an external border of the EU. Nobody really wants soldiers and border controls there. Although the Withdrawal Agreement was approved by the EU and UK negotiators, it was never approved by the British Parliament. Prime Minister Theresa May's deal was rejected three times by Parliament. Therefore, she resigned.

Boris Johnson became Prime Minister in July 2019, and promised to take Britain out of the EU by 31 October, with or without a deal, but this deadline was again extended to 31 January, 2020.
Mr. Johnson persuaded enough opposition MPs to agree to an early general election. His Conservative Party won an 80-seat majority, which in turn voted for his Withdrawal Agreement. ("Get Brexit done.") The important changes to the deal agreed by Theresa May with the EU are to do with the Irish border after Brexit.
The new agreement replaces the controversial Irish backstop plan in Theresa May's deal. Legally there now is a customs border between Northern Ireland (which is part of the UK) and the Republic of Ireland (which is part of the EU), but in practice there will be no border checks. The actual checks will be between Great Britain and the island of Ireland, with goods being checked at "points of entry" into Northern Ireland.
On 31 January 2020, Britain left the EU. There was a transition period until 31 December 2020. During this transition period, everything stayed as it was. In the meantime, there were to be negotiations on the future relationship between the UK and the EU regarding all details. The Corona crisis hit Britain in spring 2020, which did not help with the progress of the negotiations with the EU.
Finally, Britain and the EU reached a deal just in time on 24 December: The deal contains new rules for how the UK and EU will live, work and trade together. Important issues are workers' rights, social and environmental regulations, travel, fishing, and financial services. The UK will now follow its own trade policy and wishes to negotiate deals with other countries, particularly with the US, Australia, and New Zealand. What is very important is that there will no longer be freedom of movement between the UK and the EU. For longer stays, people will need visas.
Many of the EU's rules will stay in effect in Northern Ireland in order to avoid a hard border with the Republic of Ireland. Checks will be carried out on goods leaving Northern Ireland for Great Britain. At the time when Finale 2022 is being written, violence in Northern Ireland has erupted again after more than 20 years of peace. Pro-British Unionists fearing gradual alienation from the UK have started riots in the streets. For up-to-date information you should check e. g. bbc.com, guardian.com or TLDR news on YouTube, especially shortly before your English exam, in order to be able to cope with a possible task on Britain leaving the EU and its consequences.

Scotland

Scotland's First Minister, Nicola Sturgeon, said it is "democratically unacceptable" that Scotland has to leave the EU when it voted overwhelmingly to remain. There might be a second independence referendum for the country (cf. Devolution, p. 31).

Northern Ireland

The Republic of Ireland is part of the EU. Northern Ireland voted to remain. Some politicians see this as a reason for a vote on reunification. We will have to wait and see how this issue develops (see above).

Multicultural Society

Keyword:

Imperial Act (1914): Inhabitants of the colonies were given British citizenship.

- Between the 1960s and 1980s many Indians, Pakistanis and Bangladeshis immigrated to Britain. They now form the largest immigrant communities.
- Many of them settled in the Midlands or in towns in Lancashire, Yorkshire and Strathclyde, where they worked in the textile industry.

Britain today

- Britain consists of three countries (England, Scotland, Wales). Together with Northern Ireland it forms the United Kingdom. 12.4% of the population in the UK were born abroad (2013).[2]
- **Ethnic diversity** enriches Britain, not only when it comes to music, fashion and food.
- Many embrace the possibilities and advantages of ethnic diversity (such as the former Foreign Secretary Robin Cook, who said that Chicken Tikka Masala " ... is now a true British national dish ..."[3]).
- Others fear that "Britishness" will eventually be lost; they interpret multiculturalism as meaning that various cultures coexist peacefully, but without having a common basis of shared values.
- **Second generation immigrants,** i. e. children born to parents who immigrated to Britain prior to (or shortly after) their children's birth, face a variety of problems:
  - They often experience a clash of cultures. Outside their parents' home they adopt a western lifestyle, similar to that of their white friends and classmates. At home, however, they live according to values, beliefs and traditions typical of their parents' home countries, which many of these children and teenagers have never visited. Quite often they do not speak their parents' language any more, either. For some, the transition between these two different lifestyles is not easy.
  - They have difficulties when it comes to living up to the expectations of their parents, friends, teachers, etc.
  - They often have to face discrimination.

2 http://visual.ons.gov.uk/uk-perspectives-a-recent-history-of-international-migration/; see also on https://www.ons.gov.uk
3 Robin Cook's *Chicken Tikka Masala Speech*, The Guardian, April 19, 2001, http://www.guardian.co.uk/world/2001/apr/19/race.britishidentity

Glossary – Traditions and Change

act / bill / law the law	Gesetz das Gesetz
agreement	Abkommen
asylum seekers	Asylsuchende
blend in	sich einfügen, integrieren
citizenship	Nationalität, Staatsangehörigkeit
clash between/of two cultures	das Aufeinanderprallen zweier Kulturen
citizen	Bürger
conservative Conservative Party a conservative	konservativ die Conservative Party ein Konservativer
constitution	Verfassung
delegate	Delegierter
democracy	Demokratie
discriminate against someone	jemanden benachteiligen/diskriminieren
elect to be elected election electorate election period election campaign	wählen gewählt werden Wahl Wählerschaft Wahlperiode Wahlkampf
ethnic minorities	ethnische Minderheiten
ethnicity	Ethnizität, Volkszugehörigkeit
executive	die Exekutive
federal	Bundes-...
government to govern	Regierung regieren
hold racist attitudes	eine rassistische Haltung/Einstellung haben
house	Kammer des Parlaments
imperialism; imperialistic	Imperialismus; imperialistisch
indefinite leave to remain	unbeschränkte Aufenthaltserlaubnis
judiciary	die Judikative
labour	Arbeit
Labour Party	die Labour Party

legislature legislative	die Legislative gesetzgebend
loss of identity	Identitätsverlust
minister prime minister (the Prime Minister) ministry	Minister Premierminister Ministerium
MP Member of Parliament	Abgeordneter
mutual understanding and respect	gegenseitiges/beidseitiges Verständnis und Respekt
office to hold office Home Office/Foreign Office	Amt, Ministerium ein Amt innehaben Innenministerium, Außenministerium
open-minded vs. narrow-minded	aufgeschlossen vs. engstirnig
outsider	Außenseiter
parliament	Parlament
party	Partei
policy economic policy foreign policy	politisches Ziel, Maßnahmen Wirtschaftspolitik Außenpolitik
pluralistic society	eine pluralistische Gesellschaft
politics political politician	Politik politisch Politiker
poll polling-station	Abstimmung, Umfrage, Wahl, Wahllokal
racial equality	Gleichwertigkeit verschiedener Rassen
receive/be granted citizenship	die Staatsbürgerschaft erhalten
referendum	Volksbefragung, Volksentscheid
representative	(Volks-)Vertreter
secretary foreign secretary	Minister Außenminister
the people	das Volk
to support	unterstützen
vote to vote voter	Stimme stimmen, wählen Wähler
wing right/left wing	Flügel rechter/linker Flügel

Voices from the African Continent: Focus on Nigeria

From Empire to Commonwealth

Keywords:

Post-colonialism: term first used in the middle of the 20th century; refers to the time after the British had left the colonies, i. e. after their formal rule over the colonies had come to an end.
Political independence did not necessarily lead to economic independence. The withdrawal of the British often resulted in problems for the ex-colonies, e. g. in difficulties in setting up a functioning government which guaranteed the people the freedom they dreamed of.

The Commonwealth: a group of 52 states; many former British colonies joined at the end of the decolonization process; aims at racial equality and national sovereignty. The British Queen is the head of the Commonwealth.

- At the **beginning of the 17th century** Britain started to expand its empire across the globe.
- The colonizers had a huge impact on the colonies and their people, bringing new traditions, values and beliefs with them.

- **After the 2nd World War** the British Empire changed rapidly.
- Most British colonies became independent from Britain by 1970, but a large number of them stayed closely connected with their former colonizer by joining the Commonwealth.

- While the British ruled the colonies, their culture, values, traditions and language were regarded as superior to those of the colonized.
- This often caused a feeling of displacement and rootlessness on the part of the colonized, as they had grown up being constantly reminded of their inferiority.
- Now, after independence, they faced the difficult task of recreating their own identity, bridging the gap between their country's native traditions and values and British ones.
- As people from member countries of the Commonwealth were allowed to immigrate to Britain, lots of people did so in the second half of the 20th century.
- First they were welcomed, as workers were needed after the 2nd World War, but in the 1970s, when more and more workers faced unemployment because of the economic crisis, immigration came to be seen more critically.

- Much **post-colonial writing** – written both in in the former colonies and in Britain – deals with the issue of being caught between two cultures or of trying to find one's identity.

Post-Colonialism in an Anglophone Culture: Nigeria

Keywords:

The Transatlantic Slave Trade: As part of the trade triangle between Europe, Africa and America, enslaved Africans were transported by Western European slave traders to the Americas, where they had to work on tobacco, coffee, sugar, cotton and cocoa plantations. The transatlantic slave trade started in the late 15th/early 16th centuries with the Portuguese as the first nation to engage in it. They were soon followed by other European nations, in particular the British, Spanish, Dutch and French. The trade lasted until the 19th century, when most European countries prohibited slave trade and ended slavery.

Protectorate: (from Latin "protegere" = protect) a country protected and ruled by a superior power (in Nigeria's case, the British).

Republic: a country in which the power is held by representatives elected by the people.

Military rule: government by an authoritarian body controlled by the military instead of being elected by the people.

Nigerian History

A short overview of British rule in Nigeria and the country's way to independence

- Late 15th century: Nigeria starts to be affected by the transatlantic slave trade led by the Portuguese, from whom the Christian religion is initially adopted.
- 18th century: British replace Portuguese as the driving force of the slave trade.
- 1851: Lagos is invaded by British forces and formally annexed in 1865.
- 1901: Nigeria becomes a British protectorate.
- 1914: British protectorates of Northern and Southern Nigeria are joined.
- October 1, 1960: independence movement succeeds in gaining the country's independence from Britain.
- 1963: Nigeria becomes a republic but remains a member of the Commonwealth.
- 1966: Nigerian republic surrenders to military rule.
- 1967: a separatist movement leads to the "Republic of Biafra" and the three-year Nigerian Civil War breaks out with over 1 million people losing their lives.
- 1979: Nigeria becomes a single republic again, but the military seize power again in 1983.
- 1993: plans to establish a 3rd republic are dissolved by the Nigerian dictator General Sani Abacha. After his death in 1998, a 4th republic is established in 1999, after almost three decades of military rule. President Obasanjo rules until 2007, from 2004 under emergency legislation.
- In 2007 Umaru Yar'Adua is elected as President, but dies after a long illness in 2010. Goodluck Ebele Jonathan, who has already been Acting President, succeeds him.
- In 2015, Jonathan loses in the elections against Muhammadu Buhari, who is still President today.
- Obasanjo, Jonathan and Buhari were all at one time in their career military generals.

Nigeria today[1]

- **General information:** The country's official name is "Federal Republic of Nigeria"; it is located on the western coast of Africa. The capital is Abuja, the largest and most important city is Lagos. Due to its booming economy and large population it is often referred to as the "Giant of Africa." The country's geography is diverse, with climates ranging from arid to humid/equatorial.
- **Culture:** With its many languages spoken by various ethnic groups, Nigeria has a very rich and diverse national culture. Nigeria is also known for its English language literature. Among the most famous Nigerian writers are Chinua Achebe ("Things fall apart") and the winner of the Nobel Prize for Literature, Wole Soyinka. Since the 1990s, the Nigerian film-industry, also dubbed "Nollywood", has become important for the whole of Africa.
- **Society:** Nigeria is considered to be the 7th most populous country in the world and the most populous one in Africa, with the world's 3rd highest youth population after India and China. Primary education, free and compulsory, begins at age six and lasts for six years. Secondary education is free and compulsory for three years. There are 400 universities in Nigeria. The population is half urban, half rural. Over 500 languages are spoken by the more than 250 ethnic groups living in Nigeria. English serves as the official language. In addition to English, Hausa, Yoruba, Igbo, Fula, and English Creole are widely spoken. Many of the languages exist in written form. Just over 50% of the population are Muslim (mainly in the north), about 48% are Christians of various denominations.
- The Nigerian **legal and judicial system** contains three codes of law: customary law, Nigerian statute law (following English law), and Sharia (Islamic law).
- **Economy and the environment**: Nigeria is regarded as an emerging global power, due to its oil and natural gas industry, especially in the south of the country. The GDP in 2019 was 446,543 billion USD, i.e. 2,222 per capita.

Challenges

- Nigeria's rapidly growing population causes several problems, e.g. poverty, the inability to provide enough food for everyone without having to rely on food imports.
- 43% of the population are under 15, another 27% are under 30 (2018). The youth literacy rate of the age group 15–24 is 75%. However, unemployment poses a major challenge.
- inequality between men and women
- battling organized crime (especially drug trafficking), child labour and female genital mutilation, to name only a few of the problems the authorities have to deal with
- religious tension between the two major groups is rising, especially in the "middle belt" of the country. Religious fundamentalism can be noticed in both Muslim and Christian communities, a major cause being the uneven distribution of natural resources and hence wealth.

1 Statistical information based on: https://www.bpb.de/internationales/weltweit/innerstaatliche-konflikte/176466/nigeria; https://www.britannica.com/place/Nigeria; https://data.unicef.org/country/nga/; http://data.un.org/en/iso/ng.html; https://www.imd.org

- environmental problems: oil spills pose a serious environmental threat, especially in the Niger delta; inside the growing Nigerian cities, waste management is a problem and the fact that waste is often simply dumped outside the cities results in the pollution of both waterways and groundwater.
- terrorism is another major problem: the Islamic terrorist group Boko Haram is responsible for numerous attacks and the abduction of school children.
- in recent years, the Biafran conflict between the two major ethnic groups in the south of the country, the Igbo and Yoruba – which came to a head in the Biafran Civil War (1967–1970) when the Igbo population of south-east Nigeria attempted to form a republic (Biafra) of their own – has resurfaced; it remains unsolved, without any prospect of a positive outcome.

Glossary – Voices from the African continent: Focus on Nigeria

civil war	Bürgerkrieg
corruption	Korruption
to adapt to sth.	sich an etwas anpassen
to be oppressed by someone	von jemandem unterdrückt werden
citizenship	Nationalität, Staatsangehörigkeit
clash between/of two cultures	das Aufeinanderprallen zweier Kulturen
colonialism; colonizer; colonized	Kolonialismus; der Besiedler; kolonisiert
to discriminate against someone	jemanden benachteiligen/diskriminieren
empire	das Imperium
ethnic minorities	ethnische Minderheiten
ethnicity	Ethnizität, Volkszugehörigkeit
to be excluded (from)	(von) etw. ausgeschlossen sein
to hold racist attitudes	eine rassistische Haltung/Einstellung haben
hostile	feindlich, feindselig, ablehnend
imperialism; imperialistic	Imperialismus; imperialistisch
indigenous	Einheimischer eines Landes
loss of identity	Identitätsverlust
hegemony	Vorherrschaft
famine	Hungersnot
infant mortality	Kindersterblichkeit
to bribe someone	jmd. bestechen
to regain independence	Unabhängigkeit wiedererlangen
independence-minded	nach Unabhängigkeit strebend
to decolonize	in die Unabhängigkeit entlassen
to thrive and prosper	wachsen und gedeihen

Globalization and Global Challenges

Keyword:

Globalization: a worldwide movement, involving the integration of financial, economic and communications systems; often seen as an unstoppable process, affecting people all around the globe, no matter whether they live in industrialized or developing countries, in big cities or rural villages. Transfer of goods, capital and services, as well as communications, made easier, but not everyone profits from the development; smaller economies may suffer.
The world is said to be getting smaller, i.e. it has become a "global village". The term was coined by Marshall McLuhan, a Canadian philosopher and media specialist.

It is not easy to say when globalization actually started:
- Did it start with the discovery of America?
- Does it go even further back in time?
- Is it a phenomenon of the modern era?

Everyone can experience the results of globalization, e.g. when
- travelling
- keeping in touch with friends or business partners in distant countries with the help of new means of communication
- buying goods which come from far away.

Globalization is not always regarded as a positive process:
- Some people fear that individual cultures will finally blend into a single global culture, thereby losing all their characteristic features.
- Thousands of people in developing countries still suffer from malnutrition or die of curable diseases.
- Others work under cruel working conditions, producing goods which will be shipped to and sold in industrialized countries at a low price.
- The latest financial crisis, starting in the USA in 2008, shows that a crisis which starts in one country will ultimately affect other countries as well, as businesses are linked and global trade is the rule.
- Due to increased mobility, diseases like H1N1 ("Swine Flu") or the corona virus COVID-19 can easily spread all around the globe, developing into a pandemic.
- There are always two sides to a coin and there are other advantages, and of course challenges, when it comes to globalization.
- The refugee crisis in Europe can partly be seen as connected with globalization: people from all over the world want to participate in growing economic wealth. Many people from poor countries want to find a better future and leave their homes – just like people have always done over the centuries (e.g. emigration to America in the last two centuries). At the same time, civil and other wars force

people to emigrate. As more and more countries close their borders, problems in many regions are growing. Among these problems are huge refugee camps, and people drowning and starving during dangerous journeys (cf. also page 51).
- Terrorism has become an ongoing global threat which has led to a growing feeling of insecurity in many societies. In some countries (e. g. Israel) terrorist attacks have been a virtually permanent feature of life, going back six or seven decades. In most Western, as well as Middle Eastern countries, what we know as Islamist terrorism (Al Qaeda, the "Islamic State") began with the "9/11" attacks on the World Trade Center in New York and the Pentagon in Washington on September 11, 2001. This led to military reactions from the USA and its allies. Since then, the world has seen a large number of terrorist attacks connected with Islamist ideology (e. g. in France, England, Nigeria, Berlin in Germany) or with the ideology of white supremacy (e. g. in Christchurch in New Zealand or Utøya in Norway).

Aspects of Globalization

Progress
- The development of planes, fast ships and trains made fast transportation of goods from one country to another possible.
- New means of communication, especially the Internet, make the collaboration between business partners easier.
- Multinational companies have branches all over the world, and cost-effectiveness is a decisive factor when new production sites are set up.

Economic challenges

As today's customers wish to buy products at the best cost/performance ratio, the global market has become very **competitive,** with the following (and related) consequences:
- While global players consider efficiency, speed, flexibility and profits as most important, employees are increasingly unable to defend their rights.
- More and more jobs are being outsourced or off-shored to cut down production costs, thereby severely damaging local labour markets.
- When jobs are outsourced to low-wage countries, the workers often work in so-called **"sweatshops"** for long hours at a stretch, earning only minimum wages and under working conditions that are often inhumane. Safety measures in sweatshops are by no means comparable to western standards. Sadly, the lack of efficient safety measures often results in catastrophes. On April 24, 2013 a building housing several garment factories near Bangladesh's capital Dhaka collapsed, resulting in the death of more than 1.000 workers. Despite the fact that factory owners had previously been warned about deep cracks which appeared in the building's structure and had been ordered to evacuate the building, workers were sent in to work. Two weeks after the tragedy, a fire broke out in another clothing factory, killing several people.

- Critics like the Canadian journalist Naomi Klein accuse multinational companies of exploiting the poor and indirectly supporting child labour by only having their own profit in mind.
- Workers often assemble products which they will never be able to afford or do not know how to use, e. g. computers.
- People in developing countries often live under poor conditions, without a decent education or access to new means of communication. Therefore they can't reap the benefits of globalization.
- Advocates of sweatshops claim that these factories provide work for the poor, enabling them to provide for their families.
- They also say that critics of sweatshops argue from a western point of view without considering the actual situation of people in developing countries.
- In order to reduce the number of sweatshops, fair trade is becoming increasingly important. Its aim is to ensure that workers and small-scale producers in poor countries are paid a fair price for their work and products.
- Despite these attempts, a growing number of experts and laypeople alike fear that the gap between the rich and the poor is widening.
- The close links and collaboration between companies all across the globe is both a blessing and a curse.
- The financial crisis which started in the USA in 2008 shows that a national crisis can quickly develop into a global one, affecting the economies of numerous countries.

Ecological challenges and the role of customers

Environmental pollution is growing rapidly. The following factors in particular create global problems:
- **Exhaust fumes** from factories are one important factor.
- Over the last decades the number of **vehicles** on the roads has steadily increased. Cars are no longer found only in industrialized countries.
- The number of people travelling by **plane** is also greater than ever, due to the fact that plane tickets have become affordable for a larger number of people. Short-haul **flights** have become particularly popular.
- **Food-miles:** Whereas some years ago many people bought fruit and vegetables locally and ate seasonal products, they now want to eat strawberries and cherries in December. So more goods are air-freighted. Ecologically conscious customers ask themselves whether it is better to buy local products than food (even fair trade products) which has been flown across continents.
- Everyone leaves a **carbon footprint** (emission of greenhouse gases from factories, cars, trains, planes, etc) either directly or indirectly.
- **Greenhouse gases** cause chemical damage to the atmosphere (e. g. ozone hole) as well as global warming (see below).

Global warming and its consequences

- As Al Gore explains in his film *An Inconvenient Truth,* greenhouse gases form a layer around the earth trapping heat and thereby causing the temperature on the ground to rise ("global warming").
- There are many consequences of climate change, e.g. floods in coastal areas, heavy rainfall in some regions and drought in others, melting of polar ice-caps.
- Biodiversity is threatened, as many plants, flowers and animals die out. Desertification (see below) is an increasingly frequent phenomenon today.

Environmental sustainability

- Due to overgrazing[1], over-extraction (overdraft) of groundwater, unwise use of water resources, e.g. diverting rivers for industrial use or human consumption, deforestation ("slash-and-burn farming") and rising soil salinity, vast areas of land in relatively dry areas deteriorate and become useless (desertification).
- Environmental sustainability is on the agenda of many governments and has been an important topic at various summits to date.

Attempts to reduce global warming

- The **Kyoto Protocol** from 2005 aimed to reduce the emission of greenhouse gases by an annual 5.2% by the year 2012, taking 1990 levels as a basis for most countries.
- **2015: Paris UN Climate Change Conference.** A global agreement on the reduction of climate change (the Paris Agreement) has been reached and adopted by 195 countries. Among the decisions made was the resolution to limit the long-term increase of global average temperature to well below 2°C above pre-industrial levels. The agreement went into effect on 4 November 2016, as enough countries ratified it. The USA withdrew their consent to the agreement under President Trump.
- On his first day in office President Biden fulfilled a promise he made during his election campaign and returned to the Paris Climate Agreement.

Fridays for Future

- In August 2018, Greta Thunberg, a then 16-year-old Swedish climate change activist, started protesting outside the Swedish parliament in Stockholm in order to raise awareness of the dangers of climate change.
- According to Thunberg, politicians are not taking enough action against climate change, which is putting our planet's future at risk. Thunberg's solitary school strikes, which she still carries out regularly, soon caught the attention of the media in countries all over the world.
- Up to May 2019, an estimated 1.4 million teenagers and young adults worldwide have followed her example by going on strike from school every Friday and protesting against climate change. This movement is known as "Fridays for Future".
- Greta Thunberg has delivered several public speeches in which she has put pres-

1 One speaks of "overgrazing" if the number of cattle on a piece of land is too high to be sustainable (in the long term).

sure on politicians and world leaders to combat climate change more swiftly and resolutely. She spoke at various important global meetings, e.g. the United Nations Climate Change Conference in Katowice, Poland in December 2018 and at the World Economic Forum in Davos, Switzerland in January 2019.

- The speed of the reaction and the immense sums of money provided by governments during the corona crisis seem to prove Fridays for Future's point: Immediate global action is possible, but the governments all over the world do not seem to regard an effective fight against global warming as a top priority.

Conflict between economic and ecological aspects of globalization

- Companies face global competition: cost-effectiveness and profits seem more important than ecological issues.
- Some governments refrain from setting up strict laws to protect the environment, as this might drive away multinational companies that offer employment.
- As environmental pollution does not stop at borders, international cooperation is crucial – and will become even more so in future.

Corona – a virus that changed the world

- COVID-19 (Coronavirus disease, 2019) is a highly infectious disease with symptoms similar to those of common flu, e.g. fever, cough and shortness of breath. Due to intense and efficient research, several vaccines against COVID-19 have been developed, but the availability in different countries varies, as does the vaccination strategy. Most countries, e.g. Germany prioritise certain population groups regarded as vulnerable, before vaccinating other sections of the population.
- The number of people having received at least one vaccination against COVID-19 is growing rapidly. The WHO reports that "as of 20 April 2021, a total of 843,158,196 vaccine doses have been administered".
- People with a weakened immune system, as well as older persons, run a higher risk of experiencing severe symptoms, in worst cases multi-organ failure, but most cases only exhibit light symptoms.
- COVID-19 was first identified in Wuhan, China in December 2019. It is thought to have been transmitted from animals to humans at a seafood and animal market in Wuhan. On December 31, 2019 Chinese authorities informed the WHO (World Health Organization) of the outbreak of a new form of pneumonia. Since then it has spread across the world.
- On 12 January 2020, WHO named this previously unknown form of corona virus disease COVID-19, and on March 20, 2020, it was officially declared a pandemic.
- As of April 21, 2021 more than 142,238,073 cases had been reported, with outbreaks in countries around the globe.

How countries and governments attempt to tackle the virus

- Encouraging the public to take up basic protective measures for the sake of both themselves and others, e.g. frequently washing one's hands, avoid touching one's face, practise respiratory hygiene, social distancing, wearing face masks.

- In some countries wearing a mask or covering your mouth and nose with a scarf or piece of cloth is obligatory when using public transport or going shopping. Only a limited number of shoppers is allowed to enter supermarkets and shops (if they are open at all) in order to avoid too many people on the same spot, which would increase the risk of infection. In parts of Germany a negative COVID-19 test result is necessary when wishing to shop for goods not necessary for basic needs or when in need of close contact services. Undertaking rapid COVID-19 self-tests or providing a negative test result in writing twice a week is mandatory for German teachers and students (April 20221).
- In order to "flatten the curve", i.e. restrict the number of new infections so that health services can still cope, many countries have imposed restrictions: closing schools, kindergartens, restaurants and shops not necessary to fulfil basic needs, restricting or banning visitors from hospitals and nursing homes, and imposing travel restrictions, e.g. closing borders or imposing quarantine on people crossing national borders. People wishing to enter Germany face a test obligation and are only allowed to enter the country if they can provide proof of a negative test result not older than 48 hours. There are a few exemptions from this rule, e.g. for people who live in neighbouring countries but work in Germany.
- People are encouraged to work from home to limit personal contacts. Events that attract large crowds, such as concerts, theatre performances and festivals have been cancelled.
- Hospitals and clinics in some countries face difficulties meeting the increasing demand for intensive care due to COVID-19.

Consequences of these governmental measures

- Economic: Closing shops puts severe strain on shop owners and employees. Many governments, including the German, have installed programs that offer some financial compensation. It is feared that many companies will not survive the restrictions.
- Personal: The number of people working from home has increased drastically, as a result of schools and kindergartens closing when the number of new infections oversteps a certain mark. Many parents struggle to balance childcare and work. Governments have encouraged families not to visit grandparents and family members at risk or have even forbidden visits, which can lead to isolation and loneliness. Digital media play an important role in keeping in touch with one another while being physically apart.
- Neighbourly help has become more important, e.g. doing grocery shopping for those at risk and checking regularly on those affected by COVID-19.
- Among measures taken to "flatten the curve" are: limiting personal contacts to the absolutely necessary, keeping a physical distance when encountering others, keeping rooms ventilated, thoroughly cleaning your hands and wearing a mask. The increasing number of vaccinations administered is also regarded as an efficient way to battle COVID-19. (The book was written in April 2021.)

Media and communication

Many people experience the advantages of communication on the Internet on a daily basis. Social networking communities like *Facebook* and *MySpace* enable their users to find long-lost friends and to connect with people all over the world, no matter whether they live next door or on a different continent.

Founded by Harvard students Mark Zuckerberg, Eduardo Saverin, Andrew McCollum, Dustin Moskovitz and Chris Hughes in 2004, *Facebook* has become the biggest social networking community with more than 900 million users worldwide (May 2012).
Its development was also made into a film *(The Social Network,* directed by David Fincher in 2010). *Facebook* CEO Mark Zuckerberg has criticized the film for not being true to the development of Facebook.

On *Facebook,* users are able to set up their own profiles and to customize them according to their wishes, e. g. by uploading pictures and information about themselves or by adjusting the privacy settings of their profiles to restrict others from seeing them. Users can also keep track on what their friends are doing and chat with them. As there are special apps for gadgets like smartphones or tablets, users can access their *Facebook* accounts on the go.
While using *Facebook* itself is free of charge, the network has repeatedly been accused of collecting and exploiting its users' private data.
Despite being confronted with considerable criticism regarding issues like privacy protection, cyber bullying or identity theft, *Facebook* is immensely popular worldwide and made its stock market debut in May 2012.

On his own *Facebook* page, Mark Zuckerberg says that "(he's) trying to make the world a more open place[2]". Nevertheless, countries like China, Iran and Pakistan have banned people's access to Facebook.

On a political level, *Facebook* is also said to have played a role in the "Arab Spring" which started in December 2010. Generally speaking, this can be described as a series of protests and demonstrations in several countries of the Arab World, i. e. Tunisia, Egypt and Libya to force rulers from power. The success of these revolutions has partly been accredited to social media like *Facebook* and *Twitter,* as protests, marches, strikes and other examples of civil resistance were organized and coordinated with the help of social media.
Some have therefore suggested calling these revolutions 'Facebook revolutions', whereas others say that although social media might have helped to organize civil resistance and to make the state of things in Arab countries public to the western world, people's active involvement in a revolution is still the key essential for its success.

Facebook and the companies belonging to it, e. g. Instagram and WhatsApp, have

2 https://www.facebook.com/zuck (August 8, 2012)

certainly revolutionized our way of communicating and interacting with each other. Never before has it been easier to broadcast oneself and to stay in touch with people all over the globe, as well as to access news and information from anywhere around the world in real time.
Despite all these achievements, Facebook has been criticized by both opponents and users for a number of reasons. One reason is that users who report hate speech, rumours, incitement to violence and offensive posts that violate Facebook's community standards often received only standardized answers or no feedback at all. In addition to that, many users found that Facebook did not remove those posts and/or did nothing to avoid the spread of hate speech etc.
The social network's protection of its users' Internet privacy and the safekeeping and storing of personal data is another point of criticism.
In March 2018 it was revealed that Facebook had mishandled user data, enabling Cambridge Analytica, a political consulting firm, to access and evaluate the data of 87 million users and attempting to influence the presidential elections of 2016 in favour of Donald Trump.
As a consequence, Mark Zuckerberg was called to a US Senate committee hearing where he was questioned on Facebook's use and misuse of user data.
In 2018, the European Union insisted that Mark Zuckerberg should in person attend an official hearing on the same topic.

The UN and the EU

The UN

- October 24, 1945: A group of 51 countries founded the United Nations (UN) as a replacement/successor for the League of Nations.
- The UN headquarters is located in New York City and the current Secretary General is António Guterres.
- The UN has 193 member states (April 2021).
- It defends human rights and fundamental freedoms.

Five of six **main organs** of the UN (General Assembly, Security Council, Economic and Social Council, Trusteeship Council and Secretariat) are located in New York City, while the International Court of Justice is in The Hague in the Netherlands.
There are **various programs** and funds affiliated to the UN. Two of the best known are UNICEF (United Nations Children's Fund) and the UNHCR (Office of the United Nations High Commissioner for Refugees). The latter deals with the needs of refugees and displaced persons in post-conflict countries, e. g. Djibouti.

Aims of the UN

- to preserve international peace and security
- to promote friendly relations between member countries
- to support international cooperation with regard to economic, social and cultural as well as humanitarian issues

- Apart from **peacekeeping** and **peacemaking** operations, **peace-building** has become more and more important.
- Here the UN and its affiliated organizations work to equip national groups with the necessary skills in conflict management, and to ensure that lasting peace can be established.
- Currently (Spring 2021) the UN is involved in 12 peacekeeping operations, e.g. in Cyprus, Mali and South Sudan.
- **Humanitarian aid** is also of major importance, e.g. providing relief for people affected by either man-made or natural disasters, and helping refugees and displaced persons.
- Other main concerns of the UN are **international law and development** (e.g. sustainable development, agriculture, international trade).

The EU

- Currently 27 states belong to the European Union (EU). The newest members are Bulgaria and Romania, which both joined the EU on January 1, 2007, and Croatia, which became a member on July 1, 2013.
- After the 2nd World War there was a desire for a united Europe in order to prevent extreme forms of nationalism. The European Coal and Steel Community, the European Economic Community (EEC) and the European Atomic Energy Community (Euratom) were merged into the European Community (EC) in 1967.
- The EU as we know it came into existence in 1993, when the Maastricht Treaty – which among other things initiated the euro as common currency – was ratified. The individual member states came to be regarded as a single global player.
- At present the EU faces the challenge of maintaining its unity – and indeed remaining a union at all – in the face of the refugee crisis. The countries of the EU have very different attitudes to solving the refugee problem.
- In 2020, the United Kingdom left the EU ("Brexit", cf. p. 33).

Aims of the EU

- to promote prosperity and social progress with European citizenship for its peoples while still keeping their diversity alive
- to promote friendly relations between member countries
- to guarantee freedom and justice for the European peoples
- to internationally represent the member states with a single voice, tackling the various challenges of globalization, as well as respecting human rights

When it comes to defence, the individual member countries are sovereign. However, there is military cooperation in peacekeeping missions.
The three main groups which make up the EU are the **Council of Ministers,** the **European Parliament,** the **European Commission.**
Although the EU has no official capital, the official seat of the European Commission, the Council of the European Union and the second seat of the European Parliament are located in Brussels, Belgium.

International peacekeeping

International peacekeeping is one of the aims of the UN:

- Once peace has been established in a country or region, peacekeepers are sent to the country or region in question to oversee the peace process.
- This can be done by overseeing elections, providing reconstruction aid and supervising the withdrawal of combatants.
- Very often, UN peacekeepers are soldiers, but they can also be police officers or other civilian personnel.
- The UN Security Council authorizes peacekeeping missions, which are then carried out by the international community.
- Many of these missions are organized and led by the UN itself. There is no UN army. While the troops acting as peacekeepers are under the control of the UN, they still belong to the armed forces of their country of origin. The UN itself is controlled by the Security Council and the UN Secretariat.
- This reduces the risk that one peacekeeping party only follows its own interests.
- Regional organizations (e.g. NATO) can be authorized by the UN to lead peacekeeping missions. These regional organizations can also organize peacekeeping missions of their own.

Migration – a global challenge

- Migration has been a worldwide phenomenon since the beginning of human history.
- People have had a number of reasons for leaving their places of origin: poverty and the dream of a better life elsewhere, climatic reasons, wars and civil wars or religious persecution, to name only the most important.[3]
- One has to distinguish between migrants and refugees:
- **Migrants** leave their countries of origin for a limited period of time or permanently, usually for economic reasons. They might have job offers in a different country, or they might have heard of good opportunities. Examples of this are emigration from European countries to the USA in the 19th century, immigrants from Poland to the Ruhr district also during the 19th century, migrant workers inside Europe today, for example to help on farms, as carers for elderly people, or to work in hospitals, and people from Africa trying to find better living conditions in Europe.
- **Refugees** usually flee their homes in order to get away from persecution or wars. Examples of this at present are the Muslim Rohingya from Myanmar, Venezuelans to other South American and Central American countries, or Syrian or Afghan people to Europe. An important example from the past are the Jews from Germany and other countries who had to flee from the Nazis.
- The International Migration Report of the UN from 2019 states that most migrants

3 Information based on:
https://www.un.org/en/development/desa/population/migration/publications/migrationreport/docs/MigrationReport2019_Highlights.pdf
https://www.unhcr.org/figures-at-a-glance.html
https://refugeesmigrants.un.org/refugees-compact
https://www.refugeesinternational.org/reports-overview

worldwide go to countries in Asia, followed by Europe and North America. The countries with the most migrants are the USA, followed by Saudi Arabia and Germany. These migrants for the most part seek – and find – employment in the countries of destination. They are not refugees, but quite a large number of them are illegal immigrants. According to the UN, there were 272 million migrants in 2019.

- The UNHCR (United Nations refugee agency) states in its statistical report for 2020 that the world is now witnessing the highest levels of displacement on record. 79.5 million people around the world have been forced to leave their homes. Among them are nearly 26 million refugees, over half of whom are under the age of 18. 45.7 million are internal refugees, i. e. they flee from one part of the country to another (Nigeria is one example). There are 4.2 million asylum seekers worldwide. However, 73 % of refugees stay in neighbouring countries: Syrian refugees mainly flee to Turkey, Jordan and other countries close by. More than half the refugees worldwide come at present from Syria, Afghanistan and South Sudan.
- In 2020 Turkey hosted the largest refugee population worldwide, with 3.6 million refugees and asylum seekers, followed by Colombia (1.8 million), Lebanon (1.6 million) , Pakistan (1.4 million) and Uganda (1.4 million). Most refugees come from Syria (6.6 million), Venezuela (3.7 million), Afghanistan (2.7 million), South Sudan (2.2. million) and Myanmar (1.1 million).
- There are also millions of stateless people who have been denied nationality and access to basic rights such as education, healthcare, employment and freedom of movement.
- About 1 percent of the world's population have fled their homes.
- Nearly 1 person is forcibly displaced every two seconds as a result of conflict or persecution.
- The fact that most refugees seek help in neighbouring, not always wealthy countries can cause major problems there: the population of these countries has to share access to education, healthcare and jobs with the refugees. Compared to rich countries like Germany, countries like Jordan or the Lebanon find it far more difficult to cope with the situation. Colombia is another example of these conflicts: it is a country which is only just beginning to overcome the effects of a civil war. Recently it has also been the destination of over 1 million refugees from Venezuela.
- On the other hand, migration always also means enrichment: the destination country will, with time, integrate the new arrivals. Their culture, beliefs and customs will become part of the country, thus leading to a more diverse culture in general.
- Many migrants and refugees want to return to their home countries if the situation allows them to. Seasonal migrants, for example, usually leave their families behind and return when their work has finished for the year. Many refugees want to return to their old home after the end of a war, others would like to stay in their new home and build a new life there.

Glossary – Globalization

Americanization	Amerikanisierung
anti-globalist	Globalisierungsgegner/-kritiker
backwardness	Rückständigkeit
company philosophy	Geschäfts-/Firmenphilosophie
competition; to be competitive	Konkurrenz(kampf)/Wettbewerb; konkurrenzfähig sein
corporate identity	Firmenimage
crop diseases	Krankheiten von Pflanzen/Saatgut
debt relief	Schuldenerlass, Entschuldung
desertification	die Desertifikation/Wüstenbildung, das Vordringen der Wüste
developing countries	Entwicklungsländer
development aid	Entwicklungshilfe
driving forces of globalization	die Antriebskräfte der Globalisierung
drought	Dürren, Dürreperioden
earth's atmosphere	die Erdatmosphäre
economic growth	Wirtschaftswachstum
economic prosperity	ökonomischer Wohlstand
emerging markets	Schwellenländer
environmental commitment	Umwelteinsatz
environmental damage	Umweltzerstörung
environmentally friendly	umweltfreundlich
expansion of capitalism	Ausbreitung des Kapitalismus
fair trade	fairer Handel
floods	Hochwasser, Überschwemmungen
global interconnection	globale Querverbindungen
global marketplace	globaler Marktplatz
global player	Weltfirma
global super power	eine globale Supermacht
global warming	Erderwärmung
greenhouse gases	Treibhausgase
human rights	Menschenrechte
human-generated carbon dioxide	durch Menschen produziertes Kohlenstoffdioxid
increase profit margins	die Gewinnspanne erhöhen
Industrial Age	das Industriezeitalter

industrial nations	Industrieländer/-nationen
interdependence of economy and ecology	gegenseitige Abhängigkeit/Verflechtung von Ökonomie und Ökologie
international stock markets	internationale Börsenmärkte
investment climate	Investitionsbedingungen
labour laws	Arbeitsgesetze
labour market	Arbeitsmarkt
long-range goals	langfristige Ziele
low-wage countries	Niedriglohnländer
mass communication; mass media	Massenkommunikation; -medien
mass tourism	Massentourismus
melting of glaciers	das Schmelzen von Gletschern
micro-credits	Kleinkredite
NGO (non-governmental organization)	Nichtregierungsorganisation
outsourcing	Produktionsverlagerung
political turmoil	politischer Aufruhr, politische Turbulen-zen
pollution	Verschmutzung
population overshoot, overpopulation, excess of population	Überbevölkerung
poverty	Armut
reduce greenhouse gas emissions	den Ausstoß von Treibhausgasen redu-zieren
reduce the cost of production	die Produktionskosten senken
rise in global temperature	ein weltweiter Temperaturanstieg
robotized production	computergesteuerte Produktion/Ferti-gung
short-haul flights	Kurzstreckenflüge
surface transport	Bodentransport
supremacy	Vormachtsstellung, Überlegenheit
sustainability	Nachhaltigkeit, Zukunftsfähigkeit
sweatshop	ausbeuterischer Betrieb
trade	Handel
trademark policy	Markenpolitik
undernutrition, malnutrition	Unterernährung; Mangelernährung
unemployment	Arbeitslosigkeit
working conditions	Arbeitsbedingungen

The Impact of Shakespearean Drama on Young Audiences Today

The Elizabethan Age

Keyword:

The Elizabethan Age: named after Queen Elizabeth I, born 1533, crowned 1558, died 1603 (reign of 45 years)

Politics and economics

- England emerged as a world power
- international trade → rise of capitalism
- strongest naval force (defeat of Spanish Armada in 1588)
- internal problems: constant clash between Catholics and Protestants: firm establishment of Protestant Church with Elizabeth as head of the Church of England

Exploration of the New World

- Sir Francis Drake
- Sir Walter Raleigh

Culture

Keyword:

The Golden Age: term used for the Renaissance in Britain at the time of Elizabeth I

- freedom of spirit → imagination
- Greek and Roman thought
- domestic study of the Bible, widely read and heard
- opened new worlds of history and poetry, stimulated English culture
- cultural flowering: theatre, music, poetry, art, architecture
- Writers: William Shakespeare, Christopher Marlowe, Edmund Spenser
- Architect: Inigo Jones (introduced Italianate architecture to England)
- Composers: Thomas Tallis, William Byrd

The era was dominated by contrast: life for ordinary people could be hard, but economic growth also meant better conditions for many.
negative aspects:

- harsh criminal laws
- whipping and hanging for minor offences
- illiteracy
- short life-expectancy
- no rights for women

positive aspects:
- public provision for the poor (possible because of economic growth)
- few beggars

The Elizabethan World Picture

The Great Chain of Being

- vertical chain, hierarchically ordered → universal order
- every single speck of creation a link in the chain → almost infinite chain
- place in the chain determined by the relative proportion of spirit and matter
- the more spirit the higher the place in the chain

Hierarchy of the chain

God
⇩
Angels
⇩
Man
existence, life, feeling and understanding
→ the microcosm
⇩
higher animals
(having touch, memory, movement and hearing)
⇩
animals like ants
(having touch, memory, movement)
⇩
animals like shellfish
(having touch)
⇩
plants
existence and life
vegetable class
⇩
elements, liquids, metals
mere existence
inanimate class

(higher animals, animals like ants, animals like shellfish:) sensitive class – existence, life, feeling

The hierarchical order also applies within the classes:
- Water is nobler than earth.
- Gold is nobler than silver.
- The oak is nobler than the bramble.
- The lion is nobler than the dog.

The corresponding planes

Different segments of the chain are reflected in other segments. This means there is universal interdependence, i. e. correspondences.

Corresponding planes

- divine and angelic
- man or microcosm
- universe or macrocosm
- lower creation
- commonwealth or body politic

The planes were connected by an immense net of correspondences.

Keyword:

Correspondences: They existed everywhere. [...] When things were properly ordered, reason ruled the emotions, just as a king ruled his subjects, the parent ruled the child, and the sun governed the planets. But when disorder was present in one realm, it was correspondingly reflected in other realms.[1]

Examples of correspondences

macrocosm/microcosm	storms and earthquakes in the macrocosm ↔ passions of human beings
macrocosm/body politic	hierarchy of sun/moon/rainbow ↔ hierarchy of king/princes/governors
body politic/microcosm	debates of king and council ↔ commotions in a person's mind

Elizabethan thinking in terms of correspondences led to the abundance of images in Elizabethan literature.

1 Quelle: http://academic.brooklyn.cuny.edu/english/melani/cs6/ren.html

Elements and humours

As the human being was seen as a microcosm (literally, a "little world"), it reflected the structure of the world as a whole, the macrocosm. The world was composed of four "elements" (earth, water, air, fire), the qualities of which were founded on the notions of hot and cold, dry and moist.
Correspondingly, the human body was composed of four substances called "humours" with characteristics corresponding to the four elements. Imbalance or "disorder" among the humours, i. e. when they did not exist in proper proportion to each other, caused illness.

element	humour	common quality
earth	melancholy	cold and dry
water	phlegm	cold and moist
air	blood	hot and moist
fire	choler	hot and dry

Elizabethan Theatre

Theatres in Elizabethan London were venues of mass entertainment.

Theatres

- were situated outside the city
- offered performances every day
- presented plays, dances and music
- were also used for bear baiting, cruel killing of bears
- were attended by people from all social ranks.

- All performances were presented during the day.
- There was no lighting or special sound effects.
- Women's roles were played by men.
- The audience could smoke, eat, and drink.

→ Imagination depended totally on the language used in the play.

Common complaints about the theatre

- disorderly
- corrupts youth
- leads to evil and immoral ("ungodly") character and behaviour
- stage stories are morally uncontrolled and primitive, not religiously inspiring
- leads to lewdness
- keep people away from work and prayer
- attracts criminals

Elizabethan Drama

Important playwrights: William Shakespeare, Christopher Marlowe *(Dr. Faustus),* Ben Jonson *(The Alchemist),* later John Webster *(The Duchess of Malfi).*
Before the age of Elizabethan drama, plays were usually based on religious themes. Elizabethan drama focuses on more secular issues.

Types of Elizabethan play

Histories

Playgoers learned about England's 'heroic past', e.g. in *Edward II* (by Christopher Marlowe) or in Shakespeare's *Richard II, Richard III, Henry IV, Henry V,* etc.
Dramas like *Julius Caesar, Antony and Cleopatra* or *Macbeth* are not considered histories, because they do not focus on Britain's 'heroic' past but on the individual tragedies of their protagonists.

Tragedies

- end in a catastrophe (death of the character)
- catastrophe is a result of a character's flaw (Macbeth's ambition, Othello's jealousy)
- tragic hero still arouses interest in his fate, sympathy

Comedies

- happy ending
- often bawdy
- the audience went there for a good laugh
- sexual allusion and undertones very frequent even in tragedy: comic passages with strong sexual allusions often serve as comic relief (porter in *Macbeth,* Mercutio in *Romeo and Juliet)*

Romances

Shakespeare's late comedies (e.g. *The Winter's Tale, The Tempest)* are generally classified as romances. They are distinguished from comedies by certain elements:
- redemption, forgiveness, reuniting of long lost family members
- magic
- pastoral setting (beautiful nature, virgin island)

Elizabethan Poetry

Sonnets

Keyword:

Sonnet form: originally from Italy, 14th century
Sonnets were made popular by Francesco Petrarca (engl.: Petrarch)
The fashion of sonnet writing spread to France and England.

Important Elizabethan sonnet writers
- Thomas Wyatt (introduced sonnets to England, translations from Petrarca)
- Sir Philipp Sidney
- Edmund Spenser
- John Donne
- William Shakespeare X

The Italian (Petrarchan) sonnet

	rhyme scheme	
octave/octet	a b b a	quatrain
	a b b a	quatrain
turn		
sestet	c d e	*tercet*
	c d e	*tercet*

Characteristics of the sonnet
- addressed to a beloved person
- 14 lines
- clearly defined rhyme scheme (the most common seen above)
- divided into an octet and a sestet
- turn after the octave

The turn after the octave is a shift of thought or feeling, often indicated by "but" or "yet".
Variations of rhyme scheme within the conventional structure are justified by the function they serve.

The English (Shakespearean) sonnet

	rhyme scheme	
octave	a b a b	quatrain
	c d c d	quatrain
sestet	e f e f	quatrain
turn		
	g g	*couplet*

The turn in the English sonnet occurs after the third quatrain. The couplet is a conclusion or a summary. However, one should still be aware that there can be the traditional turn after the octave. A sonnet may also be structured in terms of the three quatrains. Ideally there should be "three turns of the screw" in the three quatrains, before the point is driven home in the couplet.

Shakespeare's sonnets

- Shakespeare wrote 154 sonnets.
- Sonnets 1 to 126 are addressed to a young man.
- Sonnets 127 to 154 are addressed to a "dark lady".

Main themes: love, beauty, transience, old age, death

The **basic metre** is iambic pentameter but Shakespeare does not use it slavishly. Metre is used functionally, e.g.
- regular metre: harmony, peace, tranquillity, balance, stability, etc.
- irregular metre: disharmony, confusion, parody

Shakespeare's language

Prose

Ordinary speech, no metric pattern

Visual clues

- Printed lines extend from the left to the right margin.
- Lines do not start with a capital letter (unless following a full stop).

Function of prose

- often used by low status characters (murderers, servants, craftsmen, etc.), but not as a dogmatic rule
- low comedy (especially dirty jokes) often written in prose
- suggests a realistic tone
- used for bantering, e.g. Beatrice and Benedick
- sometimes indicates madness (Lady Macbeth, Lear)

Verse

Rhymes

- usually occur as rhymed couplets (aa bb cc)
- rhyme pair in iambic pentameter called "heroic couplet"

Function of rhymes

They often serve the same function as in a sonnet: concluding a scene, hammering the point home ("capping couplet").

Rhymes are used for
- highly lyrical passages
- choruses, prologues, epilogues
- romantic passages which are slightly over the top
- supernatural beings (witches, fairies).

Blank Verse

- an **unrhymed iambic pentameter**
- the standard verse in Shakespeare's plays

Blank verse resembles prose in that the final words of the lines do not rhyme in any regular pattern.
Unlike in prose, there is a recognizable metre: most (not necessarily all) lines are in iambic pentameter, i.e. they consist of ten syllables alternating unstressed and stressed syllables: da**dum** da**dum** da**dum** da**dum** da**dum**.

Example:
Give **me** your **han**d bef**ore** this **ho**ly **fri**ar.
I **am** your **hus**band **if** you l**ike** of **me**.
(from: *Much Ado About Nothing*, Act V, Scene 4, ll. 58-59)

Visual clues

- Printed lines do not extend from left to right margin.
- Lines start with capital letters.

Function of blank verse

Unlike rhyme, which sounds artificial, blank verse comes close to the natural speaking rhythms of English. Yet it makes it sound more elevated, less ordinary.

Other types of metre

Dimeter

A ***drum*** *a* ***drum***
*Mac**beth** doth **come.** (Macbeth,* Act I, Scene 3)
→ echoing the drum

Tetrameter

Double, double toil *and* ***trouble,***
Fire burn *and* ***caul****dron* ***bubble.*** *(Macbeth,* Act IV, Scene 1)

Fair *is* ***foul*** *and* ***foul*** *is* ***fair.*** *(Macbeth,* Act I, Scene 1)

The tetrameter here is used for spells (from the witches' speeches in *Macbeth).*

Shakespeare's Relevance to Modern Audiences

Pros	Cons
timeless themes – love – hate – rejection – jealousy – envy – greed – ambition – revenge – equivocation – appearance and reality etc.	outdated world picture
authentic characters, human and understandable modern adaptation in all literary genres – opera – musical – drama – novel – film – poetry – pop song Hollywood blockbusters	outdated attitudes and values regarding – gender roles – loyalty – generations – science – religion – superstition – social hierarchies etc.
aesthetics of language ubiquitous language in – idioms – proverbs – quotations – titles – allusions	outdated language partly incomprehensible imagery allusions and jokes

Glossary – Shakespeare and the Elizabethan Age

actor actress (not in Elizabethan times)	Schauspieler Schauspielerin
aside	beiseite gesprochener Text
blank verse	Blankvers
play drama tragedy comedy history romance	Schauspiel, Drama Drama Tragödie Komödie Historiendrama Romanze
Elizabethan age/era	elisabethanisches Zeitalter
enter exit; exeunt	tritt auf (Regieanweisung) geht ab; gehen ab
fatal flaw	verhängnisvolle Schwäche (des Tragödienhelden)
groundlings	stehende Zuschauer im elisabethanischen Theater
hero heroine	Held Heldin
Jacobean	aus der Zeit James I.
Master of the Revels	für Theater zuständiger Beamter
medieval the Middle Ages	mittelalterlich Mittelalter
performance to perform	Vorstellung vorführen
playhouse	Theater
playing company troupe The Lord Chamberlain's Men The Admiral's Men	Theatertruppe (berühmte Truppen der Shakespeare-Zeit)
playwright dramatist	Bühnenautor
Renaissance	Renaissance
scenery	Kulisse
soliloquy	Monolog/Selbstgespräch
stage stage props	Bühne Requisiten
wit	Geist, Witz

Visions of the Future

Utopia and Dystopia

Keywords:

Utopian literature: a fictional text dealing with an ideal (future) society.

Dystopian literature: a fictional text dealing with a future society in which human freedom is severely limited. A dystopia often criticizes our present-day society by exposing trends and tendencies towards totalitarian control.

Extrapolation: here: fictitious description of elements of a future society on the basis of present day phenomena and developments. The writer criticizes his or her own society by demonstrating what certain trends may lead to or what point society has already reached.

School Classics – Background Knowledge

The three novels presented here are so well known (not only) in English-speaking countries that you may encounter references to any one of these works in numerous texts. They will be presented here in the order of their first publication.

Aldous Huxley: *Brave New World*

Written in 1931, set in the distant future (26th century)

Generally known elements

- total control of society by in-vitro fertilization, artificial laboratory breeding, "cloning" of work force, and conditioning
- society strictly divided into Alpha, Beta, Gamma, Delta and Epsilon people with Alphas constituting the ruling class and Epsilons constituting a slave-like work force
- natural reproduction outlawed, sex as pure entertainment, monogamy regarded as unnatural and immoral
- people kept happy by means of a drug called "soma"
- religion replaced by a strong belief in technology and science

Extrapolation of developments of 20th century society in *Brave New World*

- belief in science, technology and progress
- misuse of science
- political and economic control and manipulation
- mass production and mass consumption
- decline of religion and values
- decline of educational standards
- drugs

- mass entertainment
- sensationalism

George Orwell: *1984*

Written in 1948, hence about a future society

Generally known elements

- **Big Brother:** constant surveillance, "Big Brother is watching you." (Orwell's Big Brother: origin of the name of the popular present-day TV show)
- **Newspeak:** invention of a new, simplified form of the English language to manipulate thought, complex (i. e. critical) thinking cannot be put into words anymore Examples:
  - words like *goodthink, oldthink, crimethink:* simplify expressions of thought, make them imprecise, one-dimensional, eventually devoid of meaning
  - euphemisms like *Miniluv, Minipax, Minitrue:* sound positive, conceal their true meaning (Ministry of Love = police, Ministry of Peace = war, Ministry of Truth = propaganda)
  - **rewriting of history:** books and newspapers are manipulated

Extrapolation of elements of 20th century society in *1984*

- intrusion in people's privacy, spying on people: (Nazi Germany, Soviet Union)
- propaganda, misuse of mass media (Nazi Germany, Soviet Union)
- psychological torture

21st century relevance

- electronic surveillance
- digital tracking
- fake news

Ray Bradbury: *Fahrenheit 451*

Written in 1953, set in the future

Generally known elements

- **451 degrees Fahrenheit:** the temperature at which paper starts to burn
- society marked by entertainment, speed, restlessness and superficiality: extremely fast driving, multi-screen television at high volume with very shallow programmes, constant exposure to sound and advertising (individually by the wearing of ear-plugs or collectively by loudspeaker announcements)
- critical thought impeded as books are forbidden
- the firemen's job: to burn books

Extrapolation of elements of 20th century society in *Fahrenheit 451*

- burning of books (Nazi Germany)
- atomic bomb (Hiroshima)
- rise of television and audio media, effect on reading
- speeding-up in all areas of life: transport, communications, work, production, consumption
- dominance of entertainment
- decline of education

Science Fiction

Science fiction is a genre of fiction dealing with imaginary content such as future settings and futuristic science and technology.
As opposed to fantasy, its imaginary elements are largely possible within scientifically postulated laws of nature.
The settings for science fiction are often contrary to known reality, but most science fiction relies on potential scientific explanations or solutions to various fictional elements. There is no magic involved.

Elements of Science Fiction

- a setting in the future
- a setting in outer space (e.g. spaceflight), in other worlds, or in remote regions of the earth (underground, bottom of the sea)
- characters that include aliens, mutants, androids, or humanoid robots
- technology that is futuristic (e.g. ray guns, teleportation machines, humanoid computers, space ships, artificial planets)
- scientific principles that are new and have overcome known laws of nature, for example time travel, wormholes, or faster-than-light travel
- new and different societies, especially post-apocalyptic worlds
- paranormal abilities such as mind control, telepathy, telekinesis, and teleportation

There is considerable overlap between utopia/dystopia and science fiction.
However, one may say that science fiction is a lot more concerned with futuristic science and technology, which is central to the story, whereas utopian/dystopian narratives rather put their focus on society. Thus the element of extrapolation plays a central role in dystopian films and novels.
As an example, the films *Star Wars* or *Alien* do not really draw on extrapolation from today's society. The novels *Fahrenheit 451* and *Brave New World* or the film *Gattaca* do so extensively.

Classic Science Fiction Narratives

These classics are so well known (not only) in English-speaking countries that you may encounter references to any one of these works in numerous texts.

Mary Shelley, *Frankenstein* (1818)

Dr. Frankenstein brings to life a creature made of dead body parts and is then repulsed by what he has done. The creature becomes lonely and violent after being rejected by its creator, and turns against him.

H. G. Wells, *The Time Machine* (1895)

This story has popularized the concept of time travel, using a machine that allows an operator to travel to whatever period of history he wants. It has inspired countless science fiction stories, the most popular probably being the Hollywood production *Back to the Future*. The term "time machine", coined by Wells, is now universally used.

H. G. Wells, *The War of the Worlds* (1898)

The story of an invasion of late Victorian England by Martians. The story has become particularly famous because of its adaptation in the 1938 radio broadcast that was narrated and directed by Orson Welles. It led to widespread panic by listeners who thought the invasion was real.

20th and 21st century science fiction novels and films are so abundant that there is no use listing any of them here. For your final exam, make sure you are familiar with the texts you studied.

Glossary – Utopia and Dystopia

anti-individualist	anti-individualistisch
anti-utopian	anti-utopisch
authoritarian	autoritär
brainwashing to brainwash	Gehirnwäsche (durchführen)
dissent	abweichende Meinung haben
dissenter	Andersdenkender
dystopia	Anti-Utopie, Dystopie
extrapolation	Übertragung, Ableitung
fiction fictitious fictional	Dichtung, erzählende Literatur fiktiv, erfunden literarisch
future	Zukunft, zukünftig
futuristic	futuristisch
hierarchy	Hierarchie
imaginary	erfunden
individualist	Individualist, individualistisch
indoctrination	Indoktrination/Indoktrinierung
oppression	Unterdrückung
restriction	Einschränkung
surveillance	Überwachung
totalitarian	totalitär
utopia	Utopie

Ethical Issues of Scientific and Technological Progress

Science

> **Keyword:**
>
> **Genetics:** field of study dealing with the way living organisms inherit features from their ancestors. These features are called traits. Traits are e. g. a person's eye-colour or height.

- Genetic information is carried by a molecule called DNA which is copied and inherited across generations.
- DNA is widely known as the "double helix" and looks like a twisted ladder. It is made up of nucleotides which are the rungs of the ladder. There are four types of nucleotides (A, T, G and C). The order of the nucleotides determines the genetic code of an organism.
- Genes are segments of DNA which provide information that an organism needs so that it can build or do something. They are like sentences spelled out by means of the "letters" of the nucleotide alphabet.
- The complete set of genes in a particular organism is known as a genome.
- Genes are copied each time a cell divides into two new cells. It is through a similar process that a child inherits genes from its parents, when a copy from the mother is mixed with a copy from the father.

Genetic engineering

Putting a new piece of DNA into a cell can produce a new trait. For example, crop plants can be given a gene from an Arctic fish, so they produce an antifreeze protein in their leaves. This may prevent frost damage. Other crops can be given genes including a natural insecticide, which will protect the plant.
People with genetic disorders can be treated by means of gene therapy. The idea is to replace a malfunctioning gene with one that functions properly.

Important steps in genetic engineering

- 1953: discovery of double helix by Watson and Crick, Cambridge, UK
- 1973: blend of unrelated organisms
- 1973: production of human protein insulin
- 1981: blend of species
- 1980s: work with human genes
- 1986: open-air experimentation with plants
- 1996: commercial cultivation of genetically modified plants
- 1996: cloning of mammals (Dolly)
- 2003: sequencing of the human genome
- 2009: first transgenic primates
- 2013: use of cloning to create human embryonic stem cells

- 2016: Cultivation of crops that are modified on a large scale by means of "genetic scissors" is permitted in the US
- 2018: babies modified by means of "genetic scissors" have been allegedly born in China

Applications of GMOs (genetically modified organisms)

- biological and medical research
- production of pharmaceutical drugs
- experimental medicine (e.g. gene therapy)
- agriculture (e.g. golden rice)
- The **widest application** exists for crops resistant to herbicides or for producing pesticides from within.
- In 2018, 191.7 million hectares of biotech crops were planted by up to 17 million farmers in 26 countries.[1]

Transgenic microbes

Bacteria were the first organisms to be modified in the laboratory. These organisms are now used for several purposes, and are particularly important in producing human proteins for use in medicine.

Genetically modified bacteria are used

- to produce insulin to treat diabetes,
- to produce clotting factors to treat haemophilia,
- to produce human growth hormone to treat various forms of dwarfism,
- to facilitate crop growth in some soils or prevent crop pests.

Transgenic animals

Transgenic animals are used

- as experimental models to test genes whose function is unknown,
- for the production of human hormones such as insulin.

Transgenic mice are used to study diseases and test treatments. Mice can be grown with the same genetic disorders that occur in human beings.

First genetically modified pet: the GloFish is a patented brand of genetically modified (GM) fluorescent zebra-fish with bright red, green and orange fluorescent colours.

Transgenic plants

Transgenic plants have been engineered to

- resist pests, herbicides or harsh environmental conditions,
- improve product shelf life,
- increase their nutritional value,
- produce bigger yields, thus making farmland more efficient.

"Terminator" Technology: GM plants do not yield seeds. This means that farmers have to buy new seeds every time.

1 https://isaaa.org/resources/publications/pocketk/16/default.asp

Designer Babies (Reprogenetics)

The colloquial term "designer baby" refers to a baby whose genetic makeup has been artificially selected to ensure the presence or absence of certain characteristics, especially with regard to the sex of the child.

Cloning

Cloning is the creation of an organism that is an exact genetic copy of another. This means that every single bit of DNA is the same between the two.
Dolly: (July 5, 1996 – February 14, 2003) a female sheep (ewe), was the first mammal to be cloned from an adult body cell. She lived until the age of six, when she developed severe diseases, which has led to speculation that a clone may be born with the genetic age of the organism from which it was cloned.

Ethics

Biotechnology in agriculture

Pros	Cons
higher productivity	genes can end up in unexpected places
more efficient land use	genes can mutate with harmful effect
more ecological farming (no ploughing, no fertilizing, no insecticides, no pesticides)	"sleeper" genes could be accidentally switched on, active genes could become "silent"
solution to problem of famine in the world	interaction with wild and native populations: negative impact on birds, insects and soil
higher quality of food	transfer of allergenic genes
longer shelf life	GM products in the food chain
rehabilitation of damaged land	transfer of antibiotic resistance
	loss of farmers' control over material; "terminator" technology prevents sustainable farming → dependence on big corporations

Reprogenetics

Pros (once it is safe)	Cons
parents have a right to choose	technology is not safe yet
moral obligation to give children the best life possible	bioethical codes condemn experiments with human beings
will lead to improvement of the whole species	"super humans" may look down on normal people

	"imperfect" human beings would be discriminated against
	rich people would be at an advantage
	the human gene pool may be damaged
	"New Eugenics": people are designed to suit the needs of society
	people may be thought of as products
	human beings should not play God

Sex selection

Pros (once it is safe)	Cons
parents have a right to choose	preferences in patriarchal cultures lead to demographic imbalance
in some cultures male offspring are important to provide support for old age	members of the unwanted sex may be discriminated against
theory that having sisters (as opposed to brothers) enhances adults' quality of life	the child may not be loved if sth. goes wrong and it is not of the desired sex
	parents fulfil their own wishes, disregarding the rights of the child
	human beings are not allowed to play God

Human Cloning

Pros	Cons
medical reasons: resource of bone marrow or replaceable organs	cloning is inherently evil, an intrusion into human life
infertile couples may have children	a person who wants to clone himself/herself is self-centred
	cloning in order to produce superior beings is eugenics and eugenics is discriminatory
	using a human being as a resource for "spare parts" is unethical
	reproduction by means of cloning might have long-term consequences for human relationships
	children may be thought of as products
	Hinduism: What about the person's karma?
	dictators may become immortal

Glossary – Ethical Issues

achievement of scientists	Errungenschaft/Leistung der Wissenschaftler
artificial insemination	künstliche Befruchtung
development	Entwicklung
DNA (deoxyribonucleic acid)	DNA/DNS
double helix (DNA)	Doppelhelix, DNA
error rate	Fehlerrate
genetic disorders	genetische Funktionsstörung
genetic engineering	Gentechnik, Genmanipulation
genetic fingerprint	genetischer Fingerabdruck
genetic make-up, genetic constitution	Erbgut
genetic modification (GM)	genetische Veränderung
heredity, inheritance	Vererbung
inherit	erben
insecticide	Insektizid
in-vitro fertilization	In-vitro-Befruchtung
laboratory	Labor
to modify modification	modifizieren, verändern Modifizierung
molecule	Molekül
to mutate mutation	mutieren Mutation
non-polluting	umweltfreundlich
organ donor	Organspender
to pass on	vererben
pesticide	Unkrautvernichtungsmittel, Pestizid
progress (no article, no plural)	Fortschritt
reproductive cloning	Klonen von Menschen
research (into)	Forschung
research facility	Forschungseinrichtung
resistance	Resistenz
stem cell	Stammzelle
technology	Technologie, Technik
test-tube baby	Retortenbaby
therapeutic cloning	therapeutisches Klonen
transgenic	transgen (genetisch verändert)

Studying and Working in a Globalized World

With the world constantly becoming smaller due to globalization, it has become much easier to spend some time in a foreign country for educational reasons, both during one's time at school and/or as part of studies at a university or vocational training. Some future employers consider it an essential aspect of a prospective employee's CV (résumé) to have spent some time abroad, very often in an English-speaking country.

Benefits for oneself

- getting a personal insight into other cultures
- improving one's foreign language skills
- experiencing different educational systems
- contributing to one's personal development, e.g. to become more independent, self-confident, adaptable to different situations
- making new friends
- improving one's career opportunities
- broadening one's horizon on various levels

Studying and working abroad also has benefits for employers. A growing number of companies tend to employ people who have studied abroad, as these prospective employees are said to possess key job skills, e.g. cultural empathy, excellent foreign language skills, self-organization, adaptability, open-mindedness and flexibility.

Volunteerism and voluntourism

In the last couple of years **volunteerism** has become more popular. It means that a person volunteers to use his/her time and skills to contribute to a community without receiving any payment. An increasing number of people combine being a volunteer with spending some time abroad. There are various ways in which one can contribute to a community, e.g. humanitarian aid or teaching at a local school in a rural village. Volunteerism should not be confused with **voluntourism,** which can generally be defined as a combination of volunteering and sightseeing.
Voluntourism is a neologism based on the words "volunteer" and "tourism" and has been criticized as counterfeiting the original idea of volunteering.
Some of the arguments critics put forward against voluntourism are that it is not truly beneficial for communities, since "voluntourists" only spend a relatively short time in the communities in question and therefore often do not truly immerse. In addition to that, they are said to enjoy all the benefits of an ordinary tourist, e.g. staying in hotels far above the living-standard of the community they are helping, while not being really prepared for their placements. Whereas in the past charities and NGOs were mostly in charge of matching volunteers with the right projects, some major travel agencies now also specialize in offering placements for "voluntourists" against payment.

English as a *lingua franca*

English can be regarded as a *lingua franca,* which means that it is a language spoken by such a vast number of people all over the world that it enables speakers of different first languages to successfully communicate with each other.
These non-native speakers of English have a huge impact on the English language, e.g. when it comes to grammar or pronunciation, for when non-native speakers of English communicate with each other it is their main intention to communicate a message. As a consequence, grammatical constructions regarded as incorrect by native speakers of English are accepted by both speakers and do not impede the flow of their conversation.
Code mixing and code switching also occur.
Code mixing means that a speaker uses words, syntax etc. from his mother tongue and English words in the same sentence. In contrast to that, the term code switching is used to refer to a speaker who switches between the vocabulary, syntax etc. of his or her mother tongue and English, often in the same sentence.
Nowadays English language skills are not considered a special feature but are taken for granted in many areas of life.

The changing world of work

Past generations often spent their entire working life with one employer, retiring from the same company with which they started. But, due to globalization, the world of work has changed rapidly over the last half century. Advances in information technology have made it possible for a company's employees in different countries to work on the same project and to exchange information on the spot. Due to new technological and economic developments, new types of jobs have been created which were unheard of only half a century ago.
Still, finding one's dream job has not become easier, and employees are often expected to show a high level of flexibility and adaptability. Changing jobs and places of residence frequently is not uncommon, as there is high competition in certain jobs. Nor do the realities of the job market always match one's expectations and wishes. Despite the fact that there is employment growth in the United Kingdom, Germany and the USA, not everyone profits from it. The number of jobs for people with no or low work skills is decreasing and the gap between the rich and the poor is widening all over the world.

Minimum wage and living wage

21 countries of the European Union, and the USA, have a statutory minimum wage. In 2015 Germany introduced a minimum wage, calculated either on the basis of an hourly rate or as a monthly payment. The minimum wage varies in different fields of work. Being paid a minimum wage means that an employee receives the lowest wage his/her employer is legally allowed to pay. Some of the arguments put forward in favour of the minimum wage are that it prevents people from being exploited by

employers and from having to rely on social benefits in order to make ends meet.
In the UK some companies and institutions voluntarily pay their employees a "living wage" instead of the legal minimum wage. While a "minimum wage" is calculated in accordance with the development of the job market, a "living wage" is an hourly rate calculated on the basis of the cost of living index (e.g. accommodation, travel, food and drink, costs for heating, water and electricity), which in the UK is adjusted annually. In 2021 the voluntarily paid living wage in the UK was £9.50 an hour, with the exception of London where it is £10.85 an hour, due to higher costs of living.
In March 2021 the compulsory "national living wage" for people aged 25 or older was £8.72 per hour; lower than the living wage calculated by the Living Wage Foundation.

Living Wage Foundation

On its website, the London-based Living Wage Foundation says that it developed from a citizens' movement in 2001 when the charity "Citizens UK" brought parents together to exchange views on the ups and downs of family life: "It emerged that too many parents were working two jobs just to make ends meet and so had no time to spend with their children. They worked hard but couldn't earn enough to afford a decent standard of living."[1] The Living Wage Foundation is supported by the UK's political parties, and both Houses of Parliament are among those who pay their employees a living wage.

In January 2017, Finland launched a social experiment in which the Finnish government granted 2000 unemployed people an unconditional basic income (UBI) of €560 for 24 months, without urging them to look for employment or to accept job offers. Those who took a job during this period still received UBI.
The intention behind this social experiment was to find out whether UBI motivates unemployed people to find jobs or enter job training. UBI provides a "safety net" so that they will not feel too much financial pressure.
It is not easy to say whether this experiment has been a success or not. The number of unemployed participants in the experiment has not decreased as much as was hoped, but those who participated said that they felt more contented for the duration of the experiment.

Glossary – Studying and Working in a Globalized World

adaptability	Anpassungsfähigkeit
apprenticeship, vocational training	Berufsausbildung, Lehre
charity	Wohlfahrtsorganisation
community service	ehrenamtliche Tätigkeit
compulsory education/schooling	Schulpflicht
CV (curriculum vitae) (BE)/résumé (AE)	Lebenslauf
exchange student	Austauschschüler(in)/-student(in)

1 http://www.livingwage.org.uk (retrieved March 2021)

flexibility	Flexibilität
gap year	freiwilliges (soziales, ökologisches etc.) Jahr/Auszeit
job advertisement/job offer	Stellenanzeige/-angebot
job interview	Bewerbungsgespräch
key qualifications	Schlüsselqulifikationen
minimum wage	Mindestlohn
open-mindedness	Aufgeschlossenheit
placement/internship	Praktikum
scholarship	Stipendium
school exchange	Schüleraustausch
social commitment	soziales Engagement
social skills	soziale Kompetenz
study abroad	Auslandsstudium
to apply for (a job)	sich (für eine Stelle) bewerben
to broaden one's horizon	seinen Horizont erweitern
to climb the social ladder	Karriere machen
to donate/give sth. to charity	etw. an eine Wohltätigkeitsorganisation spenden/weiterleiten
to gain experience	Erfahrungen sammeln
to get an insight into foreign cultures	einen Einblick in fremde Kulturen erhal-ten
to speak from one's own experience	aus eigener Erfahrung sprechen
volunteer	Freiwillige(r)

Methoden der Textarbeit

Literarische Texte

Narration

Keyword:

narrative texts: narrative texts can have many forms, among them short story, novel, fairytale, satire, parable, legend, etc.
Most relevant for your final exam are the short story and the novel.

When asked to analyze a narrative text, you will have to focus on particular elements that are characteristic of short stories or novels.

Elements of narration

Structure

Plot

INFO Elements of a complete plot

exposition → rising action → climax/turning point → falling action → ending

A **plot** need not necessarily be complete (e.g. open ending).

The **sequence** need not necessarily be in chronological order.
There may be foreshadowing or flashbacks or there may be reverse narration (umgestelltes Erzählen).
In particular, an excerpt from a longer text, which is the most common sort of text in the final exam, may not contain all the elements of plot.
Certain **key events** within the action of a story will raise the tension; they will create suspense, rising to a climax or turning point. After that there will be falling tension or relief.

INFO Tension curve

rising tension → climax or turning point → falling tension or relief

Theme

The **theme** of a story is always abstract. Themes are *e.g.* love, poverty, racism, childhood, *etc.*
The **subject matter** of a story is the concrete realization of the theme.

Example
Two stories may have the same theme: racism. The subject matter of the one may be the murder of an African-American, of the other the bullying of a black schoolgirl.

Character

When asked to characterize a figure from a narrative text, you will have to be aware of different aspects. There are key questions that can guide you.

Direct characterization
- What does the narrator say about the character?
- What do other characters say about the character?
- What does the character say about himself/herself?
- How objective is what they say? Be aware of words with negative or positive connotations.

Indirect characterization
- How does the character act?
- What does the character say?
- What kind of language does he/she use?

It might help to fill in a table with the following headings:

Character's outward appearance	Character's language	Character's actions	What the character says	Other characters' statements (or actions)
...	...	...	...	...

Narrator/point of view

INFO Narrator

The narrator is either a first-person or a third-person narrator.
The first-person narrator is NOT the author!

limited point of view	unlimited/omniscient point of view
first-person narrator	third-person narrator (neutral omniscience, God-like knowledge about all facts)
third-person narrator (one character's point of view)	third-person narrator (several characters' points of view)

The narrator always works like a camera, taking a point-of-view shot through a character's eyes or looking at the characters from the outside.

Example:
In Alan Sillitoe's novel *Saturday Night and Sunday Morning* (1975), the reader is presented with an episode in a pub (p. 10). When the narrator says, "Brenda and two other women sitting at Arthur's table saw him push back his chair and stand up with a clatter, [...]", he takes Brenda's and the women's point of view: Arthur is clearly seen from outside, not by a neutral narrator but through the women's eyes: The women sitting at Arthur's table saw him push back his chair, NOT Arthur pushed back his chair.
→ limited point of view

A few lines later the point of view changes: "He felt electric light bulbs shining and burning into the back of his head."
The narrator takes Arthur's point of view, knows what Arthur feels.
→ limited point of view

Mode of presentation

Panoramic presentation (telling) vs. scenic presentation (showing)

There are two modes of presentation to be found in narratives: the **panoramic** and the **scenic** mode:

The **panoramic** mode is employed when the narrator summarizes several events, whereas **scenic** mode is used when the narrator describes scenes in great detail.

Interior monologue is a particular kind of scenic presentation, in which the thoughts and feelings passing through a character's mind are depicted. In **reported thought** the thoughts are presented as reported speech.

This is closely connected with the concepts of *narrated time and narrating* (or *acting) time:*

narrated time longer than narrating time	usually summary of events
narrated time identical with narrating time	e.g. direct speech
narrated time shorter than narrating time	e.g. stream of consciousness, interior monologue, detailed description of a scene, comparable to slow motion in film

INFO Function of mode of presentation and point of view

A neutral, omniscient narrator, who observes the action and the characters from above and who uses a panoramic mode of presentation, is more detached and thus creates a distance between the reader and the action. On the other hand, a narrator who takes a character's point of view creates immediacy, directly involves the reader in what happens.

Setting

The place and time where the action is set is called the setting. It is especially important for *atmosphere* and *symbolism.*

Atmosphere

Atmosphere is created by means of setting, objects, colours, light and darkness, but also by reference to a character's mood or the use of language.

Example:
In Kate Chopin's short story "Desirée's Baby" a "yellow stuccoed house" is described with a roof that comes down "steep and black like a cowl." (Mönchskutte). It is surrounded by "big, solemn oaks", the "thick-leaved, far-reaching branches" shadowing "it like a pall" (Leichentuch).

colour	black, dirty yellow
light/darkness	shadow of the oaks
language: similes, "like a pall", "like a cowl"	→ connotations of death, darkness, mystery.

The atmosphere created here is gloomy, sombre, sinister, threatening, eerie.

Symbolism

Symbols are part of the setting of the narrative.

INFO Established symbols

These are conventional symbols which have long been used and have a certain, traditional significance which everybody knows. Examples of established symbols: rose, cross, the colour white.

INFO Created symbols

Something becomes symbolic within a certain context, because it is closely connected to an event, a situation or a character.

Example:
In the novel *Angela's Ashes* (1996), Angela, the family's mother, vomits over the side of the ship when they leave New York harbour for Ireland and the wind from the Atlantic blows it all over the family. (p. 53)
In the course of the novel the reader will learn how unfortunate the family's decision to leave America will turn out to be and how disastrous the wind from the Atlantic will be for the family. Thus this passage from the first chapter of the book is symbolic.

INFO Symbols and metaphors

Symbols are NOT metaphors!
Symbols are really there, are part of the story. Metaphors or similes are figures of speech.

Examples:
She was a rose, so beautiful. → metaphor
She was like a rose, so beautiful. → simile/comparison
They fell in love when they first met in her father's rose garden. → symbol

Language and style

In order to determine the style of a text it is necessary to examine aspects such as register, diction (choice of words), tone, and also sentence structure.

Register is the level of language used in a particular situation. It may be formal, neutral, informal, or vulgar. There may be a lot of slang words, even taboo words, or technical terms, or jargon.

The **tone** may be ironic, sarcastic, sad, humorous, serious, playful, angry, etc., depending on the emotional attitude it expresses. This depends on the choice of words, level of speech, rhythm, sentence length, etc.

Stylistic devices will be considered at length in the chapters on poetry and non-fictional texts (pp. 89, 95)

Poetry

Poetry focuses on the **aesthetic function** of language.
Poetry appeals to the senses. It is to be enjoyed for its beauty, its cleverness, its wit, its impact. This is achieved by
- the sound of words
- the rhythm of the words and phrases
- the choice of words
- the structure of the sentences
- the composition of the poem
- the visual arrangement of words and lines
- and, above all, by means of imagery.

In your final exams, however, you will be asked not so much to enjoy the poem but to examine its meaning and the effect of the language the speaker uses.

How to proceed

Questions to be asked

- Who is the speaker of the poem?
- Where is the speaker?
- Does the speaker address somebody?
- Does the speaker contemplate something?
- Does the speaker describe something or somebody?
- Does the speaker tell a story?
- Does the speaker explain something?
- Does the speaker argue against or in favour of something?
- What is the speaker's attitude? What is he/she saying?
- How is the poem composed? Is it structured by rhyme scheme, or by division into stanzas, or by some other device?
- Is there a correspondence between the structure of the poem and the structure of the speaker's thoughts?
- What is the significance of the title?
- What words does the speaker use? What do they mean?
- What is the structure of the sentences? Simple? Complex?
- What poetic devices does the speaker use?
- And what is the effect of all this? What is the experience of reading?

In order to understand and describe poetry you need to be familiar with its most important elements.

Elements of poetry

INFO Speaker and author

The speaker of the poem is NOT the author. Poems may be autobiographical, but you must still refer to the "speaker of the poem".

Poems are composed of **stanzas** and **lines**.
Stanzas may have a certain **rhyme scheme.**

Rhyme

Rhyme schemes

rhyme pair	a a b b
alternate rhyme	a b a b
embracing rhyme	a b b a

Types of rhymes

masculine rhyme (on one syllable)	kiss/this
feminine rhyme (on two syllables)	dreary/weary
true rhyme	kiss/this, dreary/weary
slant rhyme assonance (same vowel) consonance (same consonant)	 comb/coat hope/heap

Lines may be marked by a certain rhythm. The smallest unit that determines rhythm is the foot, consisting of at least one stressed and one or two unstressed syllables. The pattern of stressed and unstressed syllables is called **metre.**

A sequence of stressed and unstressed syllables is nothing artificial. It is the natural rhythm of the English language. It is the poet's skill to choose words in a way that this pattern will constitute a regular metre.

Types of foot

foot	stresses	example
iamb/iambic	– / (da-**dum**)	compare
trochee/trochaic	/ – (**dum**-da)	lovely
spondee/spondaic	/ / **(dum dum)**	drop dead
anapest/anapestic	– – / (da-da-**dum**)	lemonade
dactyl/dactylic	/ – – (**dum**-da-da)	whispering

The number of feet or stressed syllables in a line determines its metre. The most common types are shown here:

number of feet	metre	example
1	monometer	"And find / What wind ..." (John Donne, "Song", ll. 7 – 8)
2	dimeter	"Why dost thou thus ..." (John Donne, "The Sun Rising", l. 2)
3	trimeter	"Go, Soul, the body's guest Upon a thankless errant;" (Sir Walter Raleigh, "The Lie")
4	tetrameter	"Busy old fool, unruly sun ..." (John Donne, "The Sun Rising", l. 1)
5	pentameter	"Love, all alike, no season knows, nor clime ..." (John Donne, "The Sun Rising", l. 9)
6	hexameter	"A needless alexandrine ends the song That, like a wounded snake, drags its slow length along" (Alexander Pope, "An Essay on Criticism", ll. 356 – 357)

INFO Most important metre in English poetry

Iambic pentameter:
"But thy eternal summer shall not fade" (Shakespeare, Sonnet 18).

Lines

end-stop lines	natural pause for the end of a thought at the end of a line	"Shall I compare thee to a summer's day?" (Shakespeare, Sonnet 18)
run-on lines (enjambement)	The meaning requires no pause between the lines.	"When yellow leaves, or none, or few, do hang Upon those boughs which shake against the cold ..." (Shakespeare, Sonnet 73)
caesura	The meaning requires a pause in mid-line.	"Let me not to the marriage of true minds Admit impediments; love is not love ..." (Shakespeare, Sonnet 116)

Imagery

A writer or speaker using language beyond its dictionary meaning makes use of **imagery.** All figurative use of language is imagery. Imagery appeals to all the senses, it is meant to stimulate the reader's or listener's imagination.

TIPP Watch out!

The word *imagery* is an abstract noun. There is no plural. You can only talk about single *images*.

Types of imagery

metaphor	A metaphor compares two basically dissimilar things without using the words 'like' or 'as'. Some characteristics of the one are thus transferred to the other in order to illustrate its qualities. "All the world is a stage." (W. Shakespeare)
simile/ comparison	Like a metaphor, a simile draws a comparison, but it explicitly uses the words 'like' or 'as' to do so. "My love is like a red red rose" (Robert Burns)
personification	It is a kind of metaphor in which animals, plants, inanimate objects or abstract ideas are represented as if they were human beings and possessed human qualities: "Busy old fool, unruly sun, / Why dost thou thus, / Through windows, and through curtains call on us?" (John Donne, "The Sun Rising")
symbol	see examples in previous chapter, p. 84

Other poetic devices

stylistic device	definition	example
alliteration	repetition of a sound (usually a consonant) at the beginning of adjacent words	"From forth the fatal loins of these two foes A pair of star-crossed lovers take their life." *(Romeo and Juliet,* Prologue)
onomatopoeia adj. onomatopoeic	the use of words which imitate the sound they refer to	"the stuttering rifles' rapid rattle" (Wilfred Owen, "Anthem for doomed youth")
anaphora (use: "example of anaphora/ examples of anaphora")	One or more words are repeated at the beginning of adjacent sentences or lines.	"In every cry of every man In every infant's cry of fear In every voice, in every ban" (W. Blake, "London")
chiasm	reversal of order of the words in the two parts of a sentence	"Fair is foul, and foul is fair" (Shakespeare, *Macbeth)*
oxymoron	a combination of contradictory words and meanings.	"O heavy lightness, serious vanity, Misshapen chaos of well-seeming forms," (Shakespeare, *Romeo and Juliet)*

Drama

When asked to analyze a dramatic text, you will have to focus on particular elements that are characteristic of plays or film scripts.

Elements of drama

Structure

Plot

The audience is confronted with the action on stage or on the screen directly. There is no narrator. Yet one can identify the same elements of plot as are found in narration.

INFO Elements of a dramatic plot

exposition → rising action → climax or crisis → falling action → dénouement or catastrophe

In tragedy, the opponents of the hero gain the upper hand in the falling action, which ends in the catastrophe.
Comedy has a happy ending, in which conflicts are resolved (dénouement).

Stage directions

The dramatic text consist of **two kinds of text:** the more important kind of text is the dialogue spoken by the characters (i. e. dialogue, monologue, and asides).
The stage directions are the second kind of text. They give the instructions concerning the stage design, about sounds to be heard, visual effects, the characters and also the way some of the dialogue has to be spoken.
The following visual and acoustic elements will have to be considered in your analysis of stage directions. They will help to characterize a character, create atmosphere or function as symbols. (cf. p. 84)

concerning the actors		**concerning the stage**	
visual	**acoustic**	**visual**	**acoustic**
size	voice	scenery	music
facial expression	intonation	stage design	noise
gestures	language of the play	lighting	sound
costumes	non-verbal noises	properties *(Requisiten)*	

Characters

The audience is confronted with the characters on stage directly, there is no narrator. A character is presented through action, interaction and dialogue and, of course, his outward appearance on stage (see above).
There are **flat** characters, types that act in a predictable way, and **round**, lifelike characters that are fully developed.

Language/Dialogue/Communication

When analysing the language of a play you have to keep in mind that it works on two levels:

1. The inner system of communication, i. e. the communication among the characters.
2. The outer system of communication between the playwright and the audience.

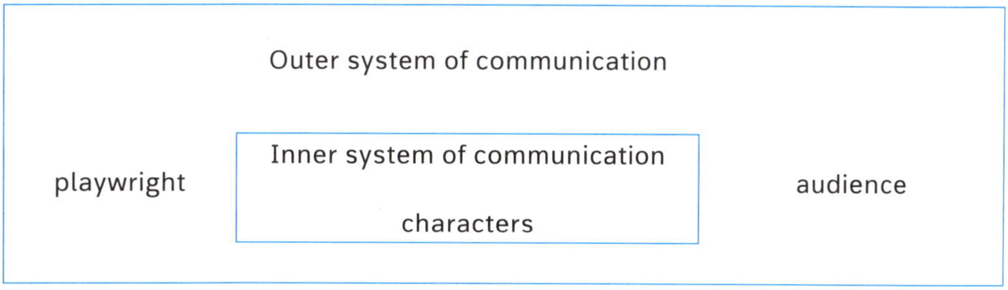

Dramatic irony

Dramatic irony is an important effect that is created by these two levels of communication. If the audience knows more than a character, an utterance will be perceived as ironic when it sharply contrasts with reality.

Example

In Shakespeare's Macbeth, King Duncan praises the peaceful atmosphere at Macbeth's castle, whereas the audience knows that Duncan will be murdered.

Comedy

On the level of communication between playwright and audience, dramatic irony, the audience's awareness of facts the characters do not know, may serve a comic effect, too.

Aside

In an aside an actor speaks to the audience in order to provide information on his thoughts and feelings or intentions. The other characters on stage supposedly do not hear what he says.

TIPP

As many of Shakespeare's plays are written in verse, you may approach their language the same way as poetry.

Glossary – Vocabulary for analysing literary texts

the narrator tells of/shows/relates/reveals
the narrator takes xy's point of view
the narrator is omniscient
the story is told in the first person/third person
the story is told from the first-person-singular point of view
the narrator uses/employs/makes use of metaphors, similes, comparisons
a metaphor shows/stands for/suggests
the narrator speaks in an ironic/satirical/detached/matter-of-fact/serious tone
the story deals with/treats of/concentrates on/focuses on ...
atmosphere is created
tension/ suspense is created/built up
a poem is written/composed
a poem is read, spoken, recited
a recital of a poem
the poem is by Shakespeare
it is a song by Genesis
the speaker of the poem/the poetic I/the poetic persona
the poem consists of/is composed of/is arranged in stanzas
the comedy ridicules/mocks/satirizes
the exposition sets the action in motion
the action moves towards and culminates in a turning-point
the play/film has a simple/complex/tight plot
it has a happy/unhappy ending
there are main/major/minor characters
the protagonist is in conflict with an opponent
the antagonist fights the protagonist
the spectator/audience follows the play
the play is performed/produced/staged
scenery is shifted
actors perform/play/enact
an actor enters/makes an entrance
an actor exits/makes his exit

Sach- und Gebrauchstexte

Argumentative Texte: *How to deal with (political) speeches*

Keyword:

(Political) speeches: aim at convincing *(überzeugen)* the audience of the speaker's position, winning them over to his/her side. Very often, the speaker tries to persuade (überreden) the listener by appealing to his/her feelings. In some cases, the orator may even attempt to manipulate *(manipulieren)* his audience. You should always keep in mind that the speaker wants to present his/her opinion/conviction/point of view as positively as possible.

When asked to analyse a political speech, you will have to focus on the topic and characteristic features.

How to proceed

Reading of the text

1. Read the (political) speech (or, more likely, an extract from it) as a whole, trying to identify the main topic of the speech (reading for gist).
2. Re-read the (political) speech (the extract) several times, paying special attention to certain characteristic features of such speeches. Mark words or phrases in the text and take notes (intensive reading).

Pay special attention to

- key words and phrases
- references to historical events
- use of symbols, key words, slogans
- references to famous people
- references to works of literature
- stylistic devices (see below)

Questions to be asked

When it comes to analysing a (political) speech, you should always ask yourself the following questions:

- What is the main topic of the speech?
- What is its political, historical and social context?
- What do I know about the speaker (biography, political orientation)?

Elements of a (political) speech

Structure

(Political) speeches can usually be divided into **introduction, main part** and **conclusion.** These parts serve different purposes:

INFO Introduction to a speech

In the introduction the orator announces the topic/purpose of the speech and explains why it is of major importance. He/she also wants to attract the audience's attention so that they will follow the speech closely and accept his/her opinion.

There are several ways to make listeners interested:
- The speaker can open by telling the audience **something about their personal history/recent experiences,** thereby underlining the fact that the topic of the speech is of personal importance to them. By relating a **little story** to the audience, the speaker will also appear more human and less flawless.
- Another common way of starting a speech is to **open it with a question** that refers to the main topic and which will be answered later in the speech. By asking the audience a question, the speaker actively involves them, indirectly asking them to think more deeply about the question.
- A speaker may also **present visuals to the audience,** e. g. pictures, concrete objects or a short extract from a film. This also helps to attract the audience's attention: listeners will become curious about how the object or visual is related to the content of the speech.

INFO Main part of a speech

In the main part of the speech the orator needs to keep the audience interested and to make sure that they can follow the train of thought.

Again, there are several ways to do this. The following techniques are particularly effective:
- **using short and simple sentences,** developing the argumentation step by step and ensuring that the audience can follow
- **quoting reliable sources/experts, referring to statistics and providing the audience with facts and necessary background information,** which shows that the speaker is well-informed and has researched the subject
- **pointing out problems, but also providing solutions** for them, thus showing that the speaker is competent
- **including personal experiences** and vivid, concrete events, again aiming for a personal relationship to the audience, **often using personal pronouns like "we", "us", "our".**

Towards the end of a speech the speaker might
- take up a question posed at the beginning of the speech;
- appeal once more to both the audience's head and heart;
- ask for support, giving the listeners the feeling that their support is important;
- develop a vision for the future.

Argumentative comments use the same stylistic means as political speeches.

Language and style

There are certain stylistic devices, which are often used in (political) speeches. They aim at making the speech more lively and interesting.

Important stylistic devices

analogy	A resemblance is established between things which are unlike.
simile	This is a direct comparison using the words "like" or "as", e.g. *He fought like a lion in the battle.*
metaphor	This is an indirect comparison without using the words "like" or "as", e.g. *He was a lion in battle.*
alliteration	A consonantal sound of two or more adjacent words is repeated, e.g. *We will win ... "We must understand that ties of trade bind nations in closest intimacy ..."* (Warren G. Harding: Inaugural address, March 4, 1921).
repetition	Repeating certain words or phrases puts emphasis on the meaning of the words and phrases in question, e.g. *"The answer to the slavery question was already embedded within our Constitution – a Constitution that had at its very core the ideal of equal citizenship under the law; a Constitution that promised its people liberty, and justice (...)."* (Barack Obama: *A More Perfect Union)*
parallelism	Two or more parts of a sentence (or two or more sentences) have the same (or similar) syntactical structure. Like repetition, parallelism puts stress on the parts of the sentence in question, intensifying the force of the statement and encouraging the audience to think about its meaning, e.g. *"Let us be our sister's keeper. Let us find that common stake we all have in one another, and let our politics reflect that spirit as well."* (Barack Obama: *A More Perfect Union)*
antithesis	Two ideas are opposed to one another, using a parallel syntactical structure to reach the desired effect, i.e. establishing a contrast, e.g. *"It's a story that hasn't made me the most conventional candidate. But it is a story that has seared into my genetic makeup the idea that this nation is more than the sum of its parts – that out of many, we are truly one."* (Barack Obama: *A More Perfect Union)*

rhetorical question	A rhetorical question is one to which no answer is expected; instead the listener is asked to think about the question and its relevance, e.g. *"How long should this suffering continue?"*
irony	Words or phrases are used to mean something different, often the opposite of their literal meaning. This is often done for rhetorical or humorous effect.

Glossary – Vocabulary for analysing speeches

By telling the listeners something about his personal history he attempts to establish a personal relationship with his audience.	Er bemüht sich, eine persönliche Beziehung zu seinen Zuhörern aufzubauen, indem er seinem Publikum etwas über seine persönliche Geschichte erzählt.
She attempts to win her listeners over to her side.	Sie versucht, das Publikum auf ihre Seite zu ziehen.
He draws a comparison between ... and ...	Er zieht einen Vergleich zwischen ... und ...
He puts emphasis on the meaning of his words by using a parallelism/repetition in l. X (line ...).	Durch den in Zeile X verwendeten Parallelismus/die in Zeile X verwendete Wiederholung verleiht er seinen Worten Nachdruck.
He refers to well-known historical events such as ...	Er bezieht sich auf allgemein bekannte historische Ereignisse wie z. B. ...
He wants to call/draw the audience's attention to the fact that ...	Er möchte die Aufmerksamkeit des Publikums auf die Tatsache lenken, dass ...
His frequent use of rhetorical questions is intended to show that ...	Sein häufiger Gebrauch rhetorischer Fragen soll verdeutlichen, dass ...
His metaphorical use of language is intended to make his speech more lively and interesting.	Sein metaphorischer Sprachgebrauch soll seine Rede interessanter und lebendiger machen.
In l. X (line ...) he directly criticizes his political opponents.	In Zeile ... kritisiert er offen seine politischen Gegner.
The frequent use of personal pronouns such as "we", "us" and "our" gives the audience the impression that he does not regard himself as superior to them, but as one of them.	Der häufige Gebrauch der Personalpronomen „wir", „uns" und „unser" soll dem Publikum das Gefühl geben, dass er sich als einer von ihnen und nicht als eine höher gestellte Person sieht.
The speaker appeals to the audience's emotions by ...	Der Redner/die Rednerin spricht die Gefühle des Publikums an, indem er/sie ...

The speaker begins by ...	Der Redner/die Rednerin beginnt mit ...
The speaker makes frequent use of metaphors/similes/symbols/examples to point out/to underline that ...	Der Redner/die Rednerin macht regen Gebrauch von Metaphern/Vergleichen/Symbolen/Beispielen, um herauszustellen/zu unterstreichen, dass ...
The speaker tries to convince his audience of his point of view by ...	Der Redner/die Rednerin versucht sein/ihr Publikum von seinem/ihrem Standpunkt zu überzeugen, indem er/sie ...
The speaker aims to convince/persuade/manipulate the audience.	Es ist das Anliegen des Redners/der Rednerin, das Publikum zu überzeugen/überreden/manipulieren.

Expositorische Texte: *How to deal with essays*

Keyword:

Essays: There are various kinds.

a) essays which reflect the author's opinion on a certain topic **(comment)**

b) essays in which the author weighs the pros and cons of a particular subject **(argumentative essay)**

c) essays in which a topic is presented in a clear and logical way and which do not contain the author's opinion **(expository essay)**

How to proceed

First you have to find out which kind of essay you are asked to analyse.

TIPP Argumentative comments

Argumentative comments use the same stylistic means as political speeches.

For details on how to analyse **comments** you can refer to the section on **political speeches** above.
Here we will focus on the **argumentative essay.**

Structure

- In the **introduction** the author expresses the main idea of the essay. Instead of giving a personal opinion, she/he might choose to provide the reader with some background information, or start with a question which will serve as a guideline and be answered in the course of the essay.

- For the **main part** of the essay the author can decide on a dialectical or an enumerative approach.
- In an **enumerative approach** the author will enumerate all the aspects of the subject in a neutral way. A **dialectical approach** can either present all the arguments in favour of a position before focusing on the counterarguments (or vice versa), or it can present the pros and cons alternately. The latter is usually considered more skilful.
- Each **new aspect** is usually presented in a new paragraph. The various **arguments** can be backed with examples from real life, established facts, an expert opinion, or other reliable sources. These pieces of evidence are very important, as they enable the author to make his argument convincing and thus to persuade the reader.
- In the **conclusion** the author sums up the arguments, frequently also restating his/her own opinion and giving an outlook on the future.

Glossary – Vocabulary for analysing essays

The author discusses the pros and cons of …	Der Verfasser/Die Verfasserin diskutiert die Vor- und Nachteile von …
The author gives his/her personal opinion on the problem of …	Der Verfasser/Die Verfasserin äußert seine/ihre eigene Meinung zum Thema …
He/she believes/is convinced/presumes that …	Er/sie glaubt/ist überzeugt/nimmt an, dass …
She/he wants to persuade the reader …	Sie/er möchte die Leser überreden …
One can easily follow his train of thought.	Man kann seinen Gedankengang leicht nachvollziehen.
At the end of her essay she draws/comes to the conclusion …	Am Ende ihres Berichts kommt sie zu dem Schluss …
His/her arguments are (not) convincing/well-chosen.	Seine/ihre Argumente sind nicht überzeugend/gut gewählt.
The main topic of the essay is …	Das Thema des Berichts ist …
The tone of this essay is humorous/neutral/ironical/serious.	Der Ton des Berichts ist humorvoll/neutral/ironisch/ernst.
The author uses real examples to convince her readers.	Die Verfasserin verwendet reale Beispiele, um ihre Leser zu überzeugen.
The author's choice of words shows/underlines that he is for …/against …	Die Wortwahl des Verfassers/der Verfasserin zeigt/unterstreicht, dass er für …/gegen … ist.

In the introductory paragraph of her essay she asks a rhetorical question which serves as a thread.	Im einleitenden Abschnitt ihres Berichts stellt sie den Lesern eine rhetorische Frage, die sich wie ein roter Faden durch den Bericht zieht.
The author uses adjectives with a positive/negative connotation to support his/her point of view.	Der Verfasser/Die Verfasserin verwendet Adjektive mit einer positiven/negativen Konnotation, um seinen/ihren Standpunkt zu verdeutlichen.
Her attempt to persuade the readers backfires/works very well.	Ihr Versuch, die Leser zu überreden, misslingt/gelingt.

Narrative Texte: *How to deal with reports*

Keyword:

Report: This is a special kind of newspaper article.
It provides answers to the five "W" questions *(Who? What? Where? When? Why?)*, as well as the *How* question (how something happened). Its aim is to inform its readers and NOT to manipulate or influence them.
A report deals with current events and only contains facts.

Sometimes students have problems when it comes to differentiating between a *report* and an *article,* which might also deal with current events but which is usually a mixture of both fact and opinion.
The style of an **article** is usually more personal and its main aim is to entertain the reader. This is ensured by using many adverbs and adjectives to make the article lively and by addressing its readers directly, often by asking them a hypothetical question, e. g. *How would you feel if you discovered that someone had stolen your brand-new car?*
The main characteristics of a **report** are outlined below.

Elements of a report

Structure

- To arouse the reader's curiosity, reports have **headlines** containing basic information without providing too much detail.
- The basic information is generally provided in the first paragraph, which serves as an **introduction.**
- The **main body** of a report consists of different paragraphs, which contain one piece of information each.
- The last paragraph serves as a kind of **conclusion.**

Language and style

- A report is written in a factual style and neither reflects the author's personal opinion nor contains any kind of speculation.
- Individual paragraphs are relatively short and consist of short sentences, which aim to ensure that the reader understands the information presented.
- Experts – or people who have first-hand experience of the topic in question – are often quoted, but no authorial comment is given about what they say.

Glossary – Vocabulary for analysing reports

The report [title] written by [author] deals with/is about/relates/ describes ...	Der Bericht [Titel] von [Verfasser] beschäftigt sich mit/handelt von/berichtet von/ beschreibt ...
The theme(s) of the report is (are) ...	Das Thema/Die Themen des Berichts ist/sind ...
In the introduction the reader learns about/gets to know ...	In der Einleitung erfährt der Leser/die Leserin ...
The report can be divided into ... paragraphs.	Der Bericht kann in ... Absätze gegliedert werden.
The report consists of ... paragraphs.	Der Bericht besteht aus ... Absätzen.
It's the author's aim to inform the reader about ...	Es ist das Anliegen des Autors/der Autorin, den Leser/die Leserin über ... zu informieren.
The 2nd/3rd paragraph contains information on ...	Der 2./3. Absatz enthält Informationen über ...
The author quotes an eye-witness/ expert who says that ...	Der Autor/die Autorin zitiert einen Augenzeugen/Experten, der sagt, dass ...
The author describes how ...	Der Verfasser/Die Verfasserin beschreibt, wie ...
The author does not give his/her personal opinion on the subject/problem/ question but merely relates facts.	Der Verfasser/Die Verfasserin äußert nicht seine/ihre eigene Meinung zum Sachverhalt/Problem/zu der Frage, sondern gibt Fakten wieder.
The factual style of writing shows that it is the author's aim to inform the reader and not to entertain him/her.	Der sachliche Sprachgebrauch verdeutlicht, dass es das Anliegen des Autors/ der Autorin ist, den Leser/die Leserin zu informieren und nicht, ihn zu unterhalten.

How to deal with cartoons, diagrams and statistics

Keywords:

Cartoons: visual images aiming at criticizing, ridiculing or commenting on current events or ideas.
Diagrams and statistics: intend to present information by comparing different items and their relations to each other. Diagram types include pie charts, bar charts, tables and line graphs.
In written exams, cartoons, diagrams and statistics will always be accompanied by a text.

Dealing with cartoons

Taking a closer look: What is shown?

Describe all the important elements of the cartoon in detail and point out the relation between them,

- start with the foreground and end with the background; of course, you can also proceed from top to bottom, or from left to right, but make sure that your reader can easily follow your train of thought,
- indicate the key features of each object or character, including captions and speech bubbles.

Analysing the message: What is the cartoonist's intention?

Explain what the artist wants to express by

- examining the use of colours if the cartoon comes in colours,
- focusing on the relation of the objects and characters presented in the cartoon (e.g. size, situation and role within the cartoon),
- interpreting the meaning of the caption or speech bubble (if the cartoon has these features).

In written exams cartoons will not have to be analysed alone, but always in combination with a text. Therefore, one should always pay close attention to the respective task.
It might also be necessary to consider the political, historical or social context and to refer to one's background knowledge.
Here it is also important to look at the task once more (What is the connection between cartoon and text?)

Evaluating the cartoon: Does the cartoonist get his message across? Is the cartoon effective?

After having described and analysed the cartoon, you should evaluate whether it is effective or not. You are free to give your own opinion, but do not forget to give reasons for it.

Dealing with diagrams and statistics

Taking a closer look:
What is the diagram/What are the statistics about?

First say what kind of diagram (table, pie chart ...) you are describing and state what it is about.
Diagrams or statistics usually come with a heading, which includes necessary information about what is being described, referred to or compared, as well as the source the information is taken from. Do not forget to mention this.

Analysing the diagram/statistics:
What can be concluded from the diagram/statistics?

Describe the relation between the different items (e. g. in bar charts and pie charts) or the development shown (e. g. in line graphs).
Then it is time to draw your conclusions from what is shown. In written exams you should also point out the connections between the diagram/statistics and the text.

Glossary – Vocabulary for analysing cartoons, diagrams and statistics

pie chart	Tortendiagramm
bar chart	Säulendiagramm
table	Tabelle
line graph	Kurvendiagramm
per cent/percentage	Prozent/prozentualer Anteil
The cartoon/pie chart etc. shows/depicts/presents/is about ...	Der Cartoon/das Tortendiagramm etc. zeigt/stellt ... dar/zeigt ... auf/handelt von ...
The cartoon/diagram etc. is taken from ...	Der Cartoon/das Diagramm stammt von/aus ...
The artist mainly uses light/bright/dark colours to achieve the desired effect.	Der Künstler verwendet überwiegend helle/strahlende/dunkle Farben, um den gewünschten Effekt zu erzielen.
The cartoonist wants the spectator to ...	Der Karikaturist möchte, dass der Betrachter ...
The artist intends to ...	Der Künstler beabsichtigt ...
The message of the cartoon is that ...	Die Botschaft des Cartoons ist, dass ...
In the foreground/background of the cartoon one can see ...	Im Vorder-/Hintergrund des Cartoons kann man ... sehen.
In the top left-hand corner/in the bottom right-hand corner ... is shown.	In der linken oberen/der rechten unteren Ecke wird ... gezeigt/dargestellt.

The bar chart compares the development of … and …	Das Säulendiagramm vergleicht die Entwicklung von … und …
The pie chart is divided into … slices, each slice representing …	Das Tortendiagramm ist in … Stücke aufgeteilt, von denen jedes … darstellt.
Looking at the size of the different slices of the pie chart/at the height of the different bars of the bar chart one can conclude that …	Wenn man die Größe der verschiedenen Stücke des Tortendiagramms/die Höhe der verschiedenen Balken des Balkendiagramms betrachtet, kann man darauf schließen/erkennen, dass …
The bar chart describes the relation between … and …	Das Säulendiagramm beschreibt die Beziehung zwischen … und …
The line graph shows the population development in … from (month/year) to (month/year).	Das Kurvendiagramm stellt die Bevölkerungsentwicklung in … von (Monat/Jahr) bis (Monat/Jahr) dar.
Over the period of time covered by the line graph the number of inhabitants/the population in … increased/decreased/remained constant from … to …	In dem Zeitraum, der durch das Kurvendiagramm abgedeckt wird, hat sich/ist die Zahl der Einwohner/die Bevölkerung in … vergrößert/verkleinert/gleich geblieben.
The horizontal axis of the line chart shows …, while the vertical axis represents …	Die horizontale Achse (x-Achse) des Kurvendiagramms zeigt …, während die vertikale Achse (y-Achse) … abbildet.
The number of … in … is compared in the pie chart/bar chart.	Das Tortendiagramm/Balkendiagramm vergleicht die Anzahl von … in …
All figures are given in per cent.	Alle Zahlen werden in Prozent angegeben.

Sprachmittlung

Im Klausurteil B, der Aufgabe zur Sprachmittlung, werden Sie dazu angehalten, die wesentlichen Inhalte von authentischen deutschen Texten sinngemäß für einen bestimmten Zweck adressatengerecht und situationsangemessen zusammenfassend in englischer Sprache wiederzugeben.

Eine Sprachmittlungsaufgabe gibt immer eine fiktive Situation vor, die eine Mittlung des deutschen Ausgangstextes verlangt. Im Gegensatz zu einer Übersetzung, die die wörtliche Übertragung eines Textes in die andere Sprache mitsamt aller möglicherweise vorhandenen Untertöne, Bildhaftigkeit, Ironie etc. erfordert, geht es bei der Sprachmittlung nur um die sinngemäße Übertragung in die Fremdsprache. In jedem Fall wird sich daher die Textform ändern.

Je nach Aufgabenstellung geht es entweder um eine Zusammenfassung des Textes, häufiger jedoch um das „Herauspicken" relevanter Informationen. Die Methodik für die inhaltliche Bearbeitung der Aufgabe gleicht also der Methodik für die Erstellung von Inhaltsangaben.

Beim Schreiben des englischen Textes berücksichtigt man die verschiedenen Aspekte der Sprachmittlung, wie sie hier in einer Übersicht dargestellt werden:

sinngemäß	– keine wortwörtliche Übersetzung – keine Übernahme von Stilmitteln oder Ton – ggf. implizierte Inhalte – nur die Inhalte des Textes, kein eigenes Wissen
situationsange-messen	– angemessener Stil – Beachtung der vorgegebenen Textform
adressatengerecht	– passendes Register (Freund? Professor? Gastmutter?) – Erläuterung von sprachlichen und kulturellen Eigenheiten[1]
zusammenfassend	– wesentliche Inhalte – ggf. wesentliche Details – nicht detailliert – nicht kommentiert (d. h. keine eigene Meinung)

TIPP zum Punktesammeln

Beachten Sie – wie immer – genau die Aufgabenstellung! Anders als bei der kreativen Teilaufgabe in Klausurteil A müssen Sie möglicherweise nicht den kompletten Zieltext erstellen, sondern nur den Teil, den die Sprachmittlung ausmacht. So kann die Aufgabenstellung z. B. lauten: "Write the part of your e-mail that is based on ..." oder "Write the part of your speech that deals with ...".

1 Viele Eigennamen oder Konnotationen werden sich dem fremdsprachlichen Adressaten nicht erschließen. Sie bedürfen daher einer Erklärung oder Umschreibung (z. B. *Rosenmontag, Abigag, Bildzeitung).*

Zieltextformate

In der anwendungs-/produktionsorientierten Teilaufgabe *re-creation of text* des Klausurteils A werden die in diesem Kapitel behandelten Textformate vorausgesetzt:
- *letter/email, letter to the editor*
- *speech script: talk, public/formal speech, debate statement*
- *newspaper/internet article*
- nur im Leistungskurs: (written) interview
- Ausgestaltung, Fortführung oder Ergänzung eines literarischen Ausgangstextes: narrative Texte; zusätzlich im Leistungskurs: dramatische Texte, *film script*

In Klausurteil B (Sprachmittlung) wird Vertrautheit mit den folgenden Zieltextformaten vorausgesetzt:
- *letter/email*
- *speech script: talk, public/formal speech*
- *newspaper/internet article*

Letter/E-mail

Formal Letter (förmlicher Brief)

Äußere Form
Adresse:
- eigene Adresse: anders als in Deutschland oben rechts, üblicherweise ohne Namen
- Empfänger: darunter auf der linken Seite

Datum:
unter der Anschrift entweder rechts oder links, Monat als Wort

persönlich bekannter Empfänger
Anrede:
Dear Mr/Mrs/Miss/Ms/Dr/Professor/ …
(*Ms* ist die neutrale Form, um *Mrs* bzw. *Miss* zu umgehen)

Schlussformel:
Yours sincerely/Kind regards

unbekannter Empfänger
Anrede:
Dear Sir/Dear Madam/Dear Sir or Madam,

Schlussformel:
Yours faithfully

Unterschrift:

persönliche Unterschrift
darunter Name in Druckschrift

Inhaltliche Gliederung

Einleitung:

Bezug und Zweck des Briefes

Hauptteil:

relevante Informationen, klar und logisch dargelegt, keine Schnörkel und Abschweifungen

Ende:

Erwartung an den Empfänger, z. B. als Bitte oder Aufforderung

Sprache

förmlich, **keine** *informal language,* d. h. **vermeiden** Sie

- *short forms*
- Interjektionen und Füllwörter wie *well, alright, okay, I see, you know*
- *question tags (isn't it, don't you, etc.)*

Benutzen Sie Wendungen wie

- *With reference to your letter of May 13th ...*
- *Thank you for your letter of ...*

- *I am writing to apply/to enquire about/to inform you/to complain about ...*
- *I should be delighted if ...*
- *I would be very glad if ...*
- *It would be very convenient if ...*
- *Please find enclosed ...* (In der Anlage finden Sie ...)

- *I should very much appreciate it if ...*
- *Please note that ...*

- *Thank you very much in advance.*

Die Regeln für die äußere Form gelten für eine E-Mail nicht. Die Form wird ja im Browser oder Client vorgegeben. Sprachlich gelten dieselben Regeln.

Letter to the Editor (Leserbrief)

Ein Leserbrief ist eher ein Zeitungsartikel als ein förmlicher Brief.
Zur sprachlichen und inhaltlichen Gestaltung siehe *Comment* (S. 111).

Äußere Form
Anrede:

Sir (bzw. *Madam)* – kein *Dear,* (gilt nicht bei einer Schülerzeitung)

Unterschrift:

Name, Stadt, ggf. Land/US-Staat

Personal Letter (persönlicher Brief)

Äußere Form
Adresse und Datum:

- eigene Adresse: anders als in Deutschland oben rechts, üblicherweise ohne Namen
- Datum darunter

Anrede:

Dear …

Schlussformel:

Yours (nicht: *your)/Best wishes/All the best/(Lots of) Love* (nicht: *in love)/Your friend …*

Unterschrift:

Vorname

Inhaltliche Gliederung
Einleitung:

Bezug zum Ausgangstext, Grund des Schreibens

Hauptteil:

z. B. Erzählung, Erklärung, Erläuterung, relevante Informationen

Ende:

z. B. Fragen, Vorschläge, Ausblick

Sprache

freundlicher Ton
informal language, d. h.:

- *short forms*
- Interjektionen und Füllwörter wie *well, alright, okay, I see, you know*

- *question tags (isn't it, don't you, etc.)*
- weitgehend einfache Satzgefüge

Alltagsvokabular, thematisches Vokabular

Speech Script (Rede)

Denkbar – und in den vergangenen Jahren im Abitur als kreative Teilaufgabe vorgekommen – sind verschiedene Formen der Rede, wie *talk* (Vortrag), *public/formal speech* (öffentliche/formelle Rede) oder *statement* (Statement, Erklärung).

Talk (Vortrag)

Einleitung:

- Begrüßung der Zuhörerschaft
- ggf. Vorstellung der eigenen Person
- Anknüpfung an den Ausgangstext
- Zusammenfassung von Inhalt und Zielen des Vortrags
- ggf. vorgesehene Gliederung

Hauptteil:
richtet sich nach dem Zweck des Vortrages:

- etwas mitteilen
- Interesse für ein Thema wecken
- für Publikation, Produkt, Dienstleistung werben
- einen Standpunkt verteidigen
- Zuhörer überzeugen
- Diskussion anregen

Strukturieren Sie ihren Hauptteil inhaltlich stringent! Ein inhaltlicher Aspekt folgt dem anderen, Argumente und Beispiele unterstreichen die einzelnen Aspekte.

Ende:

- Zusammenfassung
- Appell
- Ausblick
- Dank an die Zuhörer

Public/Formal Speech

Öffentliche Rede ist meist politische Rede und dient der Überzeugung der Zuhörerschaft.

Einleitung:

weniger sachlich als der Vortrag, d. h.:
- keine Zusammenfassung von Inhalt und Zielen
- keine Vorstellung der Gliederung
- keine persönliche Vorstellung

Begrüßung der Zuhörer

Anknüpfung an den Ausgangstext
provokative oder plakative Hinführung zum Thema
Problemstellung (und evtl. Lösung in Aussicht stellen)

Hauptteil:

klare Argumentation
Kausalketten beachten
Belege durch logische Argumente, Beispiele, Expertenmeinungen, Verweis auf Autoritäten (Regierung, Kirche, Wissenschaft)

Ende:

Zusammenfassung
Appell

Statement

Ein Statement wird gewöhnlich im Vorfeld einer Debatte abgegeben, um die Fronten zu klären. Ziel eines Statements ist es, einen Standpunkt zu verteidigen oder gar die Zuhörer zu überzeugen. So wird es den objektiven Ton eines Vortrages mit den Zielen der öffentlichen Rede verbinden.

Sprache
Anrede:

Unbedingt der vorgebenen Situation anpassen, z. B.
- *Dear Students, Dear Listeners, Dear Members of ...., (talk)*
- *Fellow Citizens, Friends, Dear Citizens of ... (public speech)*
- *Ladies and Gentlemen*
- bei Anwesenheit hochrangiger Personen oder auch nur Gastgebern:
  Mr President, Your Majesty, Prime Minister, Mr Chairman, Mr Jones

Hinführung:

plakative Aussagesätze
weitgehend einfache Satzgefüge
Fragen

public speech:
rhetorische Fragen
Anspielungen
Ironie

Hauptteil:

talk/statement:
klare, weitgehend einfache Aussagesätze
sachlicher, objektiver Stil

public speech:
emphatische Mittel: Parallelismen, Aufzählungen, Wiederholungen
(s. „Methoden der Textarbeit", S. 93)

Ende:

appellative Strukturen:
- *We must, we have to, we should*
- *It is imperative that ...*
- *Let us ...*

Dank:
- *Thank you.*
- *Thank you for your attention.*

Tipp zum Punktesammeln

Überfrachten Sie Ihre Rede nicht mit Metaphern und emphatischen Mitteln! Das kann albern wirken.

Newspaper Article/Internet Article

Report

Ein *report* ist ein Bericht, ein objektiver, sachlicher Artikel, dem eine Begebenheit oder eine Geschichte zugrunde liegt. Damit handelt es sich um einen narrativen Text. Sie können einen *report* in einer kreativen Aufgabe erwarten, wann immer eine Geschichte zu erzählen ist, insbesondere wenn der Ausgangstext gerade kein Zeitungsartikel ist.
Dramen oder Gedichte bieten häufig Stoff als Grundlage für einen Bericht.

Beachten Sie die Merkmale eines Berichtes, wie sie im Kapitel „Methoden der Textarbeit" zusammengefasst werden (S. 99).

Comment

Ein *comment* ist die Textform, die Sie besonders häufig als Sachtextvorlage Ihrer Analyseaufgabe finden. Als kreative Aufgabe sind verschiedene *comments* vorstellbar:
- ein Artikel aus Ihrer persönlichen Sicht
- ein Artikel aus der persönlichen Sicht einer Figur des Ausgangstextes
- ein Artikel aus der persönlichen Sicht des lyrischen Ichs eines lyrischen Ausgangstextes
- (ein Artikel aus der persönlichen Sicht einer Figur aus Werken, die Sie im Unterricht behandelt haben)

Immer muss ein Bezug zum Ausgangstext vorhanden sein. Stellen Sie sicher, dass Sie Ihre Erkenntnisse aus den Teilaufgaben 1 und 2 heranziehen, um die Aufgabe optimal zu lösen! Der Schlüssel zu Ihrer persönlichen Stellungnahme, aber auch zur Person eines fiktiven Verfassers und dessen persönlicher Meinung liegt genau darin.

Sprache und Aufbau

Beachten Sie die Merkmale eines Essays, wie sie im Kapitel „Methoden der Textarbeit" (S. 97) zusammengefasst werden! Für den Sprachgebrauch orientieren Sie sich an der Rhetorik der öffentlichen Rede (s. S. 93)!

(Written) Interview (nur LK)

Auch im Interview geht es um eine persönliche Stellungnahme, allerdings nicht um Ihre persönliche Meinung, sondern um die eines fiktiven Gesprächspartners.

Achtung, häufiger Fehler:
Schreiben Sie nur in Dialogform! Schreiben Sie keinen Erzähltext mit nur Anteilen von wörtlicher Rede!

Struktur
Beginn:

Aufnahme der situativen Vorgabe der Aufgabenstellung
Begrüßung, Vorstellung
Anknüpfung an den Ausgangstext
Hinführung zum Thema, ggf. Vorstellung des Anliegens

Hauptteil:

Frage/Antwort in sinnvoller Verknüpfung
Argumente und Beispiele

Schluss:

zum Beispiel:
- Zusammenfassung
- Witz
- Ausblick

Dank
Verabschiedung

Sprache

freundlicher Ton
informal language, d.h.:
- *short forms*
- Interjektionen und Füllwörter wie *well, alright, okay, I see, you know*
- *question tags (isn't it, don't you, etc.)*
- weitgehend einfache Satzgefüge

Alltagsvokabular, thematisches Vokabular

rhetorische Mittel: Wiederholungen, Aufzählungen, Anaphern, aber keine ausgefeilten Stilfiguren
Grußformel: *Good morning/afternoon/evening Mr/Mrs Jones/ Sir/Ma'am*
Schlussformel: z. B. *Thank you for your time, good bye ..., Thank you very much for the interview. Good bye ...*

Literarische Texte

Narrative Texte

Im Abitur werden Ihnen narrative Ausgangstexte meist als Roman- oder Kurzgeschichtenauszug begegnen. Folgende Varianten einer kreativen Aufgabenstellung sind denkbar:

- Lücken füllen (d. h. Begebenheiten, die im Ausgangstext nur erwähnt werden oder die der Leser nur aus dem Handlungsverlauf erschließen kann, sollen kreativ ausgestaltet werden)
- ein Ende oder eine Fortsetzung schreiben
- ein alternatives Ende schreiben
- Perspektivwechsel

Übernehmen Sie – falls die Aufgabenstellung es nicht ausdrücklich anders verlangt – die Erzählperspektive des Ausgangstextes!
Beachten Sie, dass Figuren sich weiterhin so verhalten, wie es ihrem Charakter entspricht, auch in ihrer Sprache!

Schreiben Sie keine neue Story mit einem vollständigen *plot* und einem neuen Höhepunkt. Es geht nicht um die Erfindung einer spannenden oder besonders originellen Handlung, sondern um eine logisch-konsequente Ausgestaltung des Ausgangstextes.

Sprache
Übernehmen Sie, soweit es geht, den Stil des Ausgangstextes.

Übernehmen Sie das Tempus des Ausgangstextes. In der Regel werden narrative Texte im *past tense* erzählt. Beachten Sie die Tempora der Vergangenheit.

Beispiel:
The ground ***was*** *wet because it* ***had been raining*** *all morning and although the rain* ***had stopped*** *and the sun* ***was shining*** *now, it* ***would be*** *difficult to find the track. On dry ground it* ***would have been*** *easy.*

was wet – Erzähltempus
it had been raining – vorzeitig, andauernd bis hin zum Erzählzeitpunkt
had stopped – vorzeitig
was shining – gerade ablaufende Hintergrundhandlung
it would be difficult – Zukunft aus der Sicht der Vergangenheit
it would have been easy – reine Hypothese in der Vergangenheit

Wechsel der Textform

Sollte die Aufgabenstellung eine vollständige Erzählung z. B. auf der Grundlage eines Gedichtes oder eines Zeitungsartikels verlangen, so achten Sie auf einen plausiblen inhaltlichen Bezug. Für die Ausgestaltung Ihrer Erzählung beachten Sie die Erzählelemente, wie sie im Kapitel „Methoden der Textarbeit“ (S. 80) vorgestellt werden.

Dramatische Texte (Schauspiel/Film)

Folgende Varianten einer kreativen Aufgabenstellung sind denkbar:
Bei einem dramatischen Ausgangstext:
- Lücken füllen (d. h. Begebenheiten, die im Ausgangstext nur erwähnt werden, sollen kreativ ausgestaltet werden)
- ein Ende oder eine Fortsetzung schreiben
- ein alternatives Ende schreiben

Bei anderen Ausgangstexten (z. B. Erzählung, Zeitungsartikel, Gedicht):
- Wechsel der Textform

Beachten Sie, dass Figuren sich so verhalten, wie es ihrem Charakter entspricht, auch in ihrer Sprache.

Sprache
Dialogtext:

gesprochene Sprache, d. h.
- *short forms*
- Interjektionen und Füllwörter wie *well, alright, okay, I see, you know*
- *question tags (isn't it, don't you, etc.)*
- weitgehend einfache Satzgefüge

Alltagsvokabular, thematisches Vokabular

Stage directions:

- in Klammern
- stichpunktartig
- *present tense*

Achtung, häufiger Fehler!
Erzählen Sie keine Geschichte mit wörtlicher Rede! Schreiben Sie ein Bühnenstück mit Dialogen und Regieanweisungen!

Beispiele für Prüfungsaufgaben zu den Fokusthemen

Die Beispielaufgaben sind vom Umfang und vom Schwierigkeitsgrad her teilweise für Leistungskurse, teilweise für Grundkurse konzipiert. Für Grundkurse gilt eine maximale Wortzahl von 800 Wörtern, für Leistungskurse von 1000 Wörtern. Der deutsche Text für die Sprachmittlungsaufgabe umfasst in beiden Kursen zwischen 450 und 600 Wörtern. Für ein Prüfungstraining spielt die Zuordnung keine entscheidende Rolle.
Um den verschiedenen Vorgaben für die beiden Kursarten gerecht zu werden, wurden überwiegend Texte ausgewählt, die den Vorgaben beider Kursarten entsprechen (Ausnahme: Shakespeare).

Aufgaben mit Bearbeitungsschritten und Beispiellösungen

Themenfeld *Voices from the African Continent: Focus on Nigeria*

Aufgabenbeispiel Abitur Englisch Leistungskurs
Aufgabenart gemäß KLP: 1.1: Schreiben mit Leseverstehen integriert und Sprachmittlung isoliert
Bezug zu den Vorgaben: Postkolonialismus – Lebenswirklichkeiten in einem weiteren anglophonen Kulturraum *Voices from the African Continent: Focus on Nigeria*
Englischsprachige literarische Texte (437 W. und 411 W.) (Klausurteil A, Texte 1 und 2) Auszug aus einem deutschsprachigen Sach- und Gebrauchstext (534 W.) (Klausurteil B, Text 3)
Quellenangaben: Text 1 und 2: Chimamanda Ngozi Adichie, *Americanah,* London 2013, pp. 3–4, pp. 385–386 Text 3: Lorenz Maroldt, „Image der deutschen Hauptstadt. Warum finden alle Berlin so toll – außer den Berlinern?“ *Der Tagesspiegel,* 22.04.2018, online: https://www.tagesspiegel.de/berlin/image-der-deutschen-hauptstadt-warum-finden-alle-berlin-so-toll-ausser-den-berlinern/21200348.html

Aufgabe

Klausurteil A: Leseverstehen/Schreiben (Text 1 und 2)

1. Describe Princeton and Lagos as presented in the excerpts. *(Comprehension)*

2. Examine the way the narrator presents Princeton and Lagos respectively. Consider the narrative point of view, atmosphere, characters, and the language used. *(Analysis)*

3.1 Comment on the narrator's presentation of Lagos and Ranyinudo. Assess to what extent it represents Nigeria's, as well as Africa's, social, cultural, and economic situation. *(Evalution)*

3.2 Ifemelu and Ranyinudo apparently often talk about the situation in Nigeria as compared to the western world (ll. 35–40). Write a dialogue between them considering aspects hinted at in the texts as well as aspects discussed in class. *(Re-creation of text)*

Klausurteil B: Sprachmittlung (Text 3)

4. During an exchange visit at an English school, you are doing a project in class on views people hold on various metropoles in the world. Your class comes across many English articles on Berlin. You are asked to give a short talk on what an insider's view on Berlin is like. Write your talk based on Maroldt's article. *(Mediation)*

Text 1 **Americanah** *Chimamanda Ngozi Adichie*
(excerpt from the novel, chapter 1)

Princeton, in the summer, smelled of nothing, and although Ifemelu liked the tranquil greenness of the many trees, the clean streets and stately homes, the delicately overpriced shops and the quiet, abiding air of earned grace, it was this, the lack of a smell that most appealed to her, perhaps because the other American cities she knew well had all smelled distinctly. Philadelphia had the musty scent of history. New Haven smelled of neglect. Baltimore smelled of brine, and Brooklyn of sun-warmed garbage. But Princeton had no smell. She liked taking deep breaths here. She liked watching the locals who drove with pointed courtesy and parked their latest model cars outside the organic grocery store on Nassau Street or outside the sushi restaurants or outside the ice cream shop that had fifty different flavours including red pepper or outside the post office where effusive staff bounded out to greet them at the entrance. She liked the campus, grave with knowledge, the Gothic buildings with their vine-laced walls, and the way everything transformed, in the half-light of night, into a ghostly scene. She liked, most of all, that in this place of affluent ease, she could pretend to be someone else, someone specially admitted into a hallowed American club, someone adorned with certainty.

But she did not like that she had to go to Trenton to braid her hair. It was unreasonable to expect a braiding salon in Princeton – the few black locals she had seen here so light-skinned and lank-haired she could not imagine them wearing braids – and yet as she waited at Princeton Junction station for the train, on an afternoon ablaze with heat, she wondered why there was no place where she could braid her hair. The chocolate bar in her handbag had melted. A few other people were waiting on the platform, all of them white and lean, in short, flimsy clothes. The man standing closest to her was eating an ice cream cone; she had always found it a little irresponsible, the eating of ice cream cones by grown-up American men, especially the eating of ice cream cones by grown-up American men in public. He turned to her and said. "About time," when the train finally creaked in with the familiarity strangers adopt with each other after sharing in the disappointment of a public service. She smiled at him. The greying hair on the back of his head was swept forward, a comical arrangement to disguise his bald spot. He had to be an academic, but not in the humanities or he would be more self-conscious. A firm science like chemistry, maybe.

[...]

Text 2 **Americanah** *Chimamanda Ngozi Adichie*
(excerpt from the novel, chapter 44)

At first, Lagos assaulted her; the sun-dazed haste, the yellow buses full of squashed limbs, the sweating hawkers racing after cars, the advertisements on hulking billboards (others scrawled on walls – PLUMBER CALL 080177777) and the heaps of rubbish that rose on the roadsides like a taunt. Commerce thrummed too defiantly. And the air was dense with exaggeration, conversations full of over-protestations. One morning, a man's body lay on Awolowo Road. Another morning, The Island flooded and cars became gasping boats. Here, she felt, anything could happen, a ripe tomato could burst out of solid stone. And so she had the dizzying sensation of falling, falling into the new person she had become, falling into the strange familiar. Had it always been like this or had it changed so much in her absence? When she left home, only the wealthy had mobile phones, all the numbers started with 090, and girls wanted to date 090 men. Now her hair braider had a mobile phone, the plantain seller tending a blackened grill had a mobile phone. She had grown up knowing all the bus stops and the side streets, understanding the cryptic codes of conductors and the body language of street hawkers. Now, she struggled to grasp the unspoken. When had shopkeepers become so rude? Had buildings in Lagos always had this patina of decay? And when did it become a city of people quick to beg and too enamoured of free things?

"Americanah!" Ranyinudo teased her often. "You are looking at things with American eyes. But the problem is that you are not even a real Americanah. At least if you had an American accent we would tolerate your complaining!"

Ranyinudo picked her up from the airport, standing by the Arrivals exit in a billowy bridesmaid's dress, her blusher too red on her cheeks like bruises, the green satin flowers in her hair now askew. Ifemelu was struck by how arresting, how attractive, she was. No longer a ropy mass of gangly arms and gangly legs, but now a big, firm, curvy woman, exulting in her weight and height, and it made her imposing, a presence that drew the eyes.

"Ranyi!" Ifemelu said. "I know my coming back is a big deal but I didn't know it was big enough for a ball gown."

"Idiot. I came straight from the wedding. I didn't want to risk the traffic of going home first to change."

They hugged, holding each other close. Ranyinudo smelled of a floral perfume and exhaust fumes and sweat; she smelled of Nigeria.

[...]

Annotations
Princeton – US Ivy League university
plantain – kind of banana
Americanah – *Nigerian:* emigrant to America

Text 3 **Image der deutschen Hauptstadt. Warum finden alle Berlin so toll – außer den Berlinern?** *Lorenz Maroldt*

Exzellent organisiert, erschwinglich, cool: Eine neue Begeisterung für die deutsche Hauptstadt wächst in der Welt. In Berlin dagegen überwiegt der Ärger über alltägliche Mängel. Wie passt das zusammen?

Kaum zu fassen, was da gerade so alles über Berlin geschrieben wird, vor allem in Großbritannien und den USA. Das soll unsere Stadt sein? Wir zwängen uns in übervolle Busse, quälen uns durch den Schienenersatzverkehr, lernen auf dem Bahnsteig wartend immer neue Arten von Betriebsstörungen bei der S-Bahn kennen – und lesen in der Londoner „Times": „Excellent public transport." What?

Wir erleben stark steigende Mieten und Wohnungspreise, spüren den Druck von Immobilienspekulanten, fürchten, uns die eigene Stadt nicht mehr leisten zu können – und bekommen gesagt: „Berlin is very affordable". Really?

Wir wissen nicht, wohin mit den Kindern, stehen vor gesperrten Spielplätzen, hören, dass stadtweit 500 davon demoliert sind – und lesen sprachlos in der „New York Times": „Berlin is a playground paradise." Wir stolpern über wild abgestellten Sperrmüll, lesen von Rattenalarm in heruntergekommenen Häusern, erkennen unter Tonnen von Tüten, Pappen und Flaschen nach den Wochenenden unsere Parks nicht mehr – und lassen uns von New Yorks Ex-Bürgermeister Rudy Giuliani sagen: „Berlin ist eine sehr saubere Stadt."

Die Stadt ist nicht die aus den Netflix-Serien

Haben wir, die ewigen Nörgler, eine Wahrnehmungsstörung? Finden wir nicht heraus aus unserer folkloristischen Meckerattitüde? Oder übersehen die Gäste bei ihren Stippvisiten, berauscht von was auch immer, was hier wirklich läuft – oder vielmehr: was nicht? Verwechseln sie gar die echte Stadt mit der, die in Serien von Sky, Netflix und Amazon in mehr als hundert Ländern der Welt gezeigt wird? Allein die Zahl der in Berlin lebenden US-Amerikaner ist in den vergangenen zwei Jahren um 9,6 Prozent gestiegen. 46.600 sind es jetzt, dazu kommen noch die Botschaftsangehörigen.

Auch der Blick von außen aufs große Ganze verblüfft. Im „Economist" erscheint unter dem Titel „Cool Germany" eine Hymne auf unser Land, das doch eigentlich erschöpft ist: von der Pflege-, Diesel- und Flüchtlingskrise, der quälenden Regierungsbildung, vom Aufmarsch der Rechtspopulisten, der außenpolitischen Orientierungslosigkeit. Aber auf dem Titel der „Times" steht, zu einem Bild der Hauptstadt Berlin: „A Titan of Europe".

Schließen wir mal aus, dass es eine virtuelle Parallelwelt gibt, die Berlins Stadtmarketingprofis bei Bedarf präsentieren. Woran liegt es dann, dass andere so begeistert sind von diesem Ort, Ordnung loben, wo wir Chaos sehen, Modernität erkennen, wo wir mit der Verwaltung nur analog in Kontakt treten können? Dass sie unsere Internationalität so anziehend finden, aber wir einen polyglotten belgischen Theaterintendanten nicht mal ein Jahr lang ertragen können?

[...]

In Berlin erleben wir das weitgehend klassenlose Zusammenleben zwar als spannend, aber auch als Anstrengung. Wir sind stolz auf unsere Toleranz, aber die ist stressfrei kaum zu haben. Andererseits stimmt ja auch: Wenn hier alles nur so schrecklich wäre, wie wir uns oft gegenseitig in geselliger Runde versichern, wären wir längst woanders. Die Kunst, das Theater, die Musik, Bars und Restaurants, Markthallen, die Food-Szene, relaxen an den Ufern der Spree und den zwei großen Seen – so ertragen wir das Bürgeramt, die Verkehrslenkung. Und wer an das Londoner U-Bahnnetz gewöhnt ist, wo das Schild „No Service on Victoria Line" zur Ausstattung gehört, oder die maroden, unzuverlässigen New Yorker Züge kennt, empfindet das Angebot der BVG schon eher nachvollziehbar als „excellent", relativ gesehen.

[...]

Bearbeitungsschritte und Musterlösungen

Klausurteil A
Anforderungsbereich I *(Comprehension)*

1. Describe the places and people presented in the excerpts. *(Comprehension)*

Der Operator „describe" verlangt eine gewisse Ausführlichkeit etwa im Gegensatz zu „outline" oder „sum up". Eine solche Aufgabe bietet sich an, wenn die Textvorlage selbst sehr deskriptiv ist, wenn es keine wirkliche Handlung gibt. Wenn Sie einen Blick auf die zweite Teilaufgabe werfen, so sehen Sie, dass auch die Analyse sich mit der Beschreibung der beiden Städte befasst. Beachten Sie die Trennschärfe zwischen den beiden Aufgabenstellungen! Charaktere und sprachliche Besonderheiten, Bildhaftigkeit, Erzähltechnik gehören erst in die zweite Teilaufgabe. Princeton und Lagos werden im engeren Sinne jeweils nur im ersten Textabschnitt beschrieben. Der Mann auf dem

Bahnsteig in Princeton und Ranyinudo in Lagos tragen dann als Charaktere zu der Darstellung der jeweiligen Stadt bei. Dieses sollte in Teilaufgabe 2 Erwähnung finden.

Das Isolieren von Schlüsselwörtern ist eine unabdingbare Methode, profundes Textverständnis zu erlangen. Dies geschieht normalerweise durch Markierung und Notizen im Text. Hier werden wir sie auflisten. Danach sollten sie in einen Sinnzusammenhang gebracht werden.

paragraph	**keywords**	**→**
Text 1, paragraph 1 (note: p. 3, i. e. beginning of the novel)	Princeton	place, location
	smelled of nothing	sensation
	tranquil greenness many trees clean streets stately homes delicately overpriced shops	visual appearance
	locals/pointed courtesy	people's behaviour
	latest-model cars organic grocery store sushi restaurant ice-cream shop/fifty different flavors	visual appearance
	effusive staff bounded out to greet them	people's behaviour
	campus Gothic buildings [no] braiding salon	visual appearance
Text 2, paragraph 1	Lagos	place, location
	sun-dazed haste sweating hawkers heaps of rubbish air dense with exaggeration, conversations, over-protestations	sensation
	yellow buses full of squashed limbs sweating hawkers heaps of rubbish advertisements on hulking billboards others scrawled on walls	visual appearance
	a man's body flooding	examples of visual appearance
	shopkeepers rude	behaviour
	patina of decay	visual appearance
	quick to beg	behaviour

Vor dem Verfassen des Textes rufen Sie sich die Prinzipien der Inhaltsangabe ins Gedächtnis:
Gliederung des Textes/Textverständnis
- zum besseren Textverständnis Text in Sinnabschnitte unterteilen. Meist helfen die Absätze des Textes schon dabei.

Schreiben:
- eigene Formulierungen
- einleitender Satz
- Antwort auf die geforderten W-Fragen (hier: Wo, Was und Wer)

Bei Ihrer Sammlung von Schlüsselwörtern sollten Sie prüfen, ob Inhaltsaspekte sich wiederholen (siehe Spalte 3). Ihren eigenen Text sollten Sie dann nicht anhand der Textchronologie, sondern anhand der Inhaltsaspekte strukturieren.

TIPP zum Punktesammeln

Reduzieren Sie Ihre Inhaltsangabe auf das Wesentliche (keine Ausschmückung durch besondere Adjektive, keine kleinen Details, keine Zitate, keine Metaphorik). Lassen Sie aber auch keine Merkmale, die die beiden Städte ausmachen, weg! Beschreiben Sie nur die Städte, nicht die Charaktere! Verweisen Sie nicht auf Abschnitte oder Zeilen im Ausgangstext! Zitieren Sie nicht! Nehmen Sie keine Wertung vor!
Grundtempus ist das *simple present.*

Hier eine mögliche Umsetzung:

Chimamanda Ngozi Adichie's novel "Americanah", which was published in 2013, begins with a description of Princeton as perceived by Ifemelu, apparently the main character of the novel. Unlike other American cities, Princeton has no smell, which is the most appealing feature to Ifemelu. It is presented as very green and clean, with stately houses and expensive shops, fancy restaurants, and ice-cream parlours, and an extravagant post office, but no braiding salon. The campus is marked by its Gothic buildings.
In a later chapter of the novel, Lagos, Nigeria, is described, also as perceived by Ifemelu, who is evidently from Lagos and comes back after her stay in America. Lagos is hot and moist, people are sweating, buses are overcrowded. There are large advertising billboards and informal adverts simply scribbled on walls. The roadside is full of rubbish, buildings seem to be decaying. Hawkers try to sell their merchandise to car drivers and everybody has a mobile phone. Shopkeepers seem unfriendly and there are a lot of beggars. One day there is a dead body in the street, another day the city is flooded.

Anforderungsbereich II *(Analysis)*

2. Examine the way the narrator presents Princeton and Lagos respectively. Consider the narrative point of view, atmosphere, characters, and the language used. *(Analysis)*

Prinzipiell geht es im Anforderungsbereich II immer um Struktur und/oder Sprache des Textes oder um die Analyse von Erzählelementen wie *character* oder *point of view,* nicht mehr um Inhalt, wenn auch dieses Prinzip leider nicht immer gewahrt wird.
Die Aufgabenstellung spezifiziert ausdrücklich *point of view, atmosphere, characters* und *language* (d. h. *choice of words, imagery* und *stylistic devices).* Sie sollten das dann auch ganz genau nehmen und diese Anweisung als Checkliste benutzen. Mit einer Analyse der Textstruktur sollte man sich also auch nicht aufhalten!
Passagen, in denen die Erzählperspektive *(point of view)* eine besondere Wirkung erzielt, sind ebenso im Text zu markieren, wie die für die Atmosphäre relevanten Beschreibungen des *settings* und der Charaktere sowie Besonderheiten der Sprachverwendung.
Im Zieltext muss dann nicht zwingend jeder einzelne Beleg zitiert werden, Verweise auf die entsprechenden Zeilen sollten jedoch in jedem Fall erfolgen. Wir werden im Folgenden die zu unterstreichenden Elemente benennen.

quotation	**narrative technique/ element of narration/**	**aspect of language**	**function/ effect**
Text 1			
tranquil greenness l. 3 many trees l. 3 clean streets l. 4	setting, atmosphere	choice of words: tranquil, green, clean, stately, delicately, pointed, courtesy	positive connotation: pleasant, lovely
stately homes l. 4 delicately overpriced shops ll. 4–5 locals/pointed courtesy l. 15 latest-model cars l. 16 organic grocery store l. 17 sushi restaurant l. 18 ice-cream shop/fifty different flavors ll. 19–20 effusive staff bounded out to greet them ll. 21–22	setting, atmosphere		people's lifestyle: luxurious, cosmopolitan, ecological → high class, bourgeois, academic, wealthy, quiet, white-dominated, traditional

[no] braiding salon grave with knowledge, affluent ease l. 28			
..., the lack of smell, that most appealed to her ll. 6–7	point of view		insight into character's thoughts
she knew well l. 8–9			insight into the character's pre-ferences
She liked ... She liked ... She liked ll. 13–27		anaphora	emphasis
She could pretend l. 27			insight
hallowed American club l. 30		choice of words/ imagery	exclusiveness of Princeton Uni-versity
But she did not like l. 32		antithesis	emphasis
It was unreasonable to expect ll. 33–34			character's rea-soning
She could not imagine ll. 36–37 She wondered l. 40			character's thin-king
She had always found ll. 46–47			
He had to be l. 58		reported thought	
short and flimsy clothes ll. 44–45 greying hair, swept for-ward, comical arrange-ment, academic, science ll. 55–60	character		fitting in with the setting
Text 2			
Die Beschreibung des set-ting, wie sie für Teilaufga-be 1 unterstrichen wurde.	setting, at-mosphere	choice of words: assault, sun-dazed, squas-hed, sweating, hulking, dense, heaps, exag-geration, over-protestation	atmosphere of being exposed to too much of everything: climate, popula-tion, activity: lively, diverse, overwhelming, threatening, ...
Lagos assaulted her l. 1	point of view	personification	threat

she felt l. 13			character's feeling
cars became gasping boats l. 13 a ripe tomato could burst out of solid stone ll. 14–15	setting/ atmosphere	personification/ imagery	Lagos as dynamic, unpredictable, amazing
she had the dizzying sensation of falling ll. 15–16	point of view		
Had it always been ...? ll. 18–19		reported thought	insight
When had ...? l. 30			
And when did ...? ll. 32–33			
was struck l. 46	point of view		character's perception
billowy ... dress, blusher too red, like bruises big, firm curvy exulting imposing ll.42–50	character	choice of words imagery	fitting in with Lagos
Ranyinudo smelled of ... she smelled of ... ll. 59–60	point of view		character's sensation

Es ergibt meist wenig Sinn, die Texte rein chronologisch zu beschreiben. Dies braucht viel zu viel wertvolle Arbeitszeit und Energie und führt zu Wiederholungen und einem unübersichtlichen und viel zu umfangreichen Zieltext. Viel eleganter ist es, den Zieltext inhaltlich anhand der vorgegebenen Formelemente und sprachlichen Mittel zu strukturieren und nicht Zeile für Zeile des Ausgangstextes zu behandeln. Jeder Ihrer Sinnabschnitte erhält dann aussagekräftige Zitate und ergänzende Textverweise. Wichtig sind Aussagen zur Funktion der Elemente, selbst wenn sie in der Aufgabenstellung nicht ausdrücklich genannt wird. Es reicht z. B. nicht, eine Metapher zu finden und zu benennen, man muss sie auch erläutern.
Die Aufgabenstellung verlangt die Untersuchung der Romanelemente *point of view, atmosphere* und *character*. Es bietet sich an, diese Elemente auch nacheinander zu untersuchen und dabei die Sprachverwendung im Blick zu behalten.

Da die Vorgaben einen zusammenhängenden Zieltext fordern, sollte man Teil II elegant an Teilaufgabe 1 anbinden. Ein erneuter Einleitungssatz wäre genauso unglücklich wie eine Formulierung wie „Now I am going to analyse ...“ gefolgt von einer Paraphrase der Aufgabenstellung. Es wäre ein regelrechter Bruch, keine kohärente Anbindung. Eine solche Formulierung strukturiert allenfalls einen mündlichen Vortrag, nicht jedoch einen Aufsatz. Meist ist gar keine Überleitung nötig. Wichtig ist nur Textkohärenz.

Hier eine mögliche Umsetzung:
The atmosphere created in the narrator's description of Princeton contrasts starkly with the atmosphere of Lagos. Princeton, home to one of America's Ivy League universities, appears as an extremely pleasant place with its many trees and clean streets. Positively connotated words like "tranquil", "green", "clean" (ll. 3, 4) suggest a pleasant, even graceful town. It is a wealthy environment with an atmosphere marked by people's lifestyle revealed by "stately homes", "delicately overpriced shops", "latest model cars", and "fifty different flavors" in the ice-cream shop (ll. 4, 5, 15-20.). People live an upper-class academic lifestyle of "affluent ease", buying ecologically in "organic grocery stores" (ll. 19-20), and feeling cosmopolitan by eating in "sushi restaurants" (l. 18). The lack of a braiding salon shows that Princeton society is almost exclusively white. Princeton University is referred to as a "hallowed American club", "grave with knowledge" with its "Gothic buildings" and "vine laced walls", which again expresses the exclusiveness and venerability of this place, even at night, when it becomes a "ghostly scene" (ll. 30-31).
All this is presented to the reader from Ifemelu's point of view. We participate in her perception right from the beginning, when we are told that "Princeton smells of nothing" (l. 1). We are also told how much she likes the appearance of the place. The anaphorical repetition of "She liked ..." supports this as much as the antithetical phrase "But she did not like" (ll. 13-27, 32). The reader also gets an insight into her thinking and reasoning throughout the passage: "She could pretend to be ..." (ll. 28-29), "It was unreasonable to expect ..." (ll. 33-34), "She could not imagine ..." (ll. 36-37), "She wondered ..." (l. 40), "She had always found ..." (ll. 46-47).
The characters on the platform fit in with the setting and support the atmosphere. "Short and flimsy" (l. 44) clothes and ice-cream suggest pleasant temperatures, and especially the man described fits in with the academic environment. With the "comical arrangement" of his "greying hair" he has the typical appearance of a university scientist (ll. 55-60). Again, this is observed from Ifemelu's point of view: she "had always found it a little irresponsible" to eat ice cream in public (ll. 46-50). She supposes he is an academic, expressed by the narrator by means of reported thought ("He had to be ...", l. 58)
Like Ifemelu's fondness for Princeton, her bewilderment when she returns to Lagos is expressed by the narrator's taking the third-person limited point of view: She feels "assaulted" by Lagos (text 2, l. 1). Unlike Princeton, the atmosphere created here is unpleasant, threatening, overwhelming. There is too much of everything, which is expressed in the first three sentences. The atmosphere is hectic, people are in "haste", hawkers "racing after cars" (ll. 2-4). The yellow buses, which are as characteristic of the traffic of Lagos as the yellow cabs are of New York, are full of "squashed limbs", an amorphous mass of body parts rather than people. The signs of commerce like billboards, writing on the walls, and heaps of rubbish overwhelm the observer. This idea of "too much" is also expressed in lines 1 to 15: The noises of commerce defying poverty, the noise of conversations, and exaggeration in general. Adjectives like "sun-dazed" (ll. 1-2), "squashed", "sweating" (ll. 2-3) "hulking" and "dense" give the impression that breathing is hard in Lagos. Even the cars, which metaphorically turn into boats, when part of Lagos is flooded, are personified as "gasping" (l. 13). With the image "a ripe tomato could burst out

of solid stone" (ll. 14-15) the narrator expresses how dynamic, unpredictable, amazing, and even uncanny Lagos can be.
As said above, the reader perceives this through Ifemelu's thoughts and feelings. We are told she "felt anything could happen". She is immersed into the familiar but strange culture she is coming back to. To her it is like falling (ll. 15-16), she has a "dizzying sensation of falling" with the word falling repeated twice, which suggests a certain suddenness, a certain speed but also duration. Her thinking is again expressed by reported thought, when she ponders about the changes that have occurred since she left, about mobile phones, about communication, about people's behaviour and about the condition of the buildings in Lagos (ll. 19-34).
The character of Ranyinudo fits in with the appearance and the atmosphere of Lagos and supports it. Her appearance, too, seems to be exaggerated in a "billowy" dress and her cheeks "too red" with her blusher compared to bruises (ll. 41-44). Ifemelu perceives her as a "big, firm, curvy woman, exulting in her weight and height". With Ifemelu, the reader perceives her intense smell when they hug, which – to Ifemelu – is the smell of Nigeria.

Anforderungsbereich III *(Evaluation)*

3.1 Comment on the way Lagos and Ranyinudo are presented. Assess to what extent it represents Nigeria's, as well as Africa's, social, cultural, and economic situation. *(Evalution)*

Der Operator „comment" verlangt eine persönliche Stellungnahme zum Ausgangstext, in diesem Fall nur zu Text 2. Im Unterricht erworbene Kenntnisse zu Nigeria sind hier hilfreich.
Ihre Sammlungen zu den Anforderungsbereichen I und II geben hinreichend Anlass zur Betrachtung der sozio-kulturellen Situation Nigerias bzw. Afrikas. Sie können am Anfang der Stellungnahme ganz knapp zusammenfassend darauf Bezug nehmen. Wiederholen Sie aber ja nicht konkret alles, was Sie bereits geschrieben haben! Im Hinblick auf die Anforderungen des Anforderungsbereichs III geht es hier um Verallgemeinerung. Gegebenenfalls könnten Sie diese Aspekte durch weitere Aspekte, die Sie aus dem Unterricht kennen, erweitern. Ein eleganter Bezug kann auch zum letzten Satz des Textauszuges hergestellt werden, der in der Beispiellösung ja auch am Ende von Teilaufgabe II erwähnt wird.

aspects mentioned in the texts	generally true of Nigeria
Lagos assaulted her	general impact of African megacity
sun-dazed haze	climate
exaggeration, conversations, overprotestations yellow buses full of squashed limbs sweating hawkers shopkeepers rude mobile phone	people, growing population, noise, young population, modern, affinity to modern media, class differences

a man's body flooding patina of decay quick to beg	problems: crime, infrastructure, poverty, gap between rich and poor.
advertisements on hulking billboards others scrawled on the wall heaps of rubbish mobile phone	economic situation, commerce, environmental awareness, lifestyle
Ranyinudo, clothes, smell	exuberance
Ifemelu, Americanah	problems of migration

Die Stellungnahme schließt sich ebenso nahtlos an die Analyse an, wie diese sich an die Inhaltsangabe anschließt. Wichtig ist, dass ein Bezug hergestellt wird zum bisherigen Zieltext. Da die Formulierung der Aufgabenstellung so nicht im Text erscheint, darf auf sie nicht z. B. mit Pronomen Bezug genommen werden. Ganz schlecht ist auch der sofortige Einstieg mit „I think" oder „In my opinion", denn auch die eigene Meinung erfordert eine Hinführung.

Hier eine mögliche Umsetzung:
Bearing the "smell of Nigeria" Ranyinudo is indeed a representative not only of Nigeria but of Africa, at least sub-Saharan Africa. She completely fulfils the cliché of the full-figured black lady, clothed in colourful traditional dress talking with a big smile and bright white teeth, the cliché of exuberance certainly holding a lot of truth in it.
More than just a cliché is the appearance of Lagos and its people. The passage reveals the socio-economic problems of African megacities. It hints at class differences, the large gap between rich and poor, the poor infrastructure, which is vulnerable to natural disaster and the decay of large parts of the inner cities.
Like any African megacity – be it Cairo, Nairobi or Johannesburg – it assaults the visitor as the urban nightmare that it is: the buzzing, bustling, fast-paced life of overpopulated African cities trying to come to terms with capitalist achievements and aspirations. Business, trading, advertising play an important part. Making money has become people's main concern and has infected people with selfishness and greed, some even having lost their dignity. Huge billboards and hand-scribbled adverts on the wall witness the predominant role of commerce. Nigeria is Africa's biggest economy. Lagos attracts millions of people who want to get their slice of the cake. Many of them only get a very small slice or none, as some people get the lion's share. Apparently, Nigeria has more millionaires and billionaires than any other African country with half of the population living in extreme poverty. Crime is a serious problem of African cities, the body that is mentioned in the text hints at the omnipresence of crime but also at the negligence of the authorities, the police even, which is also mirrored by the heaps of rubbish in the streets. Indeed, there are enormous sanitary problems in African cities not only concerning rubbish disposal but also sewage disposal, water shortage and poor drainage. This problem, too, is hinted at in the text when the narrator refers to flooding.

Ifemelu, as a so-called Americanah, a Nigerian emigrant to America, represents the millions of Africans who try to find a better life abroad. Apparently, Ifemelu, who has got as far as Princeton University has succeeded. She is only teased about her accent which does not seem to be properly American. Very often, however, Africans coming back to their home countries are despised as failure, a loser, somebody who got nowhere, an attitude that makes the problem of migration even bigger.
Nigeria's (and Africa's) population is young, 40 % in sub-Saharan Africa are younger than 15. Therefore, people are modern, using modern media extensively. As in many countries, mobile phones have become an indispensable accessory used in all walks of life.
Unfortunately, the text does not hint at many more positive features of Africa, apart from the presentation of Ranyinudo as a likeable person. It may slightly hint at tradition and fashion, which both play an important role in Nigeria or even Africa. Thus, the text does not do much against the negative view of African cities most of us hold.

Anforderungsbereich III ***(Evaluation/Re-creation of text)***

3.2 Ifemelu and Ranyinudo apparently often talk about the situation in Nigeria as compared to the western world (ll. 35–40). Write a dialogue between them considering aspects hinted at in the texts as well as aspects discussed in class. *(Re-creation of text)*

Für die kreative Aufgabe ist zu beachten:

Perspektivwechsel
- Wie ist die zusätzliche Sicht der Dinge aus der Perspektive Ranyinudos?
- Was für eine Art Sprache benutzt sie?

Inhaltliche Anknüpfung an Teilaufgaben 1 und 2 durch einleitenden Satz. Keine formale Anknüpfung, s. u.
Inhaltlicher Bezug zu Teilaufgaben 1 und 2, z. B. durch
- Vergleich (Ähnlichkeiten/Unterschiede)
- Kritik
- Wertung
- Gegendarstellung

Eine textkohärente Anknüpfung an Teilaufgabe 2 in diesem Fall nicht möglich, denn die Textform ist eine völlig andere.

Hier eine mögliche Umsetzung:
<u>Ifemelu:</u> Ranyinudo, I don't know what has become of Nigeria, what has become of Lagos. As if it was not hot enough in Africa, people have to squeeze into these little yellow buses; they can hardly breathe there. And the hawkers are really getting on my nerves, they harass me.
<u>Ranyinudo:</u> You're looking at all this with American eyes. You are not even a real Americanah, because you haven't got the accent.

Ifemelu: Oh, come on, I may not have the accent, but I really got used to living in the States and to the American way of life. This hassle and this noise is something I can't get used to.
Ranyinudo: Hey, you cannot compare Lagos to your beloved Princeton. Princeton is a rich university town, people living there are privileged anyway.
Ifemelu: Yes you are right, Princeton is not the place that compares with Lagos, but look at New York City. I've been to New York many times. It's just around the corner from Princeton. New York is as big as Lagos. But it is a lot better organised, a lot less chaotic.
Ranyinudo: Is it?
Ifemelu: I'm sure there must be the same number of people but half the amount of din. It is clean – at least Manhattan is – there are no rubbish heaps and people don't throw rubbish on the streets. Sure, there is a lot of crime, but you don't see dead bodies lying around for days. And the sewage system works. There is never any flooding.
Ranyinudo: Yes, I see your point. There is a lot which is not perfect in this country. But what do you expect? Lagos has become so popular among all kinds of people that they literally flock here. Lagos's infrastructure was not built for this. The city is trying hard to cope with it and to improve – for example – public transport. The sewage system and the rubbish management are important tasks that we have to tackle. And you know, corruption has always been a problem and it hasn't changed that much. Petty corruption has declined somewhat thanks to measures taken by the government, but big corruption is still increasing. The bigger the project, the greater the opportunity to divert cash. So a lot of money doesn't get where it's supposed to go.
Ifemelu: Yes, but what about the people? They've changed so much. Everybody seems to have a mobile phone.
Ranyinudo: Yes, but isn't this a phenomenon that we see all over the world? Don't tell me it's not like this in the States. And if it isn't, look at Europe. Texting is what young people do all the time. And Nigeria is extremely young. There are not so many old people like in Europe or America. And of course, that's why it's a lot more lively.
Ifemelu: But all this commerce everywhere. Everybody seems so greedy; everyone is chasing after money; shopkeepers are so unfriendly.
Ranyinudo: What do you expect? People have learned the lesson of democracy; people have learned the lesson of free enterprise and competition. This is based on your American Dream, a Nigerian Dream, Ifemelu. Look at the things that Nigeria has to offer: Our cultural diversity, our youth, our talents, our resilience and happiness. We still cherish our traditions and we still fear God. Isn't this something to be proud of?
Ifemelu: Yes, maybe you're right.

Klausurteil B
Sprachmittlung/Mediation

4. During an exchange visit at an English school, you are doing a project in class on views people hold on various metropoles in the world. Your class comes across many English articles on Berlin. You are asked to give a short talk on what an insider's view on Berlin is like. Write your talk based on Maroldt's article.

Vergegenwärtigen Sie sich die Prinzipien der Sprachmittlung, wie wir sie auf Seite 103 dargestellt haben. Für den vorliegenden Text beachten wir konkret:

Zieltext: *Talk* (vgl. Zieltextformate, S. 105)
Für eine knappe, sachliche Wiedergabe gehen wir wie bei einer Zusammenfassung vor. Der Text ist bereits vorstrukturiert, sodass Sie nur noch die einzelnen Aspekte zusammenfassen müssen:

- die positive Sicht auf die Stadt in der britischen und amerikanischen Presse hinsichtlich
  - ÖPNV
  - Lebenshaltungskosten
  - Kinderfreundlichkeit
  - Sauberkeit

- die Reflexion, ob die Wahrnehmung der Berliner oder der Besucher gestört ist
  - Berliner als notorische Meckerer
  - Touristen, die die wahren Zustände übersehen
  - Beeinflussung durch Netflix etc.

- der ebenso verblüffend positive Blick auf Deutschland als *cool Germany* und *Titan of Europe,* ungeachtet der derzeitigen Krisen
  - Pflegenotstand
  - Flüchtlingskrise
  - Dieselskandal
  - Rechtsextremismus
  - Regierungsbildung
  - außenpolitische Orientierungslosigkeit

- die Erklärung, die die Klagen der Einheimischen relativiert: Unzulänglichkeiten bei Infrastruktur und Verwaltung werden wettgemacht durch
  - Kunst, Theater, Musik
  - Gastronomie
  - Flair
  - Entspannung an Fluss und Seen
  - einen Vergleich des Berliner ÖPNV mit den U-Bahnen in New York und London

Adressatenorientiertung
In Ihrer fiktiven Situation als Teilnehmer an einem Kurs in einer englischen Schule müssen Sie dafür sorgen, dass Ihr Kurzvortrag adressatengerecht gestaltet wird. Wörter wie „Schienenersatzverkehr" oder „Betriebsstörungen", die wir unweigerlich mit nervigem Bus- und Bahnfahren assoziieren, müssen angemessen umschrieben werden, am besten in einer verallgemeinerten Beschreibung aufgehen. Das gleiche gilt für „ewige Nörgler", „Wahrnehmungsstörung" und „folkloristische Meckerattitüde". Einer kurzen Erklärung bedürfen die politischen Anspielungen, weil eine bloße

Übersetzung den fiktiven britischen Mitschülern nichts sagen würde. Einer Erklärung bedarf wohl nicht das Wort Food Szene. Auch in London spricht man von der *food scene,* wenn von trendy Restaurants oder Street Food Markets die Rede ist. Ganz schlecht ist eine Übernahme eines Wortes in Anführungsstrichen (z. B. „BVG"). Anführungsstriche helfen dem armen des Deutschen unkundigen Menschen gar nicht beim Verständnis.

Hier eine mögliche Umsetzung (305 statt 534 Wörter):

I found an article on the internet which deals with views on Berlin. It's astonishing how positive the view on Berlin is in the British and American press.

It says "Excellent transport" in the Times, whereas Berliners feel that buses are crammed and many trains do not run for all kinds of reasons. It says that "Berlin is very affordable", whereas Berliners feel that due to rising rents and property prices, they can't afford their own city anymore. The New York Times writes that Berlin is "playground paradise", whereas Berliners experience more and more closed down and vandalized playgrounds, and the ex-mayor of New York calls Berlin a clean city, whereas Berliners hear of houses full of rats and see their streets and parks as full of rubbish.

So, whose perception is disturbed? Do Berliners notoriously complain about everything, or are the visitors so impressed by whatever that they don't see the downsides? Or is the image influenced by the way Berlin is presented by series on Netflix, Sky, or Amazon?

Even Germany as a whole is presented as "cool Germany" or the "Titan of Europe" despite a catastrophic shortage of hospital staff, despite the arrival of many refugees from the Middle East and fierce controversy on their acceptance, despite a world-wide scandal on manipulated Diesel cars, despite a renaissance of the extreme right, and a government which does not seem fit to rule.

Yet, it is true, Berlin cannot be that terrible. Otherwise, people would have left. What makes up for failure of the administration and insufficient infrastructure is the large variety of theatre, art, and music events, pubs and restaurants, market halls and the food scene, and the river and the lakes, where people can relax. Even the public transport system is not too bad, if you compare it to London or New York.

Themenfeld *Globalization and Global Challenges*

Aufgabenbeispiel Abitur Englisch Grundkurs
Aufgabenart gemäß KLP: 1.1: Schreiben mit Leseverstehen integriert und Sprachmittlung isoliert
Bezug zu den Vorgaben (soziokulturelles Orientierungswissen): Chancen und Risiken der Globalisierung *Globalization and global challenges* *– The impact of globalization on culture and communication*

englischsprachiger Sachtext Text (583 W.) (Klausurteil A, Text 1) Cartoon (Klausurteil A, Text 2) Auszug aus einem deutschsprachigen Sachtext (497 W.) (Klausurteil B, Text 3)
Quellenangaben: Text 1: Neil White: "Trick or treat? The worst example of Americanisation in modern society", *Derby Telegraph*, 3.11.2014 (online) Text 2: Cartoon: Andy Singer, Saint Paul, MN Text 3: Dückers, Tanja: „Von Geburt an Multikulturalist", *Die Zeit Online*, 6.2.2015 http://www.zeit.de/gesellschaft/zeitgeschehen/2015-02/europa-identitaet-migration-einwanderung/komplettansicht (zuletzt abgerufen: 26.4.2019)

Aufgabe

Klausurteil A: Schreiben/Leseverstehen (Texte 1 und 2)

1. Sum up what the cartoon states about the impact of globalization on cultural diversity and sum up Neil White's view on the quality of this impact. *(Comprehension)*

2. Analyse the way the cartoonist and the writer try to convince the reader of their respective views. In doing this, examine the elements of the cartoon in detail and consider the structure and stylistic devices of the text. *(Analysis)*

3.1 Evaluate the view that local culture is "pitted" (l. 7) and "pock-marked" (l. 58) by American culture. Consider the cartoon, the text, and your own experience. *(Evaluation)*

3.2 Write a letter to the editor of the *Derby Telegraph* stating your personal view on the matter of globalization and Americanization with regard to White's article. *(Evaluation/re-creation of text)*

Klausurteil B: Sprachmittlung (Text 3)

4. At your Irish partner school you participate in a debate on "globalization and identity". You have done research in the German press and would like to present the views proposed in the German media. Write the part of your talk that deals with Tanja Dückers's article. *(Mediation)*

Klausurteil A

Text 1 "Trick or treat? The worst example of Americanisation in modern society" *Neil White*

WHAT sort of strange society encourages children to dress up like the undead and threaten a trick against their neighbours if they refuse to give them a treat.

Halloween has become the very worst example of the Americanisation which has pitted the British psyche.

All Hallows Eve is a religious festival at which the dead are remembered.

In the 12th century, poor children would go door-to-door and receive "soul cakes" in return for praying for the householders.

The origin of the "trick" part of trick or treat is less easy to establish.

A work colleague told me that her refusal to answer the door on Halloween resulted in eggs being thrown at her house.

Yes, that's right. She decided not to participate in this ghastly ritual and her house was attacked as a consequence.

Fortunately, she was of an age where she just cleaned up the mess and got on with life.

But what of those who are more frail and are frightened to answer the door on dark nights?

Why has it become acceptable for October 31 to be the one day a year when it is fair game to scare them out of their wits or even blackmail them by making demands with menaces?

My children are in their 20s now but, during their childhood, I refused to allow them to take part in trick or treating.

I recall that my daughter found my stance particularly hard to swallow. This wasn't entirely surprising because she saw her best friend return from a j(h)aunt along the street with a bulging basket of sweets.

One year I was away for the night and Mrs W gave in, allowing the children to knock on the doors of neighbours who she knew would be receptive to a call.

I am led to believe that a similar compromise involves children avoiding homes which have no signs of Halloween.

This seems fair to me. Stick a pumpkin in the garden if you don't mind an assault on your doorstep. If there isn't one there then trespassing laws should apply.

It strikes me as ironic that we, as a nation, should be preoccupied with trying to repel European influences and yet allow ourselves to be shrouded in Americanisation.

The latter now dominates our lives from fashion to TV, where we drink our coffee or even our government's foreign policy.

Our language is pock-marked with Americanisms and so we should not be surprised that our children aspire to mirror the behaviour of those in the United States.

The latter has been responsible for what I would call the "oh, my God" culture as seen on reality TV programmes, starring families such as the Kardashians or the Osbournes.

Their hallmark is self-obsession and "greed is good" and, in my opinion, this translates into promotion of activities such as trick or treating.

Wouldn't it be nice if role models were less shallow and keener on contributing to the greater good?

I can't see much in American culture which is worth aping and believe that Europeans tend to be a bit more civilised.

Thus, I am delighted by the advent of

German and French markets in the UK and the popularity of Italian and, more recently, Spanish restaurants as a counterpoint to American fast food.

Interestingly, the Germans just use Halloween as an excuse for a "cool" party.

They have it right. A glass of beer, a sausage cob and prancing around in fancy dress seems infinitely better than trick or treating.

Annotations
pitted – indented, pock-marked
to shroud – to cover; note: a shroud is a cloth to cover dead bodies

Text 2

Cartoon: Andy Singer, Saint Paul, MN

Klausurteil B

Text 3 **„Von Geburt an Multikulturalist"** *Tanja Dückers*

[...]

Was Europa derzeit fehlt, ist ein neuer Identitätsbegriff. Bislang haben wir unsere europäische Identität in erster Linie über Abgrenzung konstruiert: Wir sind nicht wie die Amerikaner, die Russen oder die Afrikaner. Statt sich zu einer Identität zu bekennen, haben sich Europäer nur gegen andere Nationen, Kulturen und zum Teil auch pauschal gegen nicht-christliche Religionen gerichtet.

Erinnern wir uns nur an die peinliche Leitkultur-Debatte. Sie hat es Migranten nicht leicht gemacht, sich diesem merkwürdigen, sich ständig selbst spiegelnden Goethe-und-Dieter-Bohlen-Land in der Mitte Europas zugehörig zu fühlen. Dabei wurden Trennlinien zwischen Christen und Muslimen gezogen, ungeachtet der Tatsache, dass in Deutschland mittlerweile fast die Hälfte der Menschen keiner der beiden großen christlichen Kirchen angehört. In Berlin leben mehr Muslime als Katholiken.

Viele Menschen beklagen zwar, dass die Binnenkräfte, die Europa zusammenhalten, vor allem ökonomischer Natur seien. Sie haben aber, nach ihrem Identitätsverständnis von Europa befragt, selber wenig zu bieten. Dass die Europäer sich schwer damit tun, eine europäische Identität festzulegen, ist verständlich. Zu viele Einflüsse haben historisch den Kontinent geprägt.

Der Kontinent war zwar schon immer geprägt von regem Handel und Austausch – aber auch von vielen Kriegen. Es gibt keine Region in der Welt, in der so viele von der Fläche her kleine Länder eng beieinanderliegen und keine, deren Geographie so kleinteilig und ineinandergreifend ist. Europa müsste sich jetzt auf seinen Platz in der Welt als Drehkreuz zwischen Ost und West berufen.

Denn Europa kann sich eigentlich nur als regen Marktplatz der Welt, als Vielvölkerstaat mit zahllosen kulturellen, linguistischen und ökonomischen Verbindungen zur außereuropäischen Welt verstehen. Der Europäer ist, wenn er diese Offenheit zulässt, qua Geburt ein Multikulturalist. Es war der kürzlich verstorbene deutsche Soziologe Ulrich Beck, der als einer der ersten den Europäer als Kosmopolit gedacht hat. Doch für Beck bedeutete Europa nicht das Ende der alten Nationalstaaten. Das neue Europa könne vielmehr das alte in sich bergen und zugleich sanft verändern.

Das eine – die transnationale Identität – schließt nämlich das andere – die Herkunftsidentität – nicht aus. Mit dieser Einsicht können wir die große Angst vor einem transnationalen Identitätsbegriff besiegen, die in vielen Regionen Europas geschürt wird, erst recht vor einem, der außereuropäische Fremde miteinschließt. Die Angst ist verständlich, denn es scheint zunächst schwer vorstellbar, dass die Erweiterung eines Identitätsbegriffs nicht gleichzeitig einem Verlust an anderer Stelle gleichkommt.

Berlinerin, Atheistin, Europäerin

Unsere Aufgabe ist es deshalb, einen facettenreichen, multidimensionalen Identitätsbegriff zu etablieren. Einer Identität, die sich gleichwertig aus einem nahen Herkunftsbereich („Berlinerin“) speist, einer soziokulturellen und religiösen Zugehörigkeit („atheistische Schriftstellerin“) und einem geographisch weitergefassten Bereich („Zugehörigkeit zu einem sich als heterogenes Staatengebilde verstehenden Europa“). Was bislang eher als exkludierend empfunden wurde, könnte in Zukunft integrierend verstanden werden. Wenn europäische Bürger sagen: Ich stamme aus einem Kontinent, in dem ich nicht nur jeden Tag Deutsch höre, nicht nur Nachbarn mit meiner Hautfarbe habe. Zu meiner Identität gehört es dazu, mehrere Sprachen zu sprechen und viele Sprachen ein wenig zu verstehen.

Ich lebe in einem Kontinent, der sich dem keineswegs toten, sondern von 500 Millionen Menschen täglich gelebten Multikulturalismus verschrieben hat.

Bearbeitungsschritte und Musterlösungen

Klausurteil A: Leseverstehen/Schreiben
Anforderungsbereich I *(Comprehension)*

In dieser Beispielaufgabe haben wir es im Teil A (Schreiben/integriertes Leseverstehen) mit einem Text in Verbindung mit einem Cartoon zu tun. Bei solchen Aufgaben besteht immer ein enger inhaltlicher Zusammenhang zwischen Text und Cartoon. Doch betrachten wir sie zunächst natürlich getrennt voneinander.

1. Sum up what the cartoon states about the impact of globalization on cultural diversity and sum up Neil White's view on the quality of this impact.

Obwohl Sie es gewohnt sind, ein Bild mit einer ausführlichen Bildbeschreibung anzugehen, ist dies in diesen kombinierten Aufgaben häufig nicht sinnvoll. Eine lange Beschreibung dessen, was auf dem Cartoon zu sehen ist, würde zu Doppelungen in Teilaufgabe 2 führen, und wäre deshalb wenig elegant. Vor allem aber würde eine detaillierte Beschreibung des Bildes nicht den Arbeitsauftrag „sum up what the cartoon states about the impact of globalization" erfüllen. Tun Sie also grundsätzlich nur das, was die Aufgabenstellung von Ihnen verlangt, in diesem Fall also die Aussage des Cartoons zusammenfassen.
Was den Text angeht, so verlangt der Operator „sum up" eine kurze Zusammenfassung der Behauptungen und Argumente des Autors. Die entsprechenden Schlüsselbegriffe werden im Text markiert. Hier werden wir sie auflisten:

	Key phrases
claim	worst example of Americanisation let ourselves be shrouded in Americanisation
evidence/example	strange society dress up like the undead and threaten a trick
evidence/example	Our language is pock-marked with Americanisms
evidence/example	"Oh, my God" culture, reality TV programmes, families such as the Kardashians or the Osbournes, self-obsession and "greed is good"
conclusion	I can't see much in American culture which is worth aping and believe that Europeans tend to be a bit more civilised.

Die Ausführungen des Autors zu seinen persönlichen Erfahrungen mit Halloween und sein Vorschlag zum Umgang mit den Praktiken (Z. 83–86) spielen für die Fragestellung keine Rolle und bedürfen deshalb auch keiner Zusammenfassung.

Nachdem diese Vorarbeiten abgeschlossen sind, geht es nun darum, Ihre Notizen und Markierungen in einen zusammenhängenden Text zu bringen. Es bietet sich an, eine der allgemein gehaltenen Aussagen Whites als *topic sentence* voranzustellen, dann seine Beispiele und Argumente anzuführen und mit seinem Fazit abzuschließen. Beginnen Sie mit einem Einleitungssatz, der sich auf die jeweilige Textvorlage bezieht (s. S. 205, Kapitel zur sprachlichen Leistung) und vergegenwärtigen Sie sich die Grundsätze für das Verfassen von Zusammenfassungen.

TIPP zum Punktesammeln

Vermeiden Sie Wendungen wie „In the first paragraph", „from line x to line y", „then the author says ...". Dies sind Wendungen, die eine Strukturanalyse charakterisieren, keine Zusammenfassung.

Beispiellösung (Teilaufgabe 1)

Andy Singer's Cartoon presents globalization as Americanization, the spread of American products and American culture throughout the entire world, which amounts to a military invasion and occupation of foreign countries that the indigenous people do not welcome. Also the text "Trick or Treat" from the "Derby Telegraph" of 3 November 2014 harshly criticizes Americanization. The writer, Neil White, sees American culture as shallow and not worth copying. He wonders why British people reject European influences and at the same time let themselves be strongly influenced by American culture. He sees Halloween as the worst example of Americanization in Britain, as the trick-and-treat tradition is pure blackmail and menace.
According to White, the American influence on the English language leads to British children's imitation of American behaviour, which in turn leads to the acceptance of self-obsession and greed as shown in American reality TV programmes. There is nothing the writer sees as worth copying from US culture and he is happy about the increasing influence of central and southern European culture in Britain.

Anforderungsbereich II *(Analysis)*

2. Analyse the way the cartoonist and writer try to convince the reader of their respective views. In doing this, examine the elements of the cartoon in detail and consider the structure and stylistic devices of the text.

Die Aufgabe verlangt eine Analyse des Cartoons, der Textstruktur und der Stilmittel. Diese Analysen sollten Sie getrennt voneinander angehen.
Die Grobstruktur des Textes zeigt sich schon in den Notizen zum Inhalt.

	Key phrases	function
introductory statement, ll. 1–3	WHAT sort of strange society encourages children to dress up like the undead and threaten a trick against their neighbours if they refuse to give them a treat.	get reader interested, set topic

author's claim ll. 5–7	Halloween has become the very worst example of the Americanisation which has pitted the British psyche.	
reference to peaceful religious origin, ll. 8–12	All Hallows Eve is a religious festival at which the dead are remembered. In the 12th century, poor children would go door-to-door and receive "soul cakes" in return for praying for the householders.	establish a contrast
present day example ll. 15–23	A work colleague told me that her refusal to answer the door on Halloween resulted in eggs being thrown at her house.	show contrast
evaluation ll. 24–36	Why has it become acceptable for October 31 to be the one day a year when it is fair game to scare them out of their wits or even blackmail them by making demands with menaces?	show dubious nature of the tradition
personal examples and suggestion ll. 32–49	I refused to allow them to take part in trick or treating. [...] Stick a pumpkin in the garden if you don't mind an assault on your doorstep ...	show how one can deal with this tradition
general claim ll. 55–57	The latter now dominates our lives from fashion to TV, where we drink our coffee or even our government's foreign policy.	
arguments ll. 58–67	– language is pock-marked with Americanisms – our children aspire to mirror the behaviour of those in the United States. – responsible for what I would call the "oh, my God" culture as seen on reality TV programmes, starring families such as the Kardashians or the Osbournes – self-obessesion – "greed is good" → translates into promotion of activities such as trick or treating	support
conclusion ll. 70–75	Wouldn't it be nice if role models were less shallow and keener on contributing to the greater good?	

	I can't see much in American culture which is worth aping and believe that Europeans tend to be a bit more civilised.	
example of alternative, ll. 81–86	Halloween in Germany	confirm his opinion, show resistance, contrasting light note

Bei der Umwandlung Ihrer Notizen in einen zusammenhängenden Text müssen Sie darauf achten, nicht den Inhalt, sondern die Funktion der einzelnen Abschnitte wiederzugeben. Mit dem Inhalt haben Sie sich hinreichend in Teilaufgabe 1 befasst. Inhaltliches wird hier auf ein Mindestmaß reduziert.
Überdies wird verlangt, dass Ihre Klausur aus einem zusammenhängenden Gesamttext besteht. Fangen Sie also nicht mit einem neuen Einleitungssatz an, sondern schließen Sie nahtlos an Teilaufgabe 1 an. Da Sie in Aufgabe 1 mit dem Inhalt der Textbearbeitung aufgehört haben, bietet es sich an, mit dem Text fortzufahren und den Cartoon danach zu analysieren.

TIPP zum Punktesammeln

Denken Sie daran, dass eine Analyse Belege in Form von Verweisen oder Zitaten verlangt.

Der Teil Ihrer zweiten Teilaufgabe, der sich mit der Analyse der Struktur befasst, könnte wie folgt aussehen:

White begins his text with a statement on the nature of Halloween, which arouses the reader's interest and immediately introduces the author's view of American culture as being "strange" (l. 1), a view which is explicitly confirmed in the lines that follow (ll. 3, 4). He goes on to contrast the harmless religious origin of Halloween with what it has become in modern times, by giving an example from his own experience in order to show the absurdity of this festival. He explicitly questions the dubious nature of this American tradition (ll. 24-31) and adds a passage on how Halloween can be dealt with (ll. 32-49).

In lines 27 to 69 White expands on the extent of Americanization in Britain, which, to his mind, has led to the promotion of Halloween. In order to support his view, he enumerates different fields strongly subject to Americanization: he refers to what he sees as the bad influence of American usage on the English language, and to the Kardashians and Osbournes as negative examples of American culture that influence British TV viewers.
He concludes with a rhetorical question (l. 70) stressing the superiority of European cultures. This cultural superiority is supported in his last lines (76–86), when he praises examples of Spanish, French and German culture.

Es handelt sich hier um einen persuasiven Text, einen Text, der den Leser überzeugen möchte. Ein solcher Text bedient sich neben seiner Argumente auch der Stilmittel, wie sie im Kapitel zur Analyse einer Rede dargestellt sind. Wenn Ihnen diese nicht sofort ins Auge fallen, suchen Sie gezielt nach den Ihnen bekannten Stilmitteln (Checkliste im Kopf) und markieren Sie sie im Text (vgl. Kapitel zu *political speech,* S. 94).

Im Einzelnen finden wir in diesem Text:

Zeile	Text	Stilmittel
1, 2	What sort of …	exclamatory "what"
1	strange	derogatory choice of words
2, 3, 19, 29, 30, 31, 48, 50	undead, threaten, ghastly ritual, scare out of their wits, blackmail, menace, assault, trespassing	word field of horror and crime (choice of words)
5	very worst	superlative
7	pitted	metaphor
11, 12	"soul cakes", praying	contrast to word field of horror (choice of words)
24–25	frail and are frightened	alliteration
27	Why …	(rhetorical) question
29	fair game	pun
52–54	"trying to repel" vs "allow ourselves to be shrouded"	antithesis
54	shroud	metaphor
58	pock-marked	metaphor
55–57	from fashion to TV, where we drink our coffee or even our government's foreign policy	enumeration
63	"oh-my-God" culture	derogatory choice of words
66, 67	self-obsession, "greed is good"[1]	derogatory choice of words
71	shallow	derogatory choice of words
74	aping	derogatory choice of words
76–80	German and French markets, Italian/Spanish restaurants vs American fast food	antithesis

1 Die Anspielung mit diesem Zitat auf den Film *Wall Street* und damit scharfe Kritik am amerikanischen Kapitalismus müssen Sie als Schüler nicht zwingend erkennen. Im Abitur wären dafür ggf. Zusatzpunkte zu erreichen.

Wenn Sie nun Ihren Text verfassen, ordnen Sie die Resultate wieder, anstatt textchronologisch vorzugehen. Auffällig ist die Wortwahl: Teils metaphorische, aber auch antithetische Strukturen fallen auf, was ja auch die inhaltlichen Kontraste Amerika/England bzw. England/Deutschland widerspiegelt. Sinnvollerweise beginnt man mit dem vorherrschenden Stilmittel. Es folgen dann weitere Stilmittel, deren Funktion die Emphase, die besondere Betonung ist sowie die rhetorischen Fragen. Letztere haben wir in der Strukturanalyse schon erwähnt, sodass wir sie hier weglassen können.

TIPP zum Punktesammeln

Im Anforderungsbereich II ist Ihr Thema nicht Halloween, auch nicht *Americanization*. Es geht um Wörter, Ausdrücke und Sätze. Eine Formulierung wie „The author says that ..." führt in die falsche Richtung

Der Teil Ihrer zweiten Teilaufgabe, der sich mit der Stilanalyse befasst, könnte also wie folgt aussehen:

White's bias against American culture becomes even more obvious in the way he chooses his words. Derogatory words like "strange" – enhanced by an exlamatory "what" – (l. 1) and "shallow" (l. 71) and the reinforced superlative "very worst" (l. 5) are surpassed by a large number of words and expressions from the semantic field of "horror" ("undead", "threaten", "ghastly ritual", "scare out of their wits", "blackmail", "menace", "assault", "trespassing", ll. 2, 3, 19, 29, 30, 31, 48, 50), which on the one hand refer to the example of Halloween, and on the other hand are aimed at American society. In contrast to that stand the very positive words "soul cakes" and "praying" (ll. 11, 12), which refer to the harmless and peaceful origin of the "ghastly ritual" and also the expression "frail" and "frightened" (ll. 24-25) referring to its poor victims, a fact that is additionally stressed by alliteration. Moreover, their role of hunted victims is suggested by the use of the pun in the expression "fair game" (l. 29).
Metaphors from the field of death and disease add to the gruesome tone of the text. The words "pitted" (l. 7) and "pock-marked" (l. 58) make the British mentality and the English language appear disfigured and distorted by the disease of Americanization. The metaphor "we ... allow ourselves to be shrouded" (ll. 53-54) compares British society to a dead body, which has given up its individual existence for the sake of Americanization.
The shallow nature of American culture is expressed by the term "'oh, my God' culture" (l. 63). It refers to the superficial enthusiasm for anything, uttered in a high-pitch female voice and getting on everybody's nerves, which we experience in American TV shows. White continues his derogatory choice of words with the terms "self-obsession" and "greed is good" (ll. 66, 67), the latter alluding to Gordon Gekko's speech in the 1987 film "Wall Street", and thus representing harsh criticism of the American capitalist system and greed-driven attitudes. Copying American culture is derided as "aping" (l. 74).
The writer also uses a number of emphatic means. The extent of Americanization in Britain is emphasized by enumeration. Contradictions (ll. 52-54) or pleasant contrast (ll. 76-80) are emphasized by antithesis.

Die Analyse des Cartoons verlangt nun die Interpretation der einzelnen Details. Grundsätzlich kann man sagen, dass jedes Detail eines Cartoons bedeutungstragend ist. Wie bei der Textanalyse sollten Sie sich Notizen auf Ihrem Konzeptpapier machen. Wir stellen die Detailanalyse in einer Tabelle dar.

Detail	Bedeutung
island	foreign country
palm trees, beach	idyll, beauty, paradise
invasion	Americanization
battle ships, logos of corporations	export by corporations
coke, windows,TVs	... of their products
TVs	... and their world view and culture
Disney characters – multiple Goofy – smiling Mickey Mouse	... by means of Hollywood culture, comic culture – stupid, brainless culture – superficial, hypocritical culture
natives, real people, individual faces, horrified	people, individual culture, unwilling to give it up

Die Analyse des Cartoons in ihrer zweiten Teilaufgabe könnte wie folgt aussehen:

The view presented in the cartoon coincides with White's view on Americanization.

The cartoon shows an island invaded by Disney characters who arrive on battleships and planes displaying the logos of prominent American corporations, namely Texaco, Shell, Nike, Motorola and McDonalds. They bombard the idyllic island, with its beautiful beach and palm trees, with American products like Microsoft Windows or Coca Cola. As a sign of their occupation, the invaders put up a flagpole flying the Windows flag. This alludes to the American landing on the Pacific island of Iwo Jima in World War II, which was one of the fiercest battles in the War in the Pacific[1]. Hence, globalization is here clearly presented as Americanization, the aggressive export of American products and of a culture which destroys local culture.

TV sets, which are dropped by Motorola bombers, not only represent American electronic products but also the forceful introduction of an American world-view by CNN or Fox, and by means of TV series and Hollywood films. The Disney characters in particular represent American comic book culture and Hollywood culture. Multiple Goofies, instructed by an angry Donald Duck, stress the shiftiness and stupidity of this culture. A smiling Mickey Mouse reveals superficiality and perhaps even hypocrisy.

The natives, on the other hand, are presented as people with individual faces. One of them has even been killed. Mickey Mouse in his Nike clothes and with an inviting gesture seems to promise them a good fortune, but their faces reveal fear and horror. In spite of its superficially promising attraction, Americanization is presented as not welcome in the world.

1 Die Anspielung auf das weltbekannte Foto der Besetzung von Iwo Jima, die in der Aufrichtung des Flaggenmastes zu finden ist, müssen Sie als Schüler nicht zwingend erkennen. Im Abitur wären dafür ggf. Zusatzpunkte zu erreichen.

Anforderungsbereich III *(Evaluation)*

3.1 Evaluate the view that local culture is "pitted" (l. 7) and "pock-marked" (l. 58) by American culture. Consider the cartoon, the text, and your own experience. *(Evaluation)*

Im Anforderungsbereich III wird von Ihnen eine Stellungnahme verlangt. Nachdem Sie sich intensiv mit der Textvorlage befasst haben, sollten Sie in der Lage sein, sich eine eigene Meinung zu bilden. Wichtig ist,

- dass Sie Ihre Stellungnahme auf den Ausgangstext, bzw. die Ausgangstexte beziehen,
- dass Sie Ihre eigenen Behauptungen mit Argumenten und Beispielen untermauern,
- dass Sie zu einer dezidierten persönlichen Stellungnahme gelangen, einer persönlichen Meinung, die sich aus Ihren Ausführungen ergibt.

Sammeln und ordnen Sie Ihre Gedanken auf Ihrem Konzeptblatt. Wählen Sie dazu eine Mindmap oder auch eine Liste.

Es geht um Kultur. Der Text hebt auf Unterhaltungskultur ab, was auch im Cartoon aufgegriffen wird. Stellen Sie Überlegungen an, was darüber hinaus die Kultur einer Gesellschaft ausmacht und inwieweit diese kulturellen Bereiche von der Amerikanisierung betroffen sind. Stellen Sie dem die Elemente der einheimischen beziehungsweise nicht-amerikanischen Kultur gegenüber. Wir stellen dies hier in einer Tabelle dar.

Cultural area	**Americanization**	**German/international culture**
music	English language pop music rap, etc.	British pop music German pop music German classical music
fashion	blue jeans, T-shirts, baseball caps brands: Nike, Calvin Klein, Hollister, Levis, … cosmetics	scarves, socks, other accessories
sports	basketball, American football, baseball, ice-hockey	football, handball, hockey, other world sports: e. g. rugby, cricket
food and drink	hamburgers, tex-mex, cocktails	Kebab (Döner), Currywurst, Pasta, home cooking
literature	*Hunger Games, Twilight*	German bestsellers
film and TV	high school soaps, *How I Met Your Mother, The Big Bang Theory*	German blockbusters

Entscheiden Sie dann für sich selbst, ob dies einer Dominanz der amerikanischen Kultur gleichkommt oder ob die einheimische beziehungsweise nicht-amerikanische Kultur der amerikanischen stark entgegensteht. In Ihrem Text sollten Sie dann die Ihre These unterstützenden Beispiele aussagekräftig darstellen, die Gegenbeispiele gegebenenfalls einräumen. Bereiche, die Ihre Meinung nicht belegen, müssen Sie nicht unbedingt ansprechen. Nehmen Sie anschließend auch Stellung zu der Kritik an dieser Kultur.

TIPP zum Punktesammeln

Beginnen Sie Ihre Stellungnahme nicht mit „In my opinion", „I think", etc.! Beziehen sie sich auf den Ausgangstext. Beziehen Sie sich vor allem nicht mit einem „this" oder „it" auf die Aufgabenstellung der Teilaufgabe! Ihre Gesamtaufgabe ist ein zusammenhängender Zieltext, der ohne Kenntnis der Formulierung der Teilaufgaben verständlich sein muss.

Ihre dritte Teilaufgabe könnte wie folgt aussehen:

Thus the cartoon supports White's view on American culture as being very dubious and shifty. White refers both to Halloween and to Hollywood entertainment culture, and although there may be lots of local film and TV productions in our country, there are still a large number of American TV soaps and crime series that take up a large part of TV time. In the cinema, there is no question that American films are dominant. Look at the all-time record holders "Titanic" and "Avatar" but also at the newest blockbusters like "Joker" or "1917". However, we can still see the success of German productions e.g. by Schweiger or Schweighöfer.

In other areas of culture, we find the same tendencies. Nobody would deny that American music is dominant at least as far as the popular sector is concerned. Much of the English language music is British, it is true, but still a large number of young people listen to rap, hip-hop, or black music.

In the field of fashion, jeans, T-shirts, sweatshirts, hoodies and baseball caps do not even have local counterparts. And we do not experience the introduction of traditional Asian or African clothes in the mainstream population either. There may be a German preference for scarves and other little accessories, but they remain what they are, just additional pieces.

In sports, we see a rising interest in American football and basketball. Yet football and handball are still the most popular sports here, but there are a lot more young people who are familiar with these American sports, even baseball, than there used to be.

As far as food and drink are concerned, we have seen the rise of the American fast food chains. And although Greek, Turkish and Italian food is still paramount, lots of Tex-Mex restaurants, which are American rather than really Mexican, have appeared in Germany and have become very popular among young people. 'Sausalitos' in many German cities, or 'Tijuana' not only in Aachen, are just two examples. Traditional German food has in many cases become restricted to homes and families.

As a conclusion, whether we condemn it like White and Singer, or welcome it, there is no doubt that global culture is not entirely, but largely American. It remains a matter of personal taste if you see it as foreign intrusion or rather an enrichment. Personally, I would say that as long as it does not replace or eliminate local culture completely, I would accept it as adding to the multiple options of our lifestyles.

Anforderungsbereich III *(Re-creation of text)*

3.2 Write a letter to the editor of the *Derby Telegraph* stating your personal view on the matter of globalization and Americanization with regard to White's article. *(Evaluation/re-creation of text)*

In diesem Fall ist die kreative Aufgabe der Stellungnahme inhaltlich sehr ähnlich. Indem Sie zu Whites Artikel Stellung nehmen, bewerten Sie die Frage nach der Amerikanisierung der europäischen Kulturen. Der große Unterschied zu 3.1 liegt in der Textform. Sie müssen einen Leserbrief schreiben, dessen Form wir im Kapitel Zieltextformate (s. S. 105) vorgestellt haben. Im argumentativen Teil wird sich dieser Leserbrief kaum von der Argumentation in Aufgabe 3.1 unterscheiden. Whites konkrete Beispiele (Halloween, Sprache, Reality TV) sollten mit Ihrem eigenen Land (i. d. R. Deutschland) abgeglichen werden. Wir werden uns in der Musterlösung auf den Anfang und das Ende beschränken.

TIPP zum Punktesammeln

Beachten Sie die formalen Aspeke eines *letter to the editor!* Beziehen Sie sich auf den Ausgangstext. Natürlich ist es bei der Wahl der kreativen Aufgabe nicht möglich, an die Lösung der vorhergehenden Aufgaben nahtlos anzuschließen.

Ihre dritte Teilaufgabe könnte wie folgt aussehen:

Sir,

I have read with interest Neil White's article on Halloween as the worst example of Americanization. Unfortunately, Mr White is wrong, when he says that the Germans just see Halloween as a reason for a cool party. Trick and treating has long been established in this country, too, and I hate it as much as Mr White does. To me it has always seemed like racketeering. I too see it as one of the worst examples of Americanization together with other influences. The German language, too, is "pocked-marked" by American English intruders and although there may be lots of local film and TV productions in our country, the vast number of American TV soaps and crime series still take up a large part of TV time. ... (see above)

Traditional German food has in many cases become restricted to homes and families. Thus, I would definitely agree with Mr White's view of Americanization, but I would like to

emphasize that this is not just a British, but also a European, if not a global issue.
X. Y., Aachen, Germany

Klausurteil B: Sprachmittlung

Vergegenwärtigen Sie sich die Prinzipien der Sprachmittlung, wie wir sie auf Seite 103 dargestellt haben.
Für eine knappe, sachliche Wiedergabe gehen Sie wie bei einer Zusammenfassung vor, die wir an dieser Stelle nicht ein weiteres Mal ausführlich darlegen.

Adressatenorientierung

In Ihrer fiktiven Situation als Teilnehmer an einer Debatte in einer irischen Schule müssen Sie Ihr Statement adressatengerecht gestalten. Häufig müssen Begriffe oder Eigennamen, die es im Englischen so nicht gibt, erläutert werden. In diesem Text sollte man sich überlegen, wie man mit der Erklärung der verschiedenen Identitäten umgeht. Die Erklärung der Autorin (Berlinerin, Atheistin, Schriftstellerin) zu übernehmen, wird in dem neuen Kontext merkwürdig erscheinen, denn Sie stellen die Autorin ja nicht explizit vor. Auch das Wort „Drehkreuz" in diesem übertragenen Sinne kann nicht einfach so wie im Deutschen benutzt werden. Insbesondere die Begriffe „Leitkultur" und „Goethe-und-Dieter-Bohlen-Land" könnten Probleme bereiten. In der Beispiellösung gehen sie einfach in der Zusammenfassung auf.

Ihre vierte Teilaufgabe könnte wie folgt aussehen:

Unlike Americans, Russians or Africans, we Europeans do not have a common notion of identity. Instead of acknowledging one common European identity, Europeans have always confronted other nations, other cultures or non-Christian religions, although in Germany, e.g., half of the population are not members of the Church and in Berlin there are more Muslims than Catholics.
People complain a lot about Europe being just an economic union, yet they find it hard to define a European identity. Of course, European history has always been ambivalent. There has always been internal as well as external trade but also many wars. There is no other region in the world where many countries share a relatively small geographical area. Today, Europe should really see itself as a crossroads between East and West.
Europe's self-image should be that of an international marketplace, a multi-ethnic place with cultural, linguistic, and economic ties with the rest of the world. A European is multicultural by birth. This does not mean that we have to give up our national identities. If we understand that transnational identity does not exclude national identity, we will overcome the fear that is being fuelled in many European countries and regions, especially if this notion includes non-European immigrants.
We have to establish a multidimensional notion of identity, which includes identity of origin, of sociocultural background and religion, as much as being part of a wider geographical area. In my case this would mean being German from the Rhineland, a Catholic high-school student and multicultural European. To sum up, European identity should be multilingual, multi-racial, and multicultural.

Aufgaben mit Bewertungskriterien

Themenfeld *American Myths and Realities – Freedom and Success*

Aufgabenbeispiel Abitur Englisch Grundkurs
Aufgabenart gemäß KLP: 1.1: Schreiben mit Leseverstehen integriert und Sprachmittlung isoliert
Bezug zu den Vorgaben: Amerikanischer Traum – Visionen und Lebenswirklichkeiten in den USA *American myths and realities: freedom and success*
Auszug aus einem englischsprachigen Sachtext (791 W.) (Klausurteil A, Text 1) Auszug aus einem deutschsprachigen Sachtext (452 W.) (Klausurteil B, Text 2)
Quellenangaben: Text 1: Joe Kennedy's Response to President Trump's State of the Union Address, January 30th, 2018, *Internet Archive*, San Francisco, 31.10.2018 https://archive.org/details/CSPAN_20180131_114400_State_of_the_Union_Address_Democratic_Response Text 2: Riedel, Donata: „Studie zur Chancengerechtigkeit: Sozialer Aufstieg in Deutschland bleibt die Ausnahme – OECD fürchtet Vergeudung von Talent", © Handelsblatt GmbH. Alle Rechte vorbehalten. 15.6.2018, https://www.handelsblatt.com/politik/deutschland/studie-zur-chancengerechtigkeit-sozialer-aufstieg-in-deutschland-bleibt-die-ausnahme-oecd-fuerchtet-vergeudung-von-talent/22690454.html?ticket=ST-7608828-73isM9rStOQV6VEN5bt7-ap5

Aufgabe

Klausurteil A: Leseverstehen/Schreiben (Text 1)

1. Sum up what fault Joe Kennedy finds with the present government and what issues the Democrats would target in the US. *(Comprehension)*

2. Examine Kennedy's rhetorical devices and strategies and their impact on an American listener. *(Analysis)*

3. With particular regard to lines 20–34, compare the political situation in the US to the political situation in your own country. Discuss to what extent people (or you) may also experience "a nagging, sinking feeling" that something is not right. *(Evaluation)*

Klausurteil B: Sprachmittlung (Text 2)

4. As a guest student at an American high school you are asked to give a talk on social mobility in Germany in your sociology class. Write the part of your talk that is based on the following article from Handelsblatt. *(Mediation)*

Text 1 Response to President Trump's State of the Union Address, January 30th, 2018 *Joe Kennedy*

Good evening, ladies and gentlemen. It is an absolute privilege to join you all tonight.

We are here in Fall River, Massachusetts, a proud American city.

An American city built by immigrants.

From textiles to robots, this is a place that knows how to make great things.

[...]

Like many American hometowns, Fall River has faced its share of storms. But the people here are tough. They fight for each other. They pull for their city. It is a fitting place to gather as our nation reflects on the state of our union.

This is a difficult task. Many have spent the last year anxious, angry, afraid. We all feel the fractured fault lines across our country. We hear the voices of Americans who are forgotten and feel forsaken.

We see an economy that makes stocks soar, investor portfolios bulge, and corporate profits climb, but fails to give workers their fair share of the reward. A government that struggles to keep itself open. Russia knee-deep in our democracy. An all-out war on environmental protection. A Justice Department rolling back civil rights by the day. Hatred and supremacy proudly marching in our streets. Bullets tearing through our classrooms, concerts, and congregations, targeting our safest, sacred places.

And this nagging, sinking feeling, no matter your political beliefs, that this is not right. This is not who we are.

Folks, it would be easy to dismiss this past year as chaos. Partisanship. As politics. But it's far, far bigger than that. This administration isn't just targeting the laws that protect us; they are targeting the very idea that we are all worthy of protection.

For them, dignity isn't something you're born with but something you measure, by your net worth, your celebrity, your headlines, your crowd size, not to mention the gender of your spouse, the country of your birth, the color of your skin, the God of your prayers.

Their record is a rebuke to our highest American ideal, the belief that we are all worthy, that we are all equal, that we all count, in the eyes of our law and our leaders, our God and our government. That is the American promise.

But today, ladies and gentlemen, today that promise is being broken by an administration that callously appraises our worthiness and decides who makes the cut and who can be bargained away. They are turning American life into a zero-sum game, where for one to win, another must lose, where we can guarantee America's safety if we slash our safety net, where we can extend health care in Mississippi if we gut it in Massachusetts, we can cut taxes for corporations today if we raise them on families tomorrow, where we can take care of sick kids if we sacrifice Dreamers.

We are bombarded with one false choice

after another: coal miners or single moms, rural communities or inner cities, the coast or the heartland. As if the mechanic in Pittsburgh, a teacher in Tulsa, and a daycare worker in Birmingham are bitter rivals rather than mutual casualties of a system forcefully rigged towards those at the top.

As if the parent who lies awake terrified that their transgender son or daughter will be beaten and bullied at school is any more or less legitimate than a parent whose heart is shattered by a daughter in the grips of an opioid addiction.

So here is the answer that Democrats offer tonight: We choose both.

We fight — we fight for both. Because the greatest, strongest, richest nation in the world shouldn't have to leave anyone behind.

We choose — we choose a better deal for all who call our country home. We choose a living wage, and paid leave, and affordable child care your family needs to survive. We choose pensions that are solvent, trade pacts that are fair, roads and bridges that won't rust away, a good education that you can afford.

We choose a health care system that offers you mercy, whether you suffer from cancer or depression or addiction. We choose an economy strong enough to boast record stock prices and brave enough to admit that top CEOs making 300 times their average worker is not right.

We choose Fall River. We choose the thousands of American communities whose roads aren't paved with power or privilege, but with an honest effort, with good faith, and the resolve to build something better for your kids.

That — that is our story. It began the day our founding fathers and mothers set sail for a new world, fleeing oppression and intolerance. It continued with every word of our independence, the audacity to declare that all men are created equal, an imperfect promise for a nation struggling to become a more perfect union. [...]

Annotations
State of the Union Address – annual speech presented by the President of the United States to a joint session of the United States Congress
corporate profits – profits of the big companies
to make the cut – to qualify for sth.
to gut – to take the internal parts out of an animal or a building
Dreamer – underage illegal immigrant
to rig – to manipulate

Text 2 Studie zur Chancengerechtigkeit: Sozialer Aufstieg in Deutschland bleibt die Ausnahme – OECD fürchtet Vergeudung von Talent

Donata Riedel

Für Kinder aus Arbeiterfamilien ist der soziale Aufstieg in Deutschland besonders schwer – ähnlich wie in den USA. Das hat Folgen für die Wirtschaft.

Berlin. „Der soziale Aufzug ist kaputt", schreiben die Ökonomen der Industrieländer-Organisation OECD. In einer neuen Studie vergleichen sie die soziale Mobilität in 30 Industrie- und Schwellenländern.

Die ist schwer eingeschränkt. In Deutschland kann es sechs Generationen dauern, bis die Nachkommen einer einkommensschwachen Familie das Durchschnittseinkommen erreichen, heißt es in der Studie. In Dänemark seien es nur zwei Generationen, in den übrigen skandinavischen Ländern drei Generationen. Nur in Schwellenländern wie China und Indien brauchen Menschen aus einkommensschwachen Familien noch länger – nämlich sieben bis acht Generationen.

Vergleicht man Väter und Söhne in Deutschland, dann gelingt nur neun Prozent der Söhne von Vätern mit geringem Einkommen der Aufstieg in die höchste Verdienstgruppe. Ganz anders sieht es für Kinder von Vätern mit hohem Verdienst aus: Die Hälfte von ihnen wird später einmal gut verdienen.

Ebenso schlecht sieht es bei den Bildungschancen aus: 53 Prozent der Kinder von Eltern mit hohem Bildungsstatus schaffen einen Uni-Abschluss, aber nur jedes zehnte Kind von Hauptschulabsolventen.

Ein gewisser Trost mag sein, dass es in anderen europäischen Ländern nicht besser aussieht, etwa in Frankreich und Großbritannien. Die Skandinavier allerdings haben es geschafft, Chancengerechtigkeit weitgehend herzustellen.

Die OECD-Ökonomen glauben, dass in Deutschland das Bildungssystem eine entscheidende Rolle für die fehlende soziale Mobilität spielt: Noch immer gebe es zu wenig Kitas und Ganztagsschulen, die Kindern aus sozial schwachen Familien mehr Bildung bieten könnten.

Die frühe Trennung nach der Grundschule in Gymnasien und andere Schulen verbaue zudem vielen Schülern die Chance auf Abitur und Universität.

Die OECD fürchtet, dass Deutschland damit Chancen verspielt und Talent verschwendet. Dies drücke auf die Produktivität der Wirtschaft insgesamt. Auch die Chance auf möglichst viele innovative Unternehmensgründer verspiele Deutschland so.

Die Ökonomen haben zudem die Aufstiegschancen innerhalb einer Generation verglichen, also die Frage gestellt, wie gut es gelingt, aus einem Niedriglohnjob in höhere Einkommenssphären aufzusteigen.

Auch diese Einkommensmobilität ist in Deutschland begrenzt. 58 Prozent der Geringverdiener bleiben für immer arm. Viele Teilzeitbeschäftigte blieben unter ihren Möglichkeiten, vor allem Frauen. „Ein Arbeitsplatz allein ermöglicht oftmals keine großen Schritte auf der Einkommensleiter", heißt es in dem Bericht.

Wer allerdings erst einmal einen Job mit hohem Einkommen erreicht hat, wird ihn kaum je verlieren: 74 Prozent aus dieser Gruppe steigen nicht wieder ab. Dies erhöhe die Gefahr, dass sich Vermögen in Händen weniger konzentrieren.

Die Ökonomen empfehlen als Gegenmittel eine Erbschaftsteuer mit niedrigeren Freibeträgen und weniger Ausnahmen. Gleichzeitig sollten niedrigere Einkommen von Steuern und Sozialabgaben entlastet werden. Denn je höher das Nettoeinkommen, desto eher gelingt der Bildungsaufstieg der Kinder.

Die Zahlen der OECD sind allerdings mit gewisser Vorsicht zu betrachten. Sie sind relativ alt und stammen überwiegend aus dem Jahr 2014. Seither gibt es mehr Kitas und Ganztagsschulen. Dass die Zahl allerdings bei weitem nicht ausreicht, wissen in Deutschland alle Eltern kleiner Kinder.

Bewertungskriterien

In diesem Kapitel finden Sie die Aspekte aufgelistet, die bei einer gelungenen Lösung von Ihnen erwartet werden. Sie sind für jede Teilaufgabe getrennt in einer Tabelle zusammengefasst. In der Spalte daneben sehen Sie jeweils die maximal zu erreichende Punktzahl.

Klausurteil A
Anforderungsbereich I

Der Prüfling

benennt die aktuellen Umstände, für die Kennedy die Trump-Regierung verantwortlich macht, nämlich – Spaltung der Gesellschaft – Kluft zwischen Arm und Reich – Verschlossenheit der Regierung – russische Einflussnahme auf die Wahlen – Verachtung des Umweltschutzes – Schwinden der Bürgerrechte – offener Rassismus – Amokläufe mit Schusswaffen – die politischen Maßnahmen der Regierung, die stets Menschen oder Gruppen von Menschen gegeneinander ausspielen.	4
führt an, wie Kennedy die Gesinnung der Regierung darstellt, die den Gleichheitsgrundsatz in den USA missachtet und Menschen diskriminiert hinsichtlich – ihres Vermögens – ihrer medialen Präsenz – ihrer sexuellen Orientierung – ihrer Hautfarbe – ihrer Religion	4
benennt die politischen Ziele der Democrats, die alle Amerikaner in den Blick nehmen, nämlich – ausreichende Löhne – Altersvorsorge – bezahlbare Kindertagesstätten – faire Handelsabkommen – intakte Infrastruktur – gute Bildung – funktionierende Krankenversicherung – starke Wirtschaft mit fairen Einkommen	4
	12

Anforderungsbereich II

Der Prüfling

führt aus, wie Kennedy seiner Rede eine patriotische Prägung verleiht, indem er – den (National)stolz seiner Zuhörer beschwört (Z. 3–14, Z. 82–87, Z. 109–116) – die amerikanischen Ideale denen der Regierung gegenüberstellt (Z. 37–40, Z. 48–53)	4
benennt emphatische Mittel in ihrer jeweiligen Funktion, z. B. – Alliteration und Aufzählung zur besonderen Betonung der Missstände (Z. 16, 18, 20–31, 41–47, 68–71, 77–78, 105), Aufzählungen teilweise steigernd (Z. 16, 30–31, 68–69) – Kontraste (Antithese) zusammen mit Parallelismen bzw. Anaphern zur Betonung der Widersprüchlichkeit und Unzulänglichkeit der Trump-Administration (Z. 54, 68–71, 80–81, 105–107) – Anaphern und Aufzählungen zur Betonung der Entschlossenheit der Demokraten, die Situation zu verbessern. (Z. 96–102) – Parallelismen und Wiederholung zur Betonung einzelner Kernsätze (Z. 32, 35–37, 109)	6
Erläutert verschiedene sprachliche Bilder, z. B. – „share of storms“ (Z. 10), zur Illustration der bewegten Vergangenheit und Zähigkeit der Bevölkerung – „fractured fault lines“ (Z. 17) als geologische Metapher zur Illustration der Zerrissenheit des Landes – „knee-deep“ (Z. 25) als Personifizierung Russlands und zur Assoziation mit Sumpf und Schlamm – „paved with power ...“ (Z. 105) zur Illustration der Schaffung dauerhafter, „zementierter“ Zustände	6
	16

Anforderungsbereich III

Der Prüfling

knüpft an den Ausgangstext an, indem er/sie sich auf Kennedys Aussage in Z. 20–34 bezieht	2
erläutert Tendenzen in Deutschland (oder in der EU), die dem in den USA herrschenden (Un-) Geist vergleichbar sind, z. B. unter den Stichwörtern – Rassismus, Rechtsruck, AfD, Pegida – Managergehälter – Altersarmut – Schere zwischen arm und reich – Diskriminierung von Minderheiten	10

– Macht der Konzerne – Umweltschutz (Diesel, Braunkohle, Plastik, Versiegelung) – ...	
kommt vor dem Hintergrund seiner/ihrer Überlegungen zu einer fundierten eigenen Bewertung	2
	14

Klausurteil B
Sprachmittlung

Der Prüfling gibt die wesentlichen Inhalte im Sinne der Aufgabenstellung sinngemäß zusammenfassend und adressatengerecht wieder.	18
Er stellt dar: – die OECD-Studie der sozialen Mobilität in 30 Ländern, – das schlechte Bild, das Deutschland demnach im Vergleich zu anderen Ländern abgibt (innerhalb der Generationen und über Generationen hinweg), – die Zahlen, die dies dokumentieren, (mit dem einschränkenden Hinweis auf ihr Alter), – die Gründe, die im Bildungssystem zu finden seien, • zu wenig Betreuung, • zu frühe Differenzierung, – die Folgen für die Wirtschaft, • Auswirkungen auf die Produktivität, • Vergeudung von Talenten, • Verspielen von Innovationspotential. – Lösungsvorschläge • Erbschaftssteuer, • Entlastung vom Steuern und Abgaben niedriger Einkommen.	

Themenfeld *Tradition and Change in Politics – Monarchy and Modern Democracy*

Aufgabenbeispiel Abitur Englisch Leistungskurs
Aufgabenart gemäß KLP: 1.1: Schreiben mit Leseverstehen integriert und Sprachmittlung isoliert
Bezug zu den Vorgaben: Das Vereinigte Königreich im 21. Jahrhundert – Selbstverständnis zwischen Tradition und Wandel *Tradition and change in politics: monarchy and modern democracy*
Auszug aus einem englischsprachigen literarischen Text (833 W.) (Klausurteil A, Text 1) Auszug aus einem deutschsprachigen Sach- und Gebrauchstext (481 W.) (Klausurteil B, Text 2)
Quellenangaben: Peter Morgan, *The Audience,* London 2015 (Faber and Faber), S. 80–84 Verena Mayer, „Royals in Deutschland. Immer cool bleiben“, 7.5.2019 https://www.sueddeutsche.de/panorama/royals-prinz-charles-berlin-1.4436480

Aufgabe

Klausurteil A: Leseverstehen/ Schreiben

1. Sum up what topics the Queen and the Prime Minister deal with in their audience. *(Comprehension)*
2. Examine the Queen‘s speech and behaviour with regard to her status as Head of State of the United Kingdom. *(Analysis)*

3.1 Against the backgrounds of this text, your work in class, and your own experience, discuss the suitability of a monarch in a modern democracy. *(Evaluation)*

3.2 As a member of the debating club at your British host school, you are asked to give a statement introducing an outsider‘s view on monarchy. Write your statement in favour of or against royalism. *(Evaluation/Creation of text)*

Klausurteil B: Sprachmittlung

4. Your English friend has told you that the Royals are anti-European. After you have read this article in Süddeutsche Zeitung, you write him an e-mail telling him what the article says about Royals visiting Germany. Write this part of your e-mail. *(Mediation)*

Text 1 The Audience (extract) *Peter Morgan*

It's Spring 2015. The door opens and the Equerry comes in. The sound of a mobile telephone, with an 'All About That Bass' ringtone.

Equerry Mr Cameron, Ma'am.

David Cameron, forty-eight, enters, bows respectfully.

Cameron Your Majesty.

The 'All About That Bass' ringtone continues.

Elizabeth What's that?

Cameron Not me.

The Queen looks at the Equerry.

Equerry *(hands raised in innocence)* Nor me, Ma'am.

Elizabeth *(realising)* Oh, for heaven's sake.

The Queen moves with difficulty. Searches in her pockets. Finds the phone. Tries to turn it off.

Grandchildren.

Cameron May I, Ma'am?

He takes it and switches it off for her.

Elizabeth How did you do that?

Cameron The red button, here, Ma'am.

He presses the keyboard. The Queen squints.

Elizabeth There isn't a red button.

Cameron It disappears after you touch it.

The Queen stares. Bemused. Confounded.

Cameron *(indicates)* Nice.

Elizabeth What?

Cameron The new Samsung.

Elizabeth I begged them not to give me one, but then security persuaded me it doubled as a useful tracking device in case I try to escape. I expect you have one, too?

Cameron Four.

Elizabeth How awful. Anyway, we have more important things to discuss than this. Parliament has been dissolved. The campaigns are under way. The corridors of Whitehall are empty. Everyone's up and down the country shaking hands, knocking on doorsteps. Or am I being old-fashioned? Is it just the internet now?

Cameron No, we are indeed up and down the country. I was in Leeds, Hull and Scarborough yesterday. Cardiff, Swansea and Glamorgan the day before.

Elizabeth And amid all this electioneering you've still found time for a flying visit to Bonn. Or was it Bern?

Cameron Basle. *(Heart sinks.)* Yes.

Elizabeth I seem to have done nothing *but* welcome you back from European summits. How many have you been to over the past four years?

Cameron Lost count.

Elizabeth Me, too. So ... how did it all go? In a nutshell.

Cameron Well, the desire for the single currency to survive is still there among the core countries – just. But the green shoots of recovery people had hoped for post-austerity have simply not materialised, and now the very real possibility of the Greeks packing their bags and going their own way begs the question do the creditor states bail the Greeks out again, and risk disaster, or let them go and risk disaster? It wouldn't worry me so much if I got a deeper sense of hope, or a shared mission, or ideology –

Unseen by Cameron the queen has nodded off.

– among the rest of the member states. Or anyone doing it because they actually believe in it the way the post-war generation of politicians did. 'Never again.' It's hard to understand why we British have been so resistant to Europe historically.

Cameron notices the queen is asleep.

Mostly ... I'd say it's because we're an island, and not physically part of the continent. And that we still have too vivid a memory of the war –

The Queen sits up at mention of this.

– and struggle with the languages of the Europeans. Not to mention the fact that we –

The Queen shakes herself awake.

Elizabeth Tend not to like them very much ...

Cameron Quite. But don't you think it might also be the fact that in you –

Elizabeth Oh. My fault again is it?

Cameron – we have a head of state who has such strong emotional ties with the Commonwealth that it's impossible for us subjects to commit ourselves fully to any other union. That is, until you ...

Elizabeth Drop dead?

Cameron No. No. No. *(Horrified.)* No. *(Reassuring.)*

No. *(Hesitates, thinks.)* Actually, yes, ... and it's possible for our relationship with the Commonwealth to be redrawn.

Elizabeth bristles. The basilisk stare.

Elisabeth Fifty-three member states representing three billion people, all working together productively and harmoniously in a way the Europeans could only dream of. Why on earth would you redraw that?

The Queen squints, noticing something. ...

Goodness ... Are you wearing make-up?

Cameron No.

She gets up and walks over to scrutinise Cameron ...

Elizabeth Yes, you are! It come off your neck, on to your collar.

Cameron Oh, that was from an interview this morning. In Skegness.

Elizabeth They didn't offer to take it off?

Cameron They did, but there was no time.

Elizabeth That's the excuse Mr Blair used to give. By the end, I noticed, he wore it all the time, *(Shudders.)* Along with that grin. You were a great admirer, I understand.

Cameron Of Tony's? Say what you like about the man, he was good at the game. Ran rings round us for years.

Elizabeth My husband couldn't bear him. *(Hesitates.)* Was that very indiscreet?

Cameron Yes.

Elizabeth Oops.

Cameron How is His Highness?

Elizabeth Fine, thank you. Though one can't help being just a little bit concerned for anyone his age. *(A beat.)* Our age. We're both showing wear and tear now. But still hanging on. Just.

A beat.

Elizabeth A bit like your arrangement with the Liberal Democrats. I think it was Disraeli that said the British don't care for coalition governments.

Cameron Nor you, Ma'am.

Elizabeth What?

Cameron *(louder)* Nor you, Ma'am.

Elizabeth *(terse)* Did I ever say as much?

Cameron Not in so many words. But I think all of your PM's would agree you have a way of saying nothing yet making your view perfectly clear.

Annotations
audience *here:* weekly meeting of the Queen and the Prime Minister at Buckingham Palace
Equerry: personal attendant to the Royal household
'All About That Bass': 2014 best-selling pop song
Whitehall: London area where the government buildings are
Tony Blair – Prime Minister (1997–2005)
Benjamin Disraeli – Prime Minister (1874–1880)

Text 2 Royals in Deutschland. Immer cool bleiben *Verena Mayer*

Die Ankunft des Prinzen von Wales und der Herzogin von Cornwall fällt mitten ins Brexit-Schlamassel. Zum Glück lassen sich Charles und Camilla nicht von der Hysterie anstecken und verbreiten britisches „Keep calm and carry on".

Lässt man die letzten Besuche britischer Royals Revue passieren, fällt auf, wie parallel sie zum Brexit verliefen. Im Jahr 2015, in der Planungsphase des Referendums, erinnerte die Queen bei ihrem Besuch in Deutschland an die Wunden des Krieges und daran, dass Europa den Frieden seiner Einigkeit verdanke. William und Kate kamen 2017 während der Brexit-Verhandlungen und gaben sich beim Rudern, im ICE und in einem Berliner Club als Vertreter einer europäischen Generation, die all die Veränderungen schon cool wuppen würde. „#Freundship" lautete dann auch das instagramtaugliche Motto ihres Besuchs.

Die Ankunft des Prinzen von Wales und der Herzogin von Cornwall am Dienstag in Berlin fällt nun mitten in den Brexit-Schlamassel. Da sind Pragmatismus und Gelassenheit angesagt, mit ihren 70 und 71 sind die beiden auch genau die Richtigen, um viel britisches „Keep calm and carry on" zu verbreiten.

Das Programm der viertägigen Deutschlandreise steht ganz im Zeichen der Krisen, die man schon gemeinsam durchgestanden hat. Charles hat eine Rede vorbereitet, in der er sagt, dass es hoffentlich „auf unserem Kontinent nie wieder zu Spaltungen und Konflikten wie in der Vergangenheit kommt, dass wir gemeinsam eine unentbehrliche Kraft des Guten in unserer Welt bleiben".

Kurzbesuch bei Angela Merkel

Nach einem kurzen Besuch bei Angela Merkel fahren die beiden zum alten Flughafen Tempelhof. Am Platz davor steht ein Denkmal aus Beton, das die Berliner wegen seiner wuchtigen Krümmung nur „Hungerkralle" nennen, das aber für eine historische Krise und die Rettung aus der Luft steht. Für die Flugzeuge der Westalliierten nämlich, die während der Berlin-Blockade hier landeten und die Stadt mit Nahrung versorgten. Charles tritt vor und legt einen Kranz nieder, das Denkmal erinnert auch daran, dass während der Luftbrücke vierzig Soldaten der Royal Air Force starben.

Er tut das mit der Routine eines Royals, der schon mehr als 30 Mal in Deutschland war. In Berlin war Charles schon fast überall, 1995 sogar in einer Plattenbausiedlung in Hellersdorf, wo er nach einem Besuch in „Moni's Friseursalon" mit einer Familie Rotkäppchensekt trank. Was nicht heißt, dass seine Agenda langweilig wäre. Im Gegenteil. Wenig ist derzeit so brandaktuell wie Charles' Interesse für Ökologie und nachhaltige Landwirtschaft.

Dem will auch der britische Botschafter genügen, der am Abend in seiner Residenz die traditionelle Gartenparty zu Ehren der Queen gibt. Weil Charles regionale Bio-Produkte liebt, wird es Kräuter aus einem lokalen Kräuter-Start-up geben, und der Saibling, der „nach Matjesart mit Spreewaldgurken und Wasabi-Kresse" zubereitet wird, stammt von einem Brandenburger Forellenhof. Matthias Engels züchtet die Öko-Fische und wird sich auf dem sorgfältig gestutzten Rasen unter die 600 Gäste aus Wirtschaft und Politik mischen.

Und was wird er dem Prinzen über seine Fische erzählen? „Das weiß ich noch nicht, da lasse ich lieber meine Frau reden."

Bewertungskriterien

Klausurteil A Schreiben/ Leseverstehen
Anforderungsbereich I (Teilaufgabe 1)

Der Prüfling

benennt die verschiedenen Gesprächsgegenstände	
– das neue Smartphone und seine Funktion,	2
– den anstehenden Wahlkampf samt Camerons Make-up,	3
– den EU-Gipfel, von dem Cameron gerade zurückgekehrt ist,	2
– die Problematik der Rolle der Queen in internationalen Beziehungen,	3
– Blair/Prinz Philipp/Koalitionen.	2
	12

Anforderungsbereich II (Teilaufgabe 2)

Der Prüfling

führt aus, dass die Königin unbeholfen und wenig staatsmännisch erscheint durch – ihren Umgang mit dem Handy (unbeholfene Großmutter), – den albernen hochaktuellen *bubble-gum-pop*-Klingelton als starken Kontrast zur konservativen Haltung der Queen, – die Wörter „escape“ und „tracking“, mit denen sogar Unzurechnungsfähigkeit suggeriert wird, – ihr indiskretes *gossiping* und ihre belanglose Konversation (Make-up, Blair, etc.), – verschiedene Regieanweisungen: „moves with difficulty“, „... stares. Bemused. Confounded“, „The Basilisk stare“, „squints“, „walks over to scrutinize“, „shudders“.	6
führt intellektuelle bzw. physische Defizite an – Zerstreutheit bzw. ihr Desinteresse am politischen Tagesgeschehen an (Bonn/Bern/Basel), – Einschlafen, – Vergessen ihrer Haltung zu Koalitionen.	6
führt aus, wie ihr konservatives und imperiales Denken in der Ablehnung der EU zugunsten des Commonwealth angedeutet wird.	4
	16

Anforderungsbereich III (Teilaufgabe 3.1)

Der Prüfling

knüpft an den Ausgangstext an, indem er sich auf z. B. einen oder mehrere der angesprochenen Aspekte bezieht.	2
führt Argumente für das System der konstitutionellen Monarchie in GB an, z. B. – Wert der Tradition, – Identifikation, *Britishness,* – Verehrung der *Royals,* – Stabilität, – Vorbildcharakter.	4
führt Argumente gegen das System an, z. B. – Kosten, – Privilegien (Steuern), – Personenkult, – Nutzen, – demokratische Legitimation.	4

gelangt zu einer verallgemeinernden Bewertung, indem er z. B. das System mit anderen Systemen vergleicht, z. B. Deutschland/USA.	2
kommt zu einer dezidierten eigenen Meinung.	2
	14

Anforderungsbereich III (Teilaufgabe 3.2)

Der Prüfling

nimmt die situative Vorgabe auf, indem er z. B. sich auf die an ihn gerichtete Bitte bezieht oder einen aktuellen Bezug wählt.	2
unterzieht das Königtum einer genauen Betrachtung, indem er positive und negative Aspekte anführt, z. B. – Wert der Tradition, – Identifikation, *Britishness*, – Verehrung der Royals, – Stabilität, – Vorbildcharakter, oder – Kosten, – Privilegien (Steuern), – Personenkult, – Nutzen.	5
stellt das deutsche System dem gegenüber und führt entsprechend weitere positive oder negative Aspekte an, z. B. – demokratische Legitimation, – Abwählbarkeit bzw. Absetzbarkeit, – aber auch Kosten und Sinnhaftigkeit.	5
formuliert eine klare eigene Meinung zu Monarchie oder auch allgemein zur Sinnhaftigkeit eines rein repräsentativen Staatsoberhauptes.	2
	14

Klausurteil B: Sprachmittlung

Der Prüfling gibt die wesentlichen Inhalte im Sinne der Aufgabenstellung sinngemäß zusammenfassend wieder:	18
auffallende Parallelen zu den Brexit-Ereignissen – Aussage der Queen, Europa verdanke den Frieden seiner Einigkeit, – William und Kates Auftritt als Vertreter einer europäischen Generation 2017.	
Bezüge des aktuellen Besuches und früherer Besuche zu europäischen bzw. interkulturellen Belangen – Tempelhof als Sinnbild der Luftbrücke, – das Interesse des Prinzen an der Situation nach der Wiedervereinigung, – das Interesse des Prinzen an Nachhaltigkeit und Ökologie, dem der Botschaftsempfang Rechnung trägt.	

Themenfeld *Visions of the Future*

Aufgabenbeispiel Abitur Englisch Grundkurs
Aufgabenart gemäß KLP: 1.1: Schreiben mit Leseverstehen integriert und Sprachmittlung isoliert
Bezug zu den Vorgaben: Medien in ihrer Bedeutung für den Einzelnen und die Gesellschaft *Visions of the future – utopia and dystopia*
Englischsprachiger literarischen Text (235 W., Gedicht) (Klausurteil A, Text 1) Auszug aus einem deutschsprachigen Sach- und Gebrauchstext (576 W.) (Klausurteil B, Text 2)
Quellenangaben: Roger Mc Gough, "The Lake", Fundstelle: http://www.englishdaily626.com/poetry_corner.php?047 Schäfer, Christoph, „Müll zu trennen reicht nicht“: © Alle Rechte vorbehalten. Frankfurter Allgemeine Zeitung GmbH, Frankfurt. Zur Verfügung gestellt vom Frankfurter Allgemeine Archiv http://www.faz.net/aktuell/wirtschaft/muell-zu-trennen-reicht-nicht-15376781.html#void

Aufgabe

Klausurteil A: Leseverstehen/Schreiben (Text 1)

1. Describe the physical and biological state of the lake in detail. *(Comprehension)*

2. Examine the way the speaker presents people and their environment and the results of pollution. In doing this, consider the speaker's choice of words and the syntax and imagery of the poem. *(Analysis)*

3. You have a choice here. Do either 3.1 or 3.2.

3.1 Evaluate the criticism inherent in the poem. Give arguments and examples to support or refute the author's negative view of the way people deal with their environment. *(Evaluation)*

OR

3.2 Imagine you are an environmentalist in the town where the lake is situated. Write an article for the local newspaper stating how bad the environmental situation has become. *(Re-creation of text)*

Klausurteil B: Sprachmittlung (Text 2)

4. While you are visiting your partner school in Ireland, you are praised for German awareness of environmental issues. Give a statement in class on the downsides of German rubbish production. Write your statement on the basis of the article from the "Frankfurter Allgemeine".

Text 1 The Lake *Roger McGough*

For years there have been no fish in the lake.
People hurrying through the park avoid it
like the plague. Birds steer clear
and the sedge of course has withered.
Trees lean away from it,
and at night it reflects, not the moon,
but the blackness of its own depths.
There are no fish in the lake.
But there is life there. There is life.

Underwater pigs glide between reefs of coral debris.
They love it here. They breed and multiply
in sties hollowed out of the mud
and lined with mattresses and bedsprings.
They live on dead fish and rotting things,
drowned pets, plastic and assorted excreta.
Rusty cans they like the best.
Holding them in webbed trotters
their teeth tear easily through the tin,
and poking in a snout, they noisily suck out
the putrid matter within.

There are no fish in the lake.
But there is life there. There is life.
For on certain evenings after dark
shoals of pigs surface
and look out at those houses near the park.
Where, in bathrooms,
children feed stale bread to plastic ducks,
and in attics,
toy yachts have long since run aground.
Where, in living-rooms,
anglers dangle their lines on patterned carpets,

and bemoan the fate of the ones that got away.
Down on the lake, piggy eyes glisten.
They have acquired a taste for flesh.
They are licking their lips. Listen ...

Annotations
sedge – kind of grass growing in water; G.: Schilf
shoal – G.: Schwarm

Text 2 Müll zu trennen reicht nicht *Christoph Schäfer*

China will unseren Plastikabfall nicht mehr ins Land lassen. Das teure deutsche Entsorgungssystem wird noch teurer werden. Doch Jammern hilft nichts: Um unseren Abfall müssen wir uns schon selbst kümmern.

Plastikmüll hat im Meer nichts verloren. Wenn in den Abendnachrichten Bilder gezeigt werden, wie in entfernten Weltgegenden Tausende Folien, Flaschen und Tüten auf der Wasseroberfläche treiben, ist die Empörung zu Recht groß. Glücklicherweise sind die deutschen Badeseen sauber. Das bestätigt die Deutschen darin, Klimaschützer und Recyclingmeister zu sein. Fast alle haben drei bis vier Mülltonnen vor dem Haus, um den Abfall zu trennen. Eine braune für den Bioabfall, eine blaue fürs Papier, die schwarze für den Restmüll und die gelbe für Metall und Kunststoff. Darüber hinaus gibt es Wertstoffhöfe und diverse Sammelbehälter für Elektroschrott, Altkleider und Schuhe. Gefühlt ist alles wunderbar in Ordnung.

Leider will sich eine Meldung der vergangenen Woche nicht ins harmonische Bild einfügen: Demnach droht Deutschland im Müll zu versinken, weil China unseren Plastikabfall nicht mehr haben will. Moment mal, denkt man da. Wieso exportiert Deutschland überhaupt Plastikmüll ins ferne China? Wer genauer nachliest, erfährt ganz Erstaunliches: Von den sechs Millionen Tonnen Plastikmüll, die hierzulande jedes Jahr anfallen, geht etwa ein Viertel ins Ausland. Etwa die Hälfte des exportierten Mülls landet im Reich der Mitte. Die Menge ist gigantisch: Allein im vorvergangenen Jahr kaufte China rund 750 000 Tonnen Plastikmüll aus Deutschland. Das entspricht mehr als 80 000 randvollen Müllwagen.

Was mit dem deutschen Müll in China passiert ist, will keiner so genau wissen. In die offiziellen Statistiken jedenfalls fließt das nach China verschiffte Plastik als erfolgreich recycelt ein. Dabei arbeitet laut Experten sogar die Müllverbrennung in Deutschland ökologischer als die chinesische Kunststoffverwertung. Aber weg ist weg, aus den Augen aus dem Sinn.

Müll trennen alleine reicht nicht

Bedauerlicherweise entpuppt sich die Vorstellung von den mülltrennenden Umweltchampions auch mit Blick auf andere Werte als Lüge. Der typische Bundesbürger hat laut EU-Statistikamt im vorvergangenen Jahr exakt 37,4 Kilo Plastikverpackungen als Abfall hinterlassen. Das ist dreimal mehr als ein Bulgare verursacht, und sogar sechs Kilo mehr als der durchschnittliche EU-Bürger ansammelt. Bei der Wiederverwertung sieht es besser aus, aber längst nicht vorbildlich. Das Recycling von Alt-papier, Altglas, Weißblech und Aluminium klappt gut, die Aufbereitung von Kunststoffverpackungen hingegen unzureichend. Noch immer wird in Deutschland die Hälfte der Plastikabfälle verbrannt oder landet im Ausland. Tschechien und Bulgarien hingegen erreichen Aufbereitungsquoten von 62 Prozent. Immerhin ist Besserung in Sicht. Ende dieses Jahres tritt das neue Müllgesetz in Kraft, das steigende Recyclingquoten verlangt.

Doch auch damit wird längst nicht alles gut. Der bisherige Ablasshandel (Ich trenne meinen Müll, also darf ich sorgenlos einkaufen) greift zu kurz. Hersteller wie Konsumenten müssen umdenken. Um nur ein paar Beispiele zu nennen: Muss es wirklich sein, dass in eine große Gummibärchentüte Dutzende kleine Tütchen kommen? Muss jede einzelne Gurke im Supermarkt in Plastik verpackt werden? Müssen so viele Kaffee „to go“ sein?

Auch an der Akzeptanz für wiederaufbereitete Materialien hapert es. Die Industrie ist nur in engen Grenzen bereit, bei der Qualität der Ausgangsstoffe Abstriche hinzunehmen. Die deutschen Verbraucher hingegen werden es definitiv akzeptieren müssen, dass die Preise für Plastikwaren etwas steigen. Das chinesische Importverbot für Müll wird dazu führen, dass Handel und Industrie mehr an den Grünen Punkt zahlen müssen. Das teure deutsche Entsorgungssystem wird noch teurer werden – und viele Produzenten werden die höheren Kosten durchreichen. Das ist trotzdem besser, als den alten Plastikmüll nach Fernost zu exportieren, wo er oft genug im Meer landet. Um unseren Abfall müssen wir uns schon selbst kümmern. China will unseren Plastikabfall nicht mehr ins Land lassen. Das teure deutsche Entsorgungssystem wird noch teurer werden. Doch Jammern hilft nichts: Um unseren Abfall müssen wir uns schon selbst kümmern.

Bewertungskriterien

Klausurteil A: Leseverstehen/Schreiben
Anforderungsbereich I

Der Prüfling

beschreibt, das dunkle Aussehen der Oberfläche des Sees, in der sich nicht einmal der Mond spielgelt	2
führt an, dass keine Fische darin leben und selbst Riedgras verwelkt ist.	2
führt an, dass Tiere und Menschen gleichermaßen den See meiden,	2
beschreibt, was sich an Unrat in dem See befindet, z. B. – tote Haustiere – Plastik – Fäkalien – alte Matratzen – rostige Büchsen	4
beschreibt die mutierten Monsterschweine, die den See bewohnen	2
	12

Anforderungsbereich II

Der Prüfling

analysiert die Wortwahl des lyrischen Ich, die durchgehend Abscheu, Ekel, Fäulnis, Tod und Bedrohung suggeriert *(plague, blackness, sties, mud, dead, rotting, excreta, etc.)*	4
analysiert syntaktische Merkmale des Gedichtes, insbesondere – die sich wiederholenden Zeilen 8/9 und 21/22 und die Wiederholung – innerhalb der Zeilen, die Bedrohung suggeriert – die Auslassung in der letzten Zeile, die ebenfalls bedrohlich wirkt	4
erläutert die Symbolik der sich neigenden Bäume zur Illustration der Widerwärtigkeit und die Symbolik der Schweine, – als Indikator für den Verschmutzungsgrad (Schweinestall) – als Mutanten und damit Resultat der Veränderung der Natur durch den Menschen – als Bedrohung, die eines Tages über den See hinaus spürbar wird und dem Menschen selbst gefährlich wird	4
erläutert die Bedeutung des Verhaltens der Menschen sowie die Symbolik ihrer Gegenstände, die immer wieder Widernatürlichkeit, Unappetitlichkeit, Verfall und Künstlichkeit suggeriert und so auch den Verfall der Umwelt widerspiegelt, z. B. – altes Brot – Plastikenten im Badezimmer (statt Enten in der Natur) – vergessene Spielzeugyachten (nutzlos, kaputt, als Pendant zum See) – Angeln auf dem Teppich (statt in der Natur)	4
	16

Anforderungsbereich III (Teilaufgabe 3.1)

Der Prüfling

nimmt einleitend Bezug auf die Intention des Gedichtes,	2
erläutert anhand von Beispielen den Zustand unserer Umwelt, der dem Gedicht Recht gibt oder führt an, dass allerdings auch viele Anstrengungen zum Schutz der Umwelt unternommen werden,	8
wägt die Punkte gegeneinander ab und kommt zu einer begründeten Schlussfolgerung,	4
	14

Anforderungsbereich III (Teilaufgabe 3.2)

Der Prüfling

wählt den Zustand des Sees als Aufhänger für seinen Artikel,	2
führt die Konsequenzen der Verschmutzung aus und/oder benennt und beschreibt weitere Bereiche, in denen Umweltschutz geboten ist,	6
benennt Lösungsvorschläge für das Problem des Sees und andere Probleme der Umweltverschmutzung,	4
appelliert an die Leser, mit zu einer Verbesserung beizutragen	2
	14

Klausurteil B: Sprachmittlung

1. Inhaltliche Leistung

	Anforderungen: Die Schülerin/Der Schüler gibt die wesentlichen Inhalte im Sinne der Aufgabenstellung sinngemäß zusammenfassend wieder:	**max. Punktzahl**
1	der scheinbar vorbildliche Umgang mit Plastikmüll in Deutschland	18
2	die Verschiffung ins Ausland	
3	das hohe Aufkommen trotz Recycling	
4	die Kritik an bestimmten Produkten *(coffee to go*, Gummibärchen)	
5	die mangelnde Akzeptanz recycelter Materialien	
6	die steigenden Kosten	

Themenfeld *The Impact of Shakespearean Drama on Young Audiences Today*

Aufgabenbeispiel Abitur Englisch Leistungskurs
Aufgabenart gemäß KLP: 1.1: Schreiben mit Leseverstehen integriert und Sprachmittlung isoliert
Bezug zu den Vorgaben: Literatur und Medien in ihrer Bedeutung für den Einzelnen und die Gesellschaft *The impact of Shakespearean drama on young audiences today: study of extracts and film scenes*

Auszug aus einem deutschsprachigen Sach- und Gebrauchstext (459 W.) (Klausurteil B, Text 1) Auszug aus einem englischsprachigen literarischen Text (365 W.) (Klausurteil A, Text 2)
Quellenangaben: Text 1: Frank Günther, „Sein oder Nichtsein?“, *Frankfurter Neue Presse* 19.04.2014, online http://www.fnp.de/nachrichten/kultur/Sein-oder-Nichtsein;art679,820195 Text 2: William Shakespeare, *The Taming of the Shrew*, Act V, Scene II

Aufgabe

Klausurteil B: Sprachmittlung

1. Your English teacher at your host school in England has asked you to give a talk in class on the relevance of Shakespeare in Germany. Write the part of your talk that deals with Frank Günter's view on Shakespeare's still being up-to-date. *(Mediation)*

Klausurteil A: Leseverstehen/Schreiben

2. Point out the view of a wife's duty as it is presented by Katherina. *(Comprehension)*

3. Explain the comparisons used in this monologue as well as their function. In doing this, also refer to the Elizabethan world picture. *(Analysis)*

4.1 Evaluate Katherina's speech from a 21st century point of view. *(Evaluation)*

4.2 After you have attended a performance of *The Taming of the Shrew*, write an article for an international online magazine with the title “The interest of young audiences in Shakespeare”, in which you critically discuss the relevance of Shakespeare's plays for today's audiences. Refer to the excerpt from the play, Frank Günther's article, and other texts you have studied. *(Evaluation/re-creation of text)*

Text 1 Sein oder Nichtsein? *Frank Günther*

Zum 450. Geburtstag des meistgespielten Theaterdichters der Welt fragt der Shakespeare-Experte in einem Gastbeitrag: Verstaubt oder nicht verstaubt?

Nun feiern wir also Shakespeares 450. Geburtstag. Es gibt nur wenige Autoren der Weltliteratur, bei denen man auf eine vergleichbare Wirkungsgeschichte zurückblicken kann; Dante könnte man nennen, und Cervantes, auch wenn sein „Don Quichote" – trotz Windmühlen und Dulcinea – nicht Shakespeares breitgefächerte Wirkungsmacht erreichte. Shakespeare ist eine einzigartige literarische Ikone.

Wie es euch gefällt

Was sagt man über eine 400 Jahre alte Ikone? Über Shakespeare ist dieser Tage als bewunderndes Statement häufig zu lesen, er sei „auch heute noch aktuell". Das sagt sich so leicht dahin. Unklar ist, was es bedeuten soll. Es ist nämlich ein seltsam vergiftetes Lob. Im „auch-heute-noch" schwingt als Unterton ja mit, dass solche uralten Werke nach 400 Jahren eigentlich längst zum historischen Schutt gehören müssten. Aber nein, nicht bei Shakespeare – und dann folgt dieses Wörtchen „aktuell". Shakespeare ist auch heute noch aktuell! Also wichtig, relevant, bedeutsam für unsere heutigen Probleme, für dich und mich, hier und jetzt. Noch aktuell. Also morgen vielleicht schon nicht mehr?

Es ist gut gemeint, aber etwas glitschig, dieses schlagzeilenhascherische Adjektiv „aktuell". Wir gebrauchen es gewöhnlich im Kontext der „aktuellen Nachrichten", des „aktuellen Straßenzustandsberichts", der „aktuellen Herbstmode", der „aktuellen Frühjahrsfarben", der „aktuellen Looks", der „aktuellen Trends" – also für lauter entschieden flüchtige, nur für den konkreten Moment gültige Erscheinungen, zumeist in ranschmeißerischer Werbesprache formuliert. Was „aktuell" ist, ist schnellebig; es trägt sein baldiges Ende schon in sich, denn das Wörtlein „aktuell" signalisiert, dass es alsbald von noch „Aktuellerem" abgelöst werden wird. Was heute aktuell ist, ist schon morgen von gestern.

Was ihr wollt

Shakespeare, der „auch heute noch aktuell" sein soll, soll offenbar einen entscheidenden Beitrag zum heutigen Aktuellen leisten. Was aber sind unsere aktuellen Probleme zu Shakespeares Geburtstag? Die Euro-Krise. Die Griechenland-Krise. Die Energie-Krise. Die Ukraine-Krise. Die Migrationsproblematik. Der NSU-Skandal über Nazi-Umtriebe. Der NSA-Skandal über Geheimdienstumtriebe. Die Probleme mit Very Big Data. Die Frage der sozialen Gerechtigkeit. Die Quotenregelung für Frauen in Führungspositionen. Die EU-Regelung zu Energiesparbeschränkungen bei Staubsaugern und Kaffeemaschinen. Haben Shakespeares Werke uns dazu irgendetwas zu sagen? Nein, natürlich nicht. Die Rede vom „auch heute noch aktuellen" Shakespeare entpuppt sich schnell als hilflose Hohlfloskel. Seinem Werk ist mit solchen wohlfeilen Etiketten wohl nicht beizukommen.

[...]

Unter der „Aktualität" der Oberflächenzeitumstände, die von „verstaubten" Verhältnissen erzählen mag, brodelt sehr lebendig das Eigentliche, das Shakespeares Glanz ausmacht: die niemals an ein Ende kommende, niemals auserzählbare existenzielle menschliche Werdens- und Wandlungsmöglichkeit. So kommt es, dass wir durch Shakespeares paradoxe Erzählkunst uns selbst auch hinter der verblichenen Aktualität vergangener Weltverhältnisse wiedererkennen können. In seinen zahllosen Gestalten, in ihren Leiden und Freuden, ihren Gemeinheiten und Bösartigkeiten, ihren Irrtümern und Selbsttäuschungen, ihren Egoismen und ihrer Fähigkeit zu Güte, Liebe und Mitleid erscheinen wir uns selbst, nah und vertraut.

Text 2 The Taming of the Shrew (Act V, Scene 2) *William Shakespeare*

Katherina, who is the woman to be tamed in this comedy, speaks this monologue in the final scene.

Katherina
Fie, fie! unknit that threatening unkind brow,
And dart not scornful glances from those eyes,
To wound thy lord, thy king, thy governor:
It blots thy beauty as frosts do bite the meads,
Confounds thy fame as whirlwinds shake fair buds,
And in no sense is meet or amiable.
A woman moved is like a fountain troubled,
Muddy, ill-seeming, thick, bereft of beauty;
And while it is so, none so dry or thirsty
Will deign to sip or touch one drop of it.
Thy husband is thy lord, thy life, thy keeper,
Thy head, thy sovereign; one that cares for thee,
And for thy maintenance commits his body
To painful labour both by sea and land,
To watch the night in storms, the day in cold,
Whilst thou liest warm at home, secure and safe;
And craves no other tribute at thy hands
But love, fair looks and true obedience;
Too little payment for so great a debt.
Such duty as the subject owes the prince
Even such a woman oweth to her husband;
And when she is froward, peevish, sullen, sour,
And not obedient to his honest will,
What is she but a foul contending rebel
And graceless traitor to her loving lord?
I am ashamed that women are so simple
To offer war where they should kneel for peace;
Or seek for rule, supremacy and sway,

When they are bound to serve, love and obey.
Why are our bodies soft and weak and smooth,
Unapt to toil and trouble in the world,
But that our soft conditions and our hearts
Should well agree with our external parts?
Come, come, you froward and unable worms!
My mind hath been as big as one of yours,
My heart as great, my reason haply more,
To bandy word for word and frown for frown;
But now I see our lances are but straws,
Our strength as weak, our weakness past compare,
That seeming to be most which we indeed least are.
Then vail your stomachs, for it is no boot,
And place your hands below your husband's foot:
In token of which duty, if he please,
My hand is ready; may it do him ease.

Annotations
unknit your brows ≠ knit your brows; **blot:** stain; **meads:** meadows; **confounds thy fame:** destroys your reputation; **meet:** appropriate; **moved:** bad-tempered; **bereft:** robbed; **deign:** consent, want; **froward:** hardheaded; **big:** arrogant; **haply:** perhaps; **bandy:** hit back and forth (as at tennis); **vail:** lower; **stomach:** pride, temper; **no boot:** no use

Bewertungskriterien

Klausurteil B: Sprachmittlung

Der Prüfling gibt die wesentlichen Inhalte im Sinne der Aufgabenstellung sinngemäß zusammenfassend wieder.	18
Er führt an, dass Günther den Begriff aktuell ablehnt, da er Schnelllebiges und Vergängliches bezeichnet, z. B. Modetrends oder Verkehrshinweise.	
Er führt an, dass Shakespeare auch zu den aktuellen Problemen der Welt nichts Relevantes beitragen kann, z. B. zu internationalen Krisen, humanitären Belangen oder politischen Skandalen.	
Er führt an, dass es vielmehr Shakespeares Charaktere sind, in deren Facetten wir uns immer wieder wiedererkennen, selbst vor dem Hintergrund vergangener Weltbilder.	

Klausurteil A: Leseverstehen/Schreiben
Anforderungsbereich I (Teilaufgabe 2)

Der Prüfling

führt aus, dass die Frau freundlich zu sein hat, denn nur das macht sie liebenswert und attraktiv.	4

führt aus, dass sie ihrem Mann Liebe zu erweisen, zu gefallen, zu dienen und zu gehorchen hat, als eher noch zu geringe Gegenleistung für seine Sorge und die Strapazen und Entbehrungen, die er um ihretwillen auf sich nimmt.	4
führt aus, dass diese Rolle in den natürlichen körperlichen und charakterlichen Eigenschaften der Frau begründet liegt.	4
	12

Anforderungsbereich II (Teilaufgabe 3)

Der Prüfling

analysiert den zentralen Vergleich zwischen Ehe und Staatswesen, Untertan und König ("subject vs. lord", "sovereign", "prince"), und benennt weitere Vergleiche, die Hierarchie ausdrücken: "keeper", "head" und erläutert, dass der Souverän Sorge für seine Untertanen trägt, daher sind sie zu Dienst und Loyalität verpflichtet. So ist auch die Frau, die sich gegen den Ehemann auflehnt, gleichzusetzen mit dem Rebellen und dem Verräter, der sich gegen seinen König auflehnt.	4
benennt weitere Vergleiche (Störung der Natur: "frost/meads", "whirlwinds/buds", "fountain/mud") und ihre Funktion: Weibliches Missverhalten erscheint als Auflehnung gegen die gottgewollte Ordnung.	4
erkennt und benennt weitere Vergleiche, die Schwäche und Machtlosigkeit der Frau illustrieren: "unable worms", "lances are but straws".	4
erkennt die typisch elisabethanische Sichtweise der korrespondierenden Beziehung von – Mensch und Natur, – Mensch und Staatswesen, – Mikrokosmos und Makrokosmos.	4
	16

Anforderungsbereich III (Teilaufgabe 4.1)

Der Prüfling

nimmt Bezug auf die Ungleichheit der Geschlechter, wie Katherina sie propagiert.	2
äußert sich vor dem Hintergrund der modernen demokratischen, freiheitlichen, egalitären westlichen Weltanschauung kritisch zu diesem Frauenbild, z. B. mit Verweis auf – Menschenrechte, – Menschenwürde, – Frauenbewegung des 20. Jahrhunderts, – Veränderung der Familienstrukturen, – Veränderung in der Arbeitswelt.	5

weist hin auf immer noch bestehende Ungleichheit, z. B. – im Berufsleben, – in patriarchalischen Gesellschaftsformen, – in kriminellem Kontext (Gewalt gegen Frauen).	5
formuliert eine zusammenfassende, wertende persönliche Stellungnahme zur Rolle der Geschlechter.	2
	14

Anforderungsbereich III (Teilaufgabe 4.2)

Der Prüfling

nimmt einleitend Bezug auf die vorgegebene Situation und die Textpassage als Anlass seines Artikels.	1
äußert sich vor dem Hintergrund der modernen demokratischen, freiheitlichen, egalitären westlichen Weltanschauung kritisch zu dem dargestellten Frauenbild, z. B. mit Verweis auf – Menschenrechte – Menschenwürde – Frauenbewegung des 20. Jahrhunderts – Veränderung der Familienstrukturen – Veränderung in der Arbeitswelt; hinterfragt die Aktualität und Relevanz der Dramen Shakespeares und erweitert seine Argumentation um Beispiele aus anderen Dramen z. B. je nach Schwerpunkt hinsichtlich – Geschlechterrollen – Verhältnis der Generationen – Lehnstreue – Aberglaube – etc.	5
verweist auf die sprachlichen Schwierigkeiten des vorliegenden Textes sowie anderer Dramen.	2
stellt seinen Ausführungen Argumente entgegen, die die fortwährende Aktualität und Relevanz von Shakespeares Dramen unterstreichen. Dabei bezieht er sich z. B. auf – zeitlose Problematik wie Liebe, Zurückweisung, Eifersucht, Ehrgeiz, Neid etc., – unvermindertes Interesse an Theatervorstellungen, – Erfolge von Hollywood-Produktionen, – Adaption in modernen Werken, – zeitlose Kraft und Schönheit der Sprache.	4
formuliert eine zusammenfassende persönlich wertende Stellungnahme auf der Grundlage seiner Argumentation.	2
	14

Themenfeld *Studying and Working in a Globalized World*

Aufgabenbeispiel Abitur Englisch Leistungskurs
Aufgabenart gemäß KLP: 1.1: Schreiben mit Leseverstehen integriert und Sprachmittlung isoliert
Bezug zu den Vorgaben: Lebensentwürfe, Studium, Ausbildung, Beruf international – *Englisch als lingua* franca *Studying and working in a globalised world*
Auszug aus einem englischsprachigen Sachtext (734 W.) (Klausurteil A, Text 1) Auszug aus einem deutschsprachigen Sachtext (492 W.) (Klausurteil B, Text 2)
Quellenangaben: Text 1: Julian Baggini, "If universities sacrifice philosophy on the altar of profit, what's next?" The Guardian, 21 Dec 2018, Copyright Guardian News & Media Ltd. 2021 https://www.theguardian.com/commentisfree/2018/dec/21/universities-philosophy-profit-business-partners Text 2: Bernd Kramer, „Lohnt sich das Studium noch?" *Spiegel Online,* 19.11.2017 http://www.spiegel.de/karriere/karriere-lohnt-sich-ein-studium-noch-a-1178588.html

Aufgabe

Klausurteil A: Leseverstehen/Schreiben (Text 1)

1. Point out what worries the writer considering the closure of the philosophy department at Hull University. *(Comprehension)*

2. Examine the way the writer expresses his attitude towards what is becoming of university education. In doing this, consider his choice of words and other rhetorical devices and strategies. *(Analysis)*

Choose ONE of the following tasks:

3.1. Comment on lines 106–110: "That's why Hull's fate is all our fates. Today, they're coming for philosophy. Tomorrow, they'll come for something else that isn't designed to turn a profit." In doing this, give your own view on profit-orientation in the globalised world. *(Evaluation)*

3.2. Imagine you are a leading member of the student union at Hull University. A large number of students demonstrate with you against the closure of the philosophy department. Give a speech at the end of the demonstration to clearly state the students' view. *(Evaluation/(Re-)creation of text)*

Klausurteil B: Sprachmittlung (Text 2)

4. As a guest student at a school in Ireland you have been asked to give a talk on chances and careers in Germany. You have done some research and, among others, you have found this article from Spiegel Online. Write the **part of your talk** that is based on this article.

Text 1 If universities sacrifice philosophy on the altar of profit, what's next? *Julian Baggini*

Hull says the subject doesn't meet the needs of 'business partners'. Try telling that to Thales of Miletus.

You might think that a university philosophy department facing closure in Hull is of as much interest to the average person as the shutting of a butcher's in Wolverhampton is to a vegetarian in Totnes. There are almost as many universities as high streets now, and for every closure here there's an opening somewhere else. But the events unfolding on Humberside are symptomatic of a deep malaise affecting not just universities but the wider culture. The crude pursuit of what is "practical", "efficient" or "useful" is threatening everything of value that isn't evidently profitable.

Philosophy has been taught at Hull ever since the University opened in 1928. The department has no problem with recruitment and has a good faculty. Because humanities courses are so cheap to teach and student fees so high, there is no conceivable way it could be losing money. In a letter to colleagues, Kathleen Lennon, emeritus professor of philosophy, insisted: "Philosophy at Hull is financially viable – providing a healthy return for the university."

So why is the university not accepting any more joint honours students and publicly entertaining the possibility "that we will not be recruiting new students" in 2019? A statement by Jeanette Strachan, the university's registrar, to the local newspaper suggests some worrying answers. Strachan said the university sought to offer students "a high-quality academic experience and ensure that their qualification holds value over time".

The word that screams out of that sentence is "value". The implication seems to be that a philosophy degree does not provide a sufficient financial return for those who "invest" in it. This impression is reinforced by Strachan's statement that the university "meets the needs of our students, research and business partners". The inclusion of that third party would baffle the thousands of people who have graduated with philosophy degrees without ever catching a sniff of a "business partner", let alone receiving any help from one.

You could easily demolish this economically reductive case on its own terms, as the British Philosophical Association has done in an open letter to the university protesting against the proposed cuts. It points out that "philosophy degrees equip students with a wide range of highly valued and sought-after skills, and there is compelling evidence that graduate employers have a high regard for philosophy degree-holders".

The BPA is surely right to plead with the university in the only language it understands, insisting there is "robust evidence of the value of philosophy". But we should not let the bean-counters who have captured too much of higher education set the terms of the debate. In a truly philosophical spirit, we should question the meaning of "value" that they are using as if it were common sense.

[...]

People who choose to study philosophy [...] could choose to study a course with a more reliable financial payoff. But their "investment" in three years of philosophy is not designed to maximise financial yields. This makes them wiser, not dumber, than those who allow money to entirely dictate their choices. Whereas money is only a means to an end, the pursuit of learning is intrinsically rewarding.

This is not special pleading for philosophy. The same argument holds for innumerable other subjects which don't have any direct economic benefit. I always cringe when people quote Socrates's line "the unexamined life is not worth living" as though it were an argument uniquely for philosophy. All the humanities, arts and social sciences have a role in helping us to live examined lives. If we cannot find spaces for them in our universities, education becomes nothing more than professional training, churning out people who can help run society efficiently but none who routinely and thoroughly ask what all that efficiency is in the service of.

The threat at Hull reflects a lamentable shift in education towards precisely this functional view of what universities are for. But it also reflects a crudely utilitarian worldview that infects much, much more. You see it manifest whenever arts funding is under threat or when the evident inability of GDP growth to capture what most matters fails to translate to concrete steps to replace it with better metrics. That's why Hull's fate is all our fates. Today, they're coming for philosophy. Tomorrow, they'll come for something else that isn't designed to turn a profit.

Annotations
Hull – Kingston upon Hull, Humberside, Northern English port and university city
Wolverhampton – industrial city in the English Midlands
Totnes – Southern English town associated with New Age, alternative life style, and natural health

Text 2 Lohnt sich das Studium noch? *Bernd Kramer*

Nie gab es in Deutschland mehr Studenten als heute. Viele zweifeln deshalb, ob der Abschluss von der Uni tatsächlich noch ein Garant für einen sicheren Job und ein gutes Einkommen ist.

[...]

Fest steht: In Deutschland studieren heute so viele Menschen wie noch nie zuvor, fast drei Millionen sind es. Allein zu diesem Wintersemester werden eine halbe Million Neueinschreibungen erwartet. Ein Studium galt bisher als Königsweg zu einem guten Job. Ein Uni-Abschluss war ein Versprechen auf ein gutes Einkommen, auf Status, Aufstieg – auf ein Leben in materieller Sicherheit, weitgehend zumindest.

[...]

Doch kann sich diese Hoffnung erfüllen, wenn es die Hälfte eines Altersjahrgangs in die Hörsäle und Seminarräume zieht? Verlieren die Abschlüsse dann nicht an Wert?

Diese Fragen bewegen viele Studierende in Deutschland, die Stimmung ist durchwachsen. Einerseits hat der Optimismus zugenommen. Nur eine Minderheit erwartet größere Schwierigkeiten bei der Jobsuche, das zeigt der „Studierendensurvey", für den Forscher der Uni Konstanz im Auftrag der Bundesregierung regelmäßig Studenten befragen. Andererseits ist der Wunsch nach einem stabilen Arbeitsplatz stark gestiegen. 2001 war 51 Prozent der Studierenden die Sicherheit im Job sehr wichtig, 2013 waren es bereits 67 Prozent. Deutlich mehr junge Menschen als früher richten die Entscheidung für das Studienfach nach den Arbeitsmarktchancen aus. Einfach nur drauflosstudieren, das tun heute die wenigsten – für die Forscher ein Indiz dafür, dass die „Verunsicherung der Studierenden im Hinblick auf die Zukunft" immens sein muss. Es wird schon irgendwie klappen mit dem Einstieg in den Job, aber so einfach und planbar wie früher ist es wohl nicht – so könnte man die Stimmung an den Hochschulen zusammenfassen.

Das Bundesinstitut für Berufsbildung geht sogar davon aus, dass bald mehr Akademiker einen Job suchen als in den Ruhestand gehen. Bis 2035 rechnen die Forscher mit 6,5 Millionen Hochschulabsolventen, die neu auf den Arbeitsmarkt kommen. Aber nur 3,9 Millionen Berufstätige mit Uni- oder FH-Abschluss werden im selben Zeitraum aus dem Arbeitsleben ausscheiden. Künftig suchen die Unternehmen vielleicht gar nicht mehr so dringend nach Ingenieuren, Betriebswirten und Chemikern – sondern nach Menschen mit Berufsausbildung, nach Mechatronikern oder kaufmännischen Angestellten. Pflegekräfte sind schon jetzt rar.

Ist Bildungsdeutschland manisch auf ein Studium fixiert?

Seit einigen Jahren macht daher das Wort vom Akademisierungswahn die Runde – ein Wort, das suggeriert, Bildungsdeutschland sei verrückt geworden und junge Menschen manisch auf ein Studium fixiert. In die Welt gesetzt hat es der Münchner Philosophieprofessor und ehemalige Kulturstaatsminister Julian Nida-Rümelin. Der Andrang auf die Hochschulen, so seine These, frustriere am Ende alle: die Absolventen, die nicht den Job finden, den sie sich versprochen hätten. Die Lehrlinge, die nach ihrer Ausbildung nun auch noch mit den vielen nicht untergekommenen Akademikern um Stellen konkurrieren müssten.

Und natürlich Professoren wie Nida-Rümelin selbst, die sich in den überfüllten Hörsälen voller Credit-Point-gieriger und arbeitsmarktverbissener Studenten nicht mehr so zweckfrei und leidenschaftlich wie dereinst in philosophischen Gedankenflügen verlieren könnten. Kein Wunder, dass der Beifall für die These vom Akademisierungswahn eher von der konservativen Seite kam, von Professoren, deren Selbstverständnis es ist, für eine kleine Bildungselite zuständig zu sein, nicht für den Aufstieg der Massen.

Die Frage ist: Wie berechtigt sind solche Alarmrufe? Hat das Studium wirklich an Wert verloren?

Die Antwort lautet: Es ist kompliziert. […]

Bewertungskriterien

Klausurteil A, Leseverstehen/Schreiben
Anforderungsbereich I, Teilaufgabe 1

Der Prüfling

führt an, dass die Universität Hull ihr Philosophieinstitut schließt mit der Begründung, dass die Absolventen keine nachhaltig wertvolle Qualifizierung erlangen könnten.	4
führt aus, wie der Autor diese Schließung als Symptom einer weitreichenden Krise sieht, nämlich dass sich alles der Profitorientierung unterordnet.	4
führt aus, dass der Autor die utilitaristische Bedeutung des Wortes „value“ anprangert und vor der Gefahr der profitorientierten Weltsicht warnt.	4
	12

Anforderungsbereich II, Teilaufgabe 2

Der Prüfling

benennt die tendenziöse Wortwahl des Autors, die die profitorientierte Weltsicht und ihre Vertreter scharf kritisiert („sacrifice/altar of profit“, Überschrift, „deep malaise“, „crude pursuit“, „threatening“, „the only language“ „bean-counters“, „threat“, „lamentable“, „crudely utilitarian“).	4
führt die Bildhaftigkeit an, die die Aussagen des Autors illustriert und erläutert sie: *comparison:* Wolverhampton/Totnes (ll. 4–5) *personifcation:* “scream”, l. 37 *metaphor* (erstarrt): “sacrifice on the altar of profit”, title	4
benennt rhetorische Mittel, z. B. *exaggeration:* “As many universities as high streets” (l. 6, Kritik des Verlusts der Bildungsstandards, inflationäre Universitätsabschlüsse) *parallelism:* “Hull’s fate is all our fates”; “Today they’re coming ..., tomorrow they’ll come” (ll. 107–109);	4
benennt die Adressatenorientierung: *short forms, casual tone,* trotz komplexen Satzbaus (rhetorische) Fragen. (Titel, ll. 26–30) Appell: “we should” (ll. 63–69) “we” vs. “they” (ll. 63–69): Abgrenzung gegen die “bean-counters”	4
	16

Anforderungsbereich III, Teilaufgabe 3.1

Der Prüfling

knüpft an den Ausgangstext an, durch Bezug auf die Zeilen 106–110.	2
beschreibt andere Fälle der reinen Profitorientierung in Bereichen wie Forschung, medizinischer Versorgung, Musik, Kunst, Theater, frühkindliche Bildung etc.	6
bewertet die Profitorientierung entweder in Sinne des Autors als problematisch oder als hilfreich oder als ambivalent.	4
kommt zu einem dezidierten Fazit.	2
	14

Anforderungsbereich III, Teilaufgabe 3.2

Der Prüfling

stellt einleitend die Situation an der Uni Hull dar.	4
argumentiert für Erhalt des Faches Philosophie z. B. mit Bezug auf – die Bedeutung der Philosophie in einer profitorientierten Welt, – die Bedeutung der Philosophie für die Tradition der Uni Hull, – das Überhandnehmen von Technokratie und Wirtschaft, – die individuellen Bedürfnisse angehender Studenten, – andere besorgniserregende Beispiele von Profitorientierung z. B. in Kunst und Musik, – Beispiele von Dummheit bei Entscheidungsträgern.	8
kommt zu einem dezidierten Apell.	2
	14

Klausurteil B: Mediation, Teilaufgabe 4

	Der Prüfling gibt die wesentlichen Inhalte im Sinne der Aufgabenstellung sinngemäß zusammenfassend wieder:	
1	*die Situation der Studenten* – das Studium als traditioneller Königsweg zum materiellen Erfolg – Studienwahl gezielt mit Blick auf sicheren Arbeitsplatz – trotz Verunsicherung grundsätzlicher Optimismus für Stellensuche	18
2	*die Prognose der Berufschancen für Akademiker* – mehr Hochschulabsolventen als ausscheidende Akademiker – den womöglich vermehrten Bedarf an nicht akademischen Berufen	
3	*die Fixierung auf ein Studium zum Nachteil* – sowohl von Absolventen als auch von Lehrlingen – der Professoren, die gedrängt werden, arbeitsmarktorientiert zu arbeiten, wobei die reine Forschung und Lehre auf der Strecke bleibt.	

Original-Prüfungsaufgaben 2020/2021

GK mit Beispiellösungen

Quelle der Aufgabenstellung: Qualitäts- und UnterstützungsAgentur – Landesinstitut für Schule*

Aufgabe 1

Klausurteil A: Leseverstehen und Schreiben integriert

Aufgabenstellung:

1. Describe the situation presented in the opening scene of the novel, the characters' behaviour during the conversation and the society the family lives in. *(Comprehension) (12 Punkte)*

2. Analyse how the opening scene is presented and its effect on the reader. Focus on point of view and use of language. *(Analysis) (16Punkte)*

3. Choose **one** of the following tasks:

3.1 The protagonist says that "one day [her] daughter will be expected [...] to be a devoted and dutiful wife. You need math for that, but not [...] a voice" (ll. 47 – 51). Assess the consequences that limiting people's freedom of speech can have on a society and on the individual. Refer to the extract and work done in class on dystopian literature. *(Evaluation: comment) (14 Punkte)*

3.2 "In spite of [one] year of practice" (l. 57), Jean has still not got used to her new situation. Later that day, Jean reflects on how life in the USA has changed and the impact this may have on her children. Write her interior monologue. *(Evaluation: re-creation of text) (14 Punkte)*

* Die Lösungen sind keine amtlichen Lösungen.

Klausurteil B: Sprachmittlung isoliert

Aufgabenstellung:

4. Your friend from the USA is doing a school project on gender equality in the job world. She/He has asked you for information about the situation in Germany. Write an email to your friend outlining what Sabrina Dietrich says about gender equality in Germany and how Girls'- and Boys' Days are meant to change the situation.

(Mediation) (18 Punkte)

Materialgrundlage:

Klausurteil A:
Christina Dalcher, *Vox*, New York: Berkley 2018, S. 1–2

Wortzahl: 421

Klausurteil B:
Sabrina Dietrich, „Feuerwehrfrau und Erzieher – in Deutschland eher nicht", in: *Behörden Spiegel*, Mai 2016, zitiert nach: https://initiatived21.de/feuerwehrfrau-und-erzieher-in-deutschland-eher-nicht/ (gekürzt, Zugriff: 18.06.2019)

Wortzahl: 331

Zugelassene Hilfsmittel:

- Ein- und zweisprachiges Wörterbuch
- Herkunftssprachliches Wörterbuch für Schülerinnen und Schüler, deren Herkunftssprache nicht Deutsch ist
- Wörterbuch zur deutschen Rechtschreibung

Klausurteil A

Vox *Christina Dalcher*

This is an extract from the opening scene of the novel "Vox". It is set in the USA in the near future, in a state ruled by an all-male government.

I've become a woman of few words.

Tonight at supper, before I speak my final syllables of the day, Patrick reaches over and taps the silver-toned device around my left wrist. It's a light touch, as if he were sharing the pain, or perhaps reminding me to stay quiet until the counter resets itself at midnight. This magic will happen while I sleep, and I'll begin Tuesday with a virgin slate. My daughter, Sonia's, counter will do the same.

My boys do not wear word counters.

Over dinner, they are all engaged in the usual chatter about school.

Sonia also attends school, although she never wastes words discussing her days. At supper, between bites of a simple stew I made from memory, Patrick questions her about her progress in home economics, physical fitness, and a new course titled Simple Accounting for Households.

Is she obeying the teachers? Will she earn high marks this term? He knows exactly the type of questions to ask: closed-ended, requiring only a nod or a shake of the head.

I watch and listen, my nails carving half-moons into the flesh of my palms. Sonia nods when appropriate, wrinkles her nose when my young twins, not understanding the importance of yes/no interrogatives and finite answer sets, ask their sister to tell them what the teachers are like […].

I could tell them what they want to know: All men at the front of the classrooms now. One-way system. Teachers talk. Students listen. It would cost me sixteen words.

I have five left.

"How is her vocabulary?" Patrick asks, knocking his chin my way. He rephrases. "Is she learning?"

I shrug. By six, Sonia should have an army of ten thousand lexemes, individual troops that assemble and come to attention and obey the orders her small, still-plastic brain issues. Should have, if the three R's weren't now reduced to one: simple arithmetic. After all, one day my daughter will be expected to shop and to run a household, to be a devoted and dutiful wife. You need math for that, but not spelling. Not literature. Not a voice.

"You're the cognitive linguist," Patrick says, gathering empty plates, urging Steven to do the same.

"Was."

"Are."

In spite of my year of practice, the extra words leak out before I can stop them: "No. I'm. Not."

Patrick watches the counter tick off another three entries. […]

The boys exchange worried looks, the kind of worry that comes from knowing what occurs if the counter surpasses those three digits. One, zero, zero.

Annotations
10 virgin slate – *here*: the word counter is set to zero again
42 lexeme – linguistic term for a lexical unit such as a word or expression
44 still-plastic – *here*: still in the process of developing
45 the three R's – the three basic skills reading, writing and arithmetic
52 cognitive linguist – scientist combining psychology and linguistics
53 Steven – the protagonist's eldest son

Beispiellösung

Aufgabe 1

In the opening scene of Christina Dalcher's dystopian novel "Vox", it becomes clear that the state is ruled by an all-male government, while women are only allowed to speak 100 words a day, which are counted with the help of a word counter that all female members of society have to wear around their wrist.

At midnight, the counter is reset.

The scene depicted in this extract describes dinner at the female protagonist's house. She is a cognitive linguist and mother of three children, one of them a girl called Sonia. The talk at dinner revolves around school. While the boys chatter merrily, Sonia and her mother

must count their words. To ensure that Sonia does not waste any of the words she has left for the day, her father asks her simple 'yes or no' questions that often only require her to nod, shrug her shoulders or shake her head. While Sonia does not speak at all, her younger twin brothers ask her more complex questions and want to know what school is like in more detail.
The society the protagonist and her family live in is dominated by men; women face discrimination because of their gender. They are forced to choose each word carefully in order not to be punished for talking too much. Moreover, teaching seems to be authoritarian, with the male teachers doing the talking while the students merely listen.
Female students are trained for their future role as dutiful housewives, subject to their husbands.

Aufgabe 2

The fact that the first-person narrator of Dalcher's dystopian novel "Vox" is female and therefore experiences herself the discrimination described in the extract creates a feeling of uneasiness in the reader. This feeling is intensified when readers gain an insight into life in this society for men as well as women, and the personal touch added to these descriptions by the first-person narrator forces them to take a critical look at that society.
The "[…] silver-toned device" (l. 4) that the narrator and her daughter have to wear around their wrist is not a piece of jewellery but rather a handcuff, for it counts all the words they use during the day. Exceeding the allotted number of words is punished, as becomes obvious in lines 62 to 65, when the narrator's sons exchange "[…] worried looks […] that (come) from knowing what occurs if the counter surpasses those three digits. One, zero, zero."
It is rather ironic that the narrator used to work as a cognitive linguist but now has to watch her every word and, sadly, her academic expertise is no longer needed.
When she assesses Sonia's chances as a girl, the narrator's anger, frustration and helplessness become obvious. She compares the differences in the behaviour of her twin boys, who "[…] do not wear word counters" (l. 12), and her daughter, who "[…] also attends school, although she never wastes a word discussing her days" (ll. 15-16).
The authoritarian government even extends its influence and oppression into people's homes, as Sonia and her mother have to wear their word counters nonstop, which distances them from the male family members, who chat away merrily at dinner (ll. 13-14).
While the narrator had the chance to become a cognitive linguist, Sonia's chances for the future are limited, with "[…] the three R's […] now reduced to one: simple arithmetic" (ll. 45-47), because for her intended role as a married housewife she needs only rudimentary math, "[…] but not spelling. Not literature. Not a voice" (l. 50). Not intellect or interests, but a person's sex decides what he or she can become in the future. For women and girls free choice does not exist.
That the narrator is critical and even afraid of the society she lives in is expressed in her choice of words and her often elliptical sentences (e.g. ll. 35-36, ll. 50-51, ll. 58-59).
The change within society seems to have happened fairly recently, for she states that "[she has] become a woman of few words" (l. 1) and that she has had "[one] year of practice" (l. 57). The reasons for this change are not provided in the extract from Dalcher's novel. Despite her year of practice the narrator still experiences difficulties when it comes to

limiting the number of words she speaks as "[her] nails [carve] half-moons into the flesh of [her] palms" (ll. 26-27), and when her husband talks to her "[the] extra words leak out before [she] can stop them" (ll. 57-58).

Since she cannot speak her mind, she has become an attentive observer of the scenes that unfold in front of her eyes.

Although the narrator only speaks four words in the course of the dinner scene described in this extract, her detailed and judgmental description of school, the inequality between men and women and her attitude towards having to wear a word counter indicate that she obeys the rules set up by the government but does not agree with them.

Aufgabe 3.1

In many of today's western societies we take a person's right to free speech for granted, but what would happen if people's freedom of speech were limited?

Before looking at the extract from Dalcher's novel and other pieces of dystopian literature in more detail, one has to keep in mind that even today there are societies in which people have no right to free speech, e.g. in China, where censorship prevents critical opinions from being voiced.

If one looks at the current political developments in countries like Russia or Belarus, one notices that expressing criticism of the government can be extremely dangerous, as the poisoning of Russian opposition figure Alexei Navalny or the abduction of Belarusian opposition leader Maria Kolesnikova show.

In Dalcher's novel one can see that limiting people's right to free speech also limits their ability to voice their own opinion and their chances to become an active member of society ,and prevents them from pursuing a career of their own choice. In Dalcher's novel this limitation applies only to female members of society, but in other works of dystopian fiction, e.g. in Collins's "The Hunger Games", other groups of society or minorities also experience discrimination.

In "The Hunger Games", people living in the districts of Panem usually live in poverty whereas those living in the Capitol enjoy a life of luxury. Katniss, the female protagonist living in District 12, shows resistance against the government, thereby risking her own life as well as her family's.

In "The Hunger Games" twenty-four tributes, a girl and a boy from each of the twelve districts, are chosen each year to fight for their life in a vast outdoor arena until only one candidate survives. This gruesome spectacle is used by the government as a means of exerting power over the districts and preventing any kind of rebellion.

A totalitarian government creates an atmosphere of fear. This is also pointed out in Dalcher's novel, where the female protagonist lives in constant fear of using more than the 100 words she is allowed to speak a day, and carefully weighs her words, as any violation is punished. So she cannot speak her mind and only talks when it is absolutely necessary. Limiting a person's freedom of speech in this way means that an open exchange of views no longer exists.

In "Vox" female members of society are subject to discrimination by the government. Equality between men and women is non-existent. Whereas male members of society are free to express themselves and lead their life as they want to, females are discriminated

against from an early age. Girls only receive an education that ensures that they will become dutiful wives and housewives in the future. Talent, personal interests, or freedom of choice are irrelevant.
Inequality between men and women exists not only in works of fiction but also in real life. In countries like India, girls and women are subject to discrimination and sexual exploitation, and often have to overcome barriers to get a good education, which is one of the cornerstones of emancipation.
I believe that a person's right to free speech is crucial for a democratic society in which everyone has the same chances and obligations.

Aufgabe 3.2

"Another day is over and it's only an hour until my counter resets and I have another 100 words at my disposal! 100 words – that is next to nothing! A year ago I would have joined my husband and the twin's conversation at dinner – as would Sonia. But now Sonia and I are condemned to silence. I am glad that the government does not limit the number of thoughts that I'm allowed to have a day. Otherwise, I would go crazy: my mind is the only space where I still feel free. I cannot believe that a single year has made all the difference. I feel so helpless, frustrated and angry and I have no chance to let go of my anger, because I know what the punishment feels like for those who say more words than they are allowed to. I still remember a time when I could speak my mind and when people were interested in what I had to say. It is rather ironic that I used to be a cognitive linguist. When I look at Sonia, my heart aches, for I know that she will never have the chance to choose her own future. Everything is already laid out for her. Her education ensures that she will become an obedient, dutiful housewife – no more, no less. It is hard to see all her talent wasted. I worry more about her than about the boys, as they will have every opportunity to become successful in whatever they do, just because they are male! They grow up believing that they own the world, whereas Sonia's language skills do not develop, but deteriorate, ultimately giving her the feeling that she is worth less than the boys. Of course, this fits the government's plan to make gender inequality the norm.
I remember a time when our country's constitution guaranteed equal rights for everyone. It is even part of our country's Declaration of Independence, but obviously this does not count anymore.
I try to stay hopeful despite the circumstances, but it gets harder every day."

Klausurteil B

Feuerwehrfrau und Erzieher – in Deutschland eher nicht *Sabrina Dietrich*

Das Mädchen möchte zur Feuerwehr, der Junge Erzieher werden. In unserer modernen Gesellschaft sollten diese beruflichen Entscheidungen selbstverständlich sein. Dennoch sind tradierte Rollenbilder noch immer fest verankert und damit auch das Spektrum für die Berufswahl junger Menschen eingeschränkt.

Seit über zehn Jahren gibt es den bundesweiten Girls' Day und Boys' Day. Dieser Tag soll Schülerinnen und Schüler ermutigen, Berufe auszuprobieren, die typischerweise nicht ihrem Geschlecht zugeordnet werden. Beim Girls' Day geht es um die Bereiche Technik und Naturwissenschaften, Forschung und Wissenschaft, Informatik und Handwerk, beim Boys' Day um die Bereiche Pädagogik, Soziales und Erziehung, Pflege und medizinische Versorgung. Die sogenannten Zukunftstage wollen erreichen, dass junge Menschen ihren Blick für die Vielfalt der Möglichkeiten öffnen und Berufe wählen, die ihrem Können und ihrer Vorliebe entsprechen. […]

Wo der Girls(- wie Boys)' Day hilft, das Thema Chancengleichheit und Chancengerechtigkeit ins gesellschaftliche Bewusstsein zu heben, macht er ebenso bewusst, wie defizitär die Situation in Deutschland noch immer ist. So sind es noch immer Frauen. die den Großteil der unbezahlten Arbeit übernehmen und sich um Kinderbetreuung und Pflege von Familienangehörigen kümmern. Nur 5,5 Prozent der Männer mit minderjährigem Kind arbeiten in Teilzeit, Frauen zu 67,8 Prozent. Diese Zahlen weisen zudem deutlich auf die Lohnlücke zwischen Mann und Frau. Bei gleicher Arbeit verdienen Frauen im Schnitt 21 Prozent weniger als Männer. Dies konnte auch die sukzessive Wandlung der Geschlechterrollen in der Gesellschaft nicht merklich verringern. Für Frauen wäre es attraktiv, in den deutlich besser bezahlten MINT-Berufen zu arbeiten. Männer schrecken die niedrigen Löhne im sozialen Bereich oftmals ab. Es ist an der Zeit, Frauen und auch Berufe, die eher weiblich konnotiert sind, weil hauptsächlich von Frauen ausgeführt, besser zu stellen. Erst diese Schritte würden zu wirklicher Gerechtigkeit führen. […]

Die gute Bilanz des Girls' Day zeigt, dass Schülerinnen offen sind für den Blick über den Tellerrand und es oftmals nur an Ideen und einem kleinen Schubs fehlt. Knapp 80 Prozent der teilnehmenden Mädchen befinden ihre Teilnahme am Girls' Day als hilfreich für die berufliche Orientierung. Inzwischen nennen 21 Prozent der Teilnehmerinnen einen Wunschberuf im MINT-Bereich.

Anmerkung:
60 MINT-Berufe – Berufe in den Bereichen Mathematik, Informatik, Naturwissenschaften oder Technik

Beispiellösung

Aufgabe 4

Hey Betty,

Thanks for your email. It is good to hear that you and your family are doing well. Your school project on gender equality in the job world sounds quite interesting and I have done some research on what the situation is like in Germany. On the internet I came across an article which offers insights into gender equality when it comes to boys and girls choosing a future career.

Sadly, gender equality in the job world does not exist here in Germany. Even if a woman does the same job as a man, this does not mean that she will earn the same money as her male colleague. On the contrary, women earn up to 21% less for the same workload. As far more women than men take care of their children, elderly or sick family members and do household chores, 67.8% of all working women work part-time, in contrast to 5.5% of all men with non-adult children.

Many women still opt for jobs that are assumed to be "traditionally female", e.g. caring for children or working as nurses in hospitals, and these jobs are not as well paid as "traditionally male" jobs like engineering.

In order to eradicate this gender inequality, women should make different career choices and should be encouraged to choose a job that fits their interests, talents and skills – even if this job is still regarded as "typically male".

Of course, boys should also be encouraged to revise gender stereotypes and go for the job that best suits them.

Stereotypes need to be revised and everyone needs to become aware that there is stinn a lot of gender inequality in the job world.

To achieve this, we have an annual "Girls' and Boys' Day" here in Germany, where boys and girls can try out jobs that are traditionally regarded as typical of the opposite sex.

I hope all this information helps you with your school project. If you have any questions, just send me an email and I'll do my best to answer them.

Kindest regards,
Simon

Vorgaben für die Bewertung der Schülerleistungen

Aufgabe 1 *(Comprehension)*

Es können maximal 12 Punkte erreicht werden. Um die maximale Punktzahl zu erreichen, werden folgende inhaltliche Aspekte erwartet:

- Beschreibung der dargestellten familiären Alltagssituation: Unterhaltung über die Schule während des Abendessens, Austausch der Eltern über die sprachliche Entwicklung der Tochter *(2 Punkte erreichbar);*
- Darstellung des Verhaltens der Familienmitglieder während des Gesprächs, insbesondere den lebhaften Austausch der Söhne, die wohlüberlegte und gezielte Fragetechnik des Vaters gegenüber seiner Frau und seiner Tochter, die minimalistische, durch Mimik und Gestik geprägte Kommunikation der Tochter, das zunächst stille

Beobachten und Zuhören der Mutter (das sie später durchbricht), die sorgenvollen Blicke der Zwillinge angesichts der Äußerungen ihrer Mutter *(6 Punkte erreichbar);*
- Nennung der im Textauszug dargestellten Merkmale der Gesellschaft: die Begrenzung der täglich erlaubten Wortzahl von Frauen und Mädchen auf 100, Kontrolle der Wortzahlen durch Messgeräte am Handgelenk und Konsequenzen bei Überschreitung, autoritär ausgerichteter Schulunterricht durch eine ausschließlich männliche Lehrerschaft, geschlechterdifferenzierende Schulbildung und ausschließliche Vorbereitung der Mädchen auf die Rolle als Haus- und Ehefrau *(4 Punkte erreichbar).*

Aufgabe 2 *(Analysis)*

Es können maximal 16 Punkte erreicht werden. Um die maximale Punktzahl zu erreichen, werden folgende inhaltliche Aspekte erwartet:
- Ausarbeitung, dass bei den Leserinnen und Lesern ein Gefühl des Unbehagens hinsichtlich der Situation der diskriminierten Mädchen und Frauen und eine kritische Haltung gegenüber der dargestellten Gesellschaft erzeugt werden, und zwar mithilfe der durch die Wahrnehmungen und Reflexionen der Protagonistin geprägten Erzählperspektive und durch eine die Wirkung intensivierenden sprachlichen Gestaltung *(4 Punkte erreichbar);*
- Herausarbeitung der Art und Weise, wie durch den Einsatz eines Ich-Erzählers Einblick in die Gedanken- und Gefühlswelt der Protagonistin gewährt und dadurch Verständnis für ihre Situation erzeugt wird, z. B. durch ihre Reflexionen über ihre Tochter und deren Ausbildung, die Gegenüberstellung ihrer erzwungenen Sprachlosigkeit mit ihrem ausgeprägten Beobachtungs- und Reflexionsvermögen und durch den Ausdruck ihrer Frustration *(6 Punkte erreichbar);*
- Analyse der Art und Weise, wie durch den gezielten Einsatz sprachlicher Mittel eine systemkritische Grundhaltung gegenüber der dargestellten Gesellschaft erzeugt wird, z. B. durch eine die eingeschränkten Kommunikationsmöglichkeiten spiegelnde Syntax, eine bildhafte Sprache, Wiederholungen und Aufzählungen und durch eine wertende Wortwahl *(6 Punkte erreichbar).*

Aufgabe 3.1 *(Evaluation: comment)*

Es können maximal 14 Punkte erreicht werden. Um die maximale Punktzahl zu erreichen, werden folgende inhaltliche Aspekte erwartet:
- eine kritisch-wertende Darlegung – ausgehend vom Romanauszug und unter funktionalem Rückgriff auf im Unterricht erworbenes Wissen zu dystopischer Literatur – welche gesellschaftlichen Implikationen die Einschränkung der Meinungsfreiheit haben kann, unter Bezug z. B. auf die Unterdrückung bestimmter gesellschaftlicher Gruppen, Zensur als Merkmal totalitärer Regimes, die Manipulation des öffentlichen Diskurses, das Schaffen eines gesellschaftlichen Klimas der Angst und aktuelle politische Entwicklungen weltweit *(6 Punkte erreichbar);*
- eine kritisch-wertende Erläuterung – unter funktionalem Rückgriff auf im Unterricht erworbenes Wissen zu dystopischer Literatur –der Faktoren, die eine Einschränkung des Rechts auf freie Meinungsäußerung für das Individuum hat, unter Einbe-

ziehung z. B. individueller Entfaltungs- und Ausdrucksmöglichkeiten, veränderter zwischenmenschlicher Beziehungen, Diskriminierungserfahrungen und politischer und gesellschaftlicher Teilhabe *(6 Punkte erreichbar);*
- eine begründetes und nachvollziehbares Fazit auf der Basis der eigenen Ausführungen, in dem z.B. Meinungsfreiheit als Grundvoraussetzung für eine Demokratie herausgestellt und angesichts aktueller Entwicklungen die Notwendigkeit zur Wachsamkeit betont wird *(2 Punkte erreichbar).*

Aufgabe 3.2 ***(Evaluation: re-creation of text)***

Es können maximal 14 Punkte erreicht werden. Um die maximale Punktzahl zu erreichen, werden folgende inhaltliche Aspekte erwartet:
- Verfassung eines rollen- und situationsgerechten inneren Monologs auf Grundlage des Textauszugs, in dem die Rollenvorgabe konsequent beachtet und schlüssig umgesetzt und wesentliche Inhalte aufgegriffen und nachvollziehbar ausgestaltet werden *(2 Punkte erreichbar);*
- Einblick in die von Besorgnis und Frustration geprägte Gedankenwelt der Protagonistin bezogen auf die gesellschaftlichen Veränderungen in den USA und auf ihre eigene veränderte Situation, unter Einbeziehung z. B. ihrer Erinnerungen an ihr vorheriges Leben, des Bruchs mit den in der Verfassung der USA verankerten Werten und Rechten und ihrer Wut auf die Verantwortlichen *(6 Punkte erreichbar);*
- aus der Sicht der Protagonistin formulierte Sorgen und Ängste angesichts der Zukunft ihrer Kinder, z. B. im Hinblick auf die Konsequenzen der reduzierten Kommunikationsmöglichkeiten für die geistige und sprachliche Entwicklung ihrer Tochter, die begrenzten Möglichkeiten der Selbstverwirklichung des Mädchens, die Rollenbilder ihrer Söhne und auf die gesamtgesellschaftliche Entwicklungen der USA *(6 Punkte erreichbar).*

Aufgabe 4 (***Mediation)***

Es können maximal 18 Punkte erreicht werden. Um die maximale Punktzahl zu erreichen, werden folgende inhaltliche Aspekte erwartet:
Verfassen einer situations- und adressatengerechte persönliche E-Mail, in der
- die durch einen Mangel an Gleichberechtigung im beruflichen und familiären Bereich geprägte Situation in Deutschland beschrieben wird, insbesondere die ungleiche Bezahlung von Frauen für gleiche Arbeit, der hohe Anteil an Teilzeitbeschäftigung bei weiblichen Arbeitskräften aufgrund der Übernahme von familiären Aufgaben im Bereich von Pflege und Erziehung, die vergleichsweise niedrigen Gehälter in häufig von Frauen ausgeübten Berufen
- die Darstellung der Intention der Girls'- und Boys'-Days, insbesondere die Möglichkeit zu Einblicken in und das Wecken von Interesse für traditionell dem anderen Geschlecht zugeschriebene Berufe, die Bestärkung der Jugendlichen in einer auf Interessen und Fähigkeiten basierenden Berufswahl und die Sensibilisierung für Chancengleichheit.

Aufgabe 2
Klausurteil A: Leseverstehen und Schreiben integriert

Aufgabenstellung:

1. Outline Lucy Pasha-Robinson's views on multiculturalism in the UK and on the public debate. *(Comprehension) (12 Punkte)*

2. Analyse how the author presents her views. Consider communicative strategies and use of language. *(Analysis) (16 Punkte)*

3. Choose **one** of the following tasks:

3.1 The author claims that the British "should be turning [their] attention to what it means to be British today" (ll. 55–56). Comment on this statement, focussing on the concept of national identities in a globalised world. Refer to the text as well as to work done in class on culture and communication. *(Evaluation: comment) (14 Punkte)*

3.2 At the end of her article Pasha-Robinson states that "[m]ulticulturalism has happened – deal with it" (ll. 64–65). Write a letter to the editor in which you respond to her views.
Refer to the text and work done in class on multiculturalism in the UK. *(Evaluation: re-creation of text) (14 Punkte)*

Klausurteil B: Sprachmittlung isoliert

Aufgabenstellung:

4. You are doing an internship with an organisation that runs the website www.multicultural-germany.de. On this website, published in English, young people from all over Europe find interesting information and facts about Germany. You are doing a special feature on *Diversity in the Media and in Journalism.*
   Based on Aurora Lushtaku's article you have been asked to write a report outlining the situation of migrants in German media and ways to improve their position in journalism. *(Mediation) (18 Punkte)*

Materialgrundlage:

Klausurteil A:
Lucy Pasha-Robinson, "British Culture Wouldn't Exist Without Multiculturalism – It's Time To Take This Tired Debate Off The Table", in: *HuffPost*, 17 September 2018
https://www.huffingtonpost.co.uk/entry/multiculturalism-immigration_uk_5b9fbdeee4b046313fbd728f?guccounter=2; from *HuffPost* (2018) Oath Inc. All rights reserved. Used under licence. (gekürzt, Zugriff: 10.10.2019)

Wortzahl: 417

Klausurteil B:
Aurora Lushtaku, „Warum mehr Migranten Journalisten werden sollten", in: *Kurt*, 07. Oktober 2019
http://kurt.digital/2019/10/07/kommentar-warum-mehr-migranten-journalisten-werden-sollten/ (gekürzt, Zugriff: 19.12.2019)

Wortzahl: 313

Zugelassene Hilfsmittel:

- Ein- und zweisprachiges Wörterbuch
- Herkunftssprachliches Wörterbuch für Schülerinnen und Schüler, deren Herkunftssprache nicht Deutsch ist
- Wörterbuch zur deutschen Rechtschreibung

Klausurteil A

British Culture Wouldn't Exist Without Multiculturalism – It's Time To Take This Tired Debate Off The Table *Lucy Pasha-Robinson*

As a born and bred product of British multiculturalism, it's hard for me to comprehend the ongoing demonisation of immigrants. Growing up in a mixed-race family was getting a new pencil case before the start of term; plastering Spice Girls posters on my wall; eating fish and chips on a Friday in the school canteen; Sundays spent wrapped in the love of my nana's chicken curries, gulab jaman and jalebis.

My childhood feels typically British because multiculturalism is my norm – something that, in my lifetime, has been the bedrock of British culture and, historically, a source of great pride. Yet, in this post-Brexit climate, it's hard not to notice the mood shifting.

At a time when global anti-immigrant sentiment is reaching fever pitch, a study claiming that four in 10 people believe multiculturalism has undermined British culture feels like sticking the knife in. It's just another reminder to the UK's migrant or minority ethnic communities that they will never be British enough.

It's baffling to me that a sizeable minority of people could feel that British culture is being stifled by multiculturalism. [...]

To those who don't support multiculturalism, I'd love to ask: do you know any immigrant families? Have you taken the time to understand who they are or their stories? Or do you just hate people who don't look like you? People are scared of what they don't know but surely it's time we stopped indulging ignorance. It's hurtful and alienating to the millions of us whose legitimacy is placed second to the views of the xenophobic.

This constant othering of migrants, first-generation or otherwise, is tiring. I know immigration – and it's not something to fear. [...]

The researchers did find a majority (59%) of those surveyed felt diversity brought by immigration had enriched British culture and 63% felt migrant workers supported the economy and brought valuable skills to the UK, so clearly all is not lost. These are the stats we need to be focusing on – the resounding consensus that multiculturalism is important and continues to make a valuable contribution to our society.

Instead of continuing this tired debate, we should be turning our attention to what it means to be British today, in all its richness and difference, and celebrating what makes our culture so unique. That's where representation in media and popular culture becomes so important, along with social mobility in education and employment. It's time the multiculturalism debate is taken off the table, because it's already here. Multiculturalism has happened – deal with it.

[...]

Annotations
6 **Spice Girls** – British female pop group from the 1990s
9 **nana** – a child's word for "grandmother"
10 **gulab jaman and jalebis** – sweets from the Indian subcontinent
22 **to stick the knife in** – to criticize someone very strongly, especially when they are already weak
50 **stats** – statistics

Beispiellösung

Aufgabe 1

In her article "British Culture Wouldn't Exist Without Multiculturalism – It's Time To Take This Tired Debate Off The Table", Lucy Pasha-Robinson criticizes the ongoing debate on the diversity of British culture. Having grown up in a family of mixed ethnicity, she sees diversity as typically British. Multiculturalism is the norm and British society should be proud of it. She complains about recent tendencies that foreground nationalist and xenophobic attitudes. To her, it is astonishing that a sizeable minority opposes multiculturalism in Britain, and she wonders if they really know what they are saying, and if they have ever taken time to give cultural diversity a thought. She rather suspects that they just fear what they do not know and thus hurt millions of British compatriots. She claims she knows immigration and it is nothing to be afraid of.
Still, she is relieved that a majority of people regard cultural diversity positively.
Pasha-Robinson demands an end to this debate and calls for a growth in awareness of what it means to be British today. People should realize the enriching benefits of multiculturalism and be proud of it. Representation of people of colour in the media, equality in education and social equality play an important role here. People must accept the fact that multiculturalism is not a threat but an aspect of society which has long been established in Britain.

Aufgabe 2

This critical view is presented in a very subjective way. The author's bias becomes clear right from the beginning, when she refers to her own biography. She presents her inter-ethnic background by mentioning various cultural elements that illustrate the two sides of that background (ll. 4–10), proving that she is "a born and bred product of British multiculturalism", the alliteration in this phrase giving it an extra stress. Later in the text (ll. 40–43) she refers to her own experience in very a matter-of-fact way: "I know immigration and it's not something to fear."
She supports her view with facts and figures (l. 20, ll. 44–48). 59 percent of the population share her view, a consensus which she also emphasises in a matter-of-fact way.
Her bias becomes still more obvious in her other communicative strategies. Her questions to those who are opposed to multiculturalism are provocative, suggest narrow-mindedness or even stupidity on their part and insinuate ignorance (ll. 30–34). From line 50 she vehemently appeals to the reader, using expressions like "we need to" (l. 50), "we should" (l. 55), "it's time" (l. 62), and the imperative "deal with it" (ll. 64–65).
Her choice of words is also strongly biased: she uses a large number of words with negative connotations when she refers to attitudes towards people of colour or to the current mood of the country. She speaks of the "demonisation" (l. 3) and "othering" (l. 40) of immigrants, who are said to "undermine" (l. 21) or "stifle" (l. 28) British culture. To immigrants, this sentiment is "hurtful" and "alienating" (ll. 36–37), and she sees the whole debate as "tiring" (l. 41) or "tired" (l. 54; headline). Those who oppose diversity are accused of "ignorance", which opponents of immigration simply "indulge" (l.36).
Imagery is another stylistic device. The use of the idiom "fever pitch" (l. 19) suggests an extreme rise in anti-immigrant sentiment and at the same time the sickness of this attitude and the danger it presents to society's health and well-being. The use of the idiom "sticking

the knife in" (l. 22) shows the pain that is inflicted on legitimate British people who are still seen as foreign. These hurtful images find their counterpart in Pasha-Robinson's tells the perfectly multicultural story of her own childhood, when she was "wrapped in the love" of her grandmother's food – a phrase which suggests warmth, protection, harmony, something which British society presently does not exactly offer to migrants.

Aufgabe 3.1

Against this background, the author claims (in lines 55–65) that the British should really "be turning their attention to what it means to be British today". For years, Britain was Europe's role model as far as multiculturalism, tolerance and integration were concerned. Racism and xenophobia, still widespread in the 1970s, seemed to have been overcome. Britain had become a modern, global place. A visit to London, and just a glimpse of the food section of Camden Market showed how much Britain had become a nation of diversity. Interaction between indigenous Britons and immigrants was normal. People of colour had entered the world of British culture, on television, in theatre, literature, film and art. Britishness seemed an overarching identity in a complex supra-ethnic, supra-national society. Unfortunately, in recent years, trends in the opposite direction have become only too visible. Racist assaults have shocked a seemingly tolerant society. Tendencies towards secluded communities of immigrants, inner cities dominated by Asians, suggest that the idea of a multicultural nation has failed. The rise of nationalism, culminating in the unfortunate 2016 Brexit referendum and finally in Brexit last January, is a sad fact. And we have seen the development of similar trends in many other countries.
I believe that these tendencies are very un-21st century. In a globalized world, which is interconnected in so many ways, nationalism or national pride as demonstrated by Brexiteers or people like Donald Trump, Victor Orban, Recep Erdogan, or Vladimir Putin and, of course, by members of the German right-wing party AFD, is an anachronism beyond comprehension and beyond reason. The world has become small, tiny really, with people being able to travel across borders in no time. Modern communication on social networks, which has taken on a new dimension over the last decade with the rise of smartphones, should not really promote thinking in terms of national borders. International trade, cultural globalization with the mutual influence of diverse ethnic cultures should reduce xenophobia. And especially the climate crisis and the Corona pandemic should tell people how ridiculous thinking in terms of national pride is today. Still, nationalism is on the rise pretty much everywhere. Looking at the protagonists, who are mostly stupid old white men just appealing to people's emotional instincts, I place my hope in generations Y and Z, who have grown up in a digital globalized world and who have long been showing their opposition to traditional structures. This is especially visible in the Fridays-for-Future and the Black-Lives-Matter movements, but also in our classroom discussions. It's time for them to take over.

Aufgabe 3.2

Sir,

I am writing to you in response to Lucy Pasha-Robinson's article "British Culture Wouldn't Exist Without Multiculturalism – It's Time To Take This Tired Debate Off The Table". In the light of Brexit and the Brexit campaign, which have fuelled anti-immigrant sentiment, I can perfectly understand her annoyance. As an outsider from Germany, I have always regarded Britain as a role model of integration. There are so many examples of working multiculturalism. Britain has always seemed to me a modern, global place. A visit to London and just a glimpse of the food section of Camden Market shows how much Britain has become a nation of diversity. Interaction between indigenous Britons and immigrants seems normal. A glance at British television reveals diversity in the media. News readers, actors, comedians – people of colour have been the norm for years. In school we have read short stories written by and dealing with immigrants, we have analysed films starring Asians and dealing with their integration. Bringing up the old idea of immigration as undermining true Britishness is – to me – a reactionary thought. It simply does not fit in our globalized age. As Ms Pasha-Robinson says, multiculturalism has happened. People just have to deal with it, just accept it as a fact and stop whining. In an age when there is access to world-wide communication in everybody's pocket, when there is international exchange through social media but also – due to easy access to air travel – where there is international trade and mutual cultural exchange, xenophobia is a ridiculous leftover from bygone times. The likes of Farage, Cummings and Johnson and their cronies, as much as Trump, Erdogan and Orban, or also Höcke in my own country, seem to me like knuckle-dragging Neanderthals – which may even be an offence to the Neanderthals. I can only support Ms Pasha-Robinson's appeal: Wake up, forget this myth of white Anglo-Saxon Britishness. Britishness has long been an overarching identity tying many ethnicities. Britishness today, as seen by an outsider, applies to a nation of diversity embracing British values of democracy, liberty and tolerance. This includes gender relations as much as ethnic relations. British people can be proud of being British, proud of a nation a majority of which believe that immigrants and diversity enrich British culture. Proud of a country which is a modern, global place. London's cultural diversity makes it an attractive city to international companies and hence it contributes to London's wealth. What hurts me as much as it does Ms Pasha-Robinson is that there is rising fear of multiculturalism fuelled by the above-mentioned political circles. Let me appeal to the 60 percent in favour of multiculturalism and to the young, who oppose Brexit but have messed it all up by being too passive. Take back control!

NN, Aachen, Germany

Klausurteil B

Warum mehr Migranten Journalisten werden sollten *Aurora Lushtaku*

Laut dem Statistischen Bundesamt lebten im Jahr 2017 rund 19,3 Millionen Menschen mit einem Migrationshintergrund in der Bundesrepublik – das ist ein Anteil von 23,6 Prozent. Deutschland hat sich zu einer Migrationsgesellschaft entwickelt. Diese wird wiederum durch die Medien abgebildet. Rainer Gaißler, emeritierter Professor für Soziologie an der Universität Siegen, beschreibt das Phänomen wie folgt: „Was die Bevölkerung über die Bedeutung von Migration und Integration und über die Situation der MigrantInnen in Deutschland weiß, das weiß sie in der Regel vor allem aus den Massenmedien." Wenn aber nur rund fünf Prozent der Journalisten einen interkulturellen Hintergrund besitzen, mangelt es an interkultureller Perspektive: Migranten im Journalismus haben einen anderen Blick auf die Dinge als der Herkunftsdeutsche. [...]

Das Thema findet bereits auf mehreren Ebenen Zuspruch: Der „Nationale Aktionsplan Integration" der Bundesregierung etwa ist um die sogenannte mediale Integration bemüht und fordert „eine angemessene Beteiligung von Migranten in den Medienberufen". Initiativen wie die Talentwerkstatt „Grenzenlos" des WDR oder der Verein „Neue deutsche Medienmacher*innen" haben sich die Förderung von Journalisten mit Migrationshintergrund zur Aufgabe gemacht und sind laut eigener Angabe an größerer Vielfalt in den Medien interessiert. Das Begabtenförderungswerk der Heinrich-Böll-Stiftung unterstützt seit 2008 mit seinem Stipendienprogramm „Medienvielfalt, anders" Migranten auf ihrem Weg in den Journalismus [...].

Sowohl auf der Seite der Medienbetriebe als auch auf der Seite der Migranten gibt es Faktoren, die für die geringen Zahlen verantwortlich sind. Nur einer Gruppe die Schuld zuzuschreiben, wäre problematisch, erklärt Horst Pöttker: „Auf beiden Seiten muss ein starkes Umdenken stattfinden." Der Sozialwissenschaftler setzt sich in seiner Forschung unter anderem mit dem Verhältnis von Medien, Migration und Integration auseinander. Er betont, dass in der „Migrantencommunity" Berufe wie Arzt oder Ingenieur, die mit einem sicheren Einkommen verbunden sind, sehr viel angesehener sind – besonders bei Eltern, die häufig aus Ländern stammen, in denen ein anderes Verständnis vom Journalismus herrscht als in Deutschland. Die sind meist wenig begeistert, wenn ihre Kinder den Berufswunsch des Journalisten äußern. Auch, was die Sprache anbetrifft, haben viele die Angst, sie nicht gut genug zu beherrschen.

Anmerkung:
Alle die Sprachrichtigkeit betreffenden Fehler im Originaltext wurden berichtigt.

Beispiellösung

Aufgabe 4

There should be more journalists among immigrants in Germany

by NN

Almost a quarter of the population in Germany has an immigrant background. Germany has become an immigration society, which in turn is reflected in the media. Yet only 5 percent of journalists have an immigration background. One result of this is that the media lack an intercultural perspective. Immigrant journalists view matters differently from indigenous Germans.

The issue is on various agendas. The federal government demands appropriate participation of immigrants in the media business. Other initiatives, which are interested in greater diversity in the media, support journalists with an immigration background; still others offer scholarships specifically for immigrants.

Both the media business and the immigrants themselves are responsible for the low numbers. Professions like physician or engineer are a lot more prestigious in ethnic communities, and especially parents from countries with a different concept of journalism do not really appreciate their children's wish to become journalists. Moreover, many fear that their command of the German language may not be sufficient.

LK mit Beispiellösungen

Aufgabe 1

Klausurteil A: Leseverstehen und Schreiben integriert

Aufgabenstellung:

1. Point out what Amy and Archie are each occupied with.
(Comprehension) (12 Punkte)

2. Analyse how Archie and his state of mind are presented. Focus on point of view and use of language. *(Analysis) (16 Punkte)*

3. Choose **one** of the following tasks:

3.1 In the excerpt, the events taking place in the USA in 1963 are described as an "endless tangle of horror and hope that seemed to define the American landscape" (ll. 28–30). Evaluate to what extent this might also be a valid description of the situation in the USA today. Refer to the text and work done in class on American myths and realities then and now. *(Evaluation: comment) (14 Punkte)*

3.2 Having devoted her life to a "cause" (l. 70), Amy, now 73 years old, has agreed to give an interview to *The New York Times* on crucial causes young people should fight for in the 21st century. Write the interview, taking into account the text and work done in class on economic, ecological and political issues of globalisation.
(Evaluation: re-creation of text) (14Punkte)

Klausurteil B: Sprachmittlung isoliert

Aufgabenstellung:

4. Your English friend is a member of a political youth organisation. They are interested in young people's social commitment across Europe. She/He has asked you specifically for information on volunteering in Germany.
   Based on Julia Emmrich and Theresa Martus' article, write her/him an email in which you present the situation of volunteering and ways to encourage more young people to participate. *(Mediation) (18 Punkte)*

Materialgrundlage:

Klausurteil A:
Paul Auster, *4 3 2 1*, New York: Henry Holt 2017, S. 140–142

Wortzahl: 559

Klausurteil B:
Julia Emmrich und Theresa Martus, „Wie sinnvoll wäre ein Pflichtdienst für junge Leute?", in: *NRZ*, 8. August 2018
http://www.nrz.de/politik/wie-sinnvoll-waere-ein-pflichtdienst-fuer-junge-leute-id215037271.html (gekürzt, Zugriff: 27.05.2019)

Wortzahl: 434

Zugelassene Hilfsmittel:

- Ein- und zweisprachiges Wörterbuch
- Herkunftssprachliches Wörterbuch für Schülerinnen und Schüler, deren Herkunftssprache nicht Deutsch ist
- Wörterbuch zur deutschen Rechtschreibung

Klausurteil A

4 3 2 1 *Paul Auster*

Archie Ferguson meets Amy Schneiderman, daughter of his parents' friends, at a Labor Day barbecue party at his home in Montclair, New Jersey. It is September 2, 1963.

They were the same age, or very nearly the same age, two hundred months old as opposed to a hundred and ninety-eight months old, but because Amy had been born at the end of 1946 (December 29) and Ferguson at the beginning of 1947

(March 3), she was a full year ahead of him in school, which meant that she was about to start her senior year at Hunter while he was still stuck in the trenches as a lowly junior. College was no more than a nebulous anywhere to him at that point, a far-flung destination that had yet to be given a name, whereas she had been studying maps for the better part of a year and was almost ready to begin packing her bags. She would be applying to several schools, she said. Everyone had told her she would need backups, second and third options, but Barnard was her first choice, her only choice, really [...].

[A]s he sat in the room with Amy and later walked through the streets with her, they talked about any number of things, mostly about the roller-coaster summer that had started with the killing of Medgar Evers and ended with Martin Luther King's speech, the endless tangle of horror and hope that seemed to define the American landscape, and also about the books and records on the shelves and floor of Ferguson's room, not to mention schoolwork, SATs, and even baseball, but the one question he did not ask her, was determined at all costs to refrain from asking, was whether she had a boyfriend, for he had already decided he was going to do everything in his power to make her the next one, and he had no interest in learning how many rivals were standing in his way.

On September fifteenth, less than two weeks after the Labor Day barbecue, which was exactly six days before they were supposed to get together again in New York, she called him, and because he was the one she called and no one else, he understood that there was no boyfriend in the picture, no rival to be afraid of, and that she was with him now in the same way he was with her. He knew that because he was the person she chose to call when she heard the news about the bombing of a black church in Birmingham, Alabama, and the murder of four little girls inside, another American horror, another battle in the race war spreading across the South, as if the March on Washington two and a half weeks earlier had to be avenged with bombs and murder, and Amy was crying into the phone, struggling not to cry as she told him the news, and bit by bit, as she slowly pulled herself together, she began to talk about what could be done, about what she felt had to be done, not just laws passed by politicians but an army of people to go down there and fight the bigots, and she would be the first one to join up, the day after she graduated from high school she would hitchhike to Alabama and work for the cause, bleed for the cause, make the cause the central purpose of her life. It's our country, she said, and we can't let the bastards steal it from us.

Annotations

9	**Hunter** – Hunter College High School in Manhattan, New York
20	**Barnard** – Barnard College in New York City, a college for women only
25–26	**Medgar Evers** – an American civil rights activist in Mississippi
32	**SATs** – Scholastic Assessment Test; standardised tests used for college admissions in the USA
53	**16th Street Baptist Church bombing, Birmingham, Alabama, 1963** – a terrorist act committed by the Ku Klux Klan

Beispiellösung

Aufgabe 1

The extract from Paul Auster's novel "4321" (pp. 140–142), published in 2017 by Henry Holt, New York, is set in the USA in the 1960s and focuses on the lives and plans of two 16-year-olds, Archie Ferguson and Amy Schneiderman.

It is early September 1963 and Archie and Amy, the daughter of a friend of his parents, meet for the first time at a Labor Day barbecue party at Archie's home in Montclair, New Jersey.

As Amy is a few months older than Archie, she is a full year ahead of him at college and already about to become a senior at Hunter College High School, New York. On the day of the barbecue party, her plans for the future revolve around sending out college applications. She hopes to be accepted at Barnard College in New York City, a college for women only.

While Amy and Archie talk about many things that day, ranging from the civil rights movement to books, records and school, the thing Archie is most interested in is finding out whether Amy has a boyfriend or not. In order not to ruin his hopes of having her as his girlfriend, however, he refrains from asking her about relationships.

When Amy calls him less than two weeks after the barbecue party, Archie considers this to be a sign that she is also interested in him, but her motivation for calling him is entirely different: The 16th Street Baptist Church bombing in Birmingham, Alabama, committed by the Ku Klux Klan, has changed her future plans and she needs to talk to someone about the emotional upheaval caused by this attack.

Amy has abandoned all plans to go to college and is set on hitchhiking to Alabama on the very day she leaves high school in order to actively support the civil rights movement.

Aufgabe 2

Unlike Amy, who cares about what is going on around her and seems to have a clear plan of what to do with her life, Archie seems immature and self-centred.

The story is told by a third-person narrator who allows the reader to experience Archie's thoughts and feelings while keeping a critical distance from him. One instance where this becomes clear is when the narrator compares Amy's plans for going to college (ll. 14-21) with Archie's situation, stating that he "[is] still stuck in the trenches as a lowly junior […] no more than a nebulous anywhere to him at that point […]" (ll. 10-11).

Their first meeting on September 2, 1963 is recapitulated in a matter-of-fact way (ll. 14-17) by enumerating the various topics of their conversation but finally stating that for Archie only one question is relevant: He intends to find out "[…] whether she [has] a boyfriend; he had already decided he [is] going to do everything in his power to make her the next one, and he had no interest in learning how many rivals were standing in his way" (ll. 35-40).

Another instance of Archie's self-centredness and determination becomes apparent in his reaction to Amy's phone call two weeks after the Labor Day barbecue. When he answers the phone, he does not care about her reasons for contacting him but interprets it as a sign that "[…] because he [is] the one she [calls] and no one else […] there [is] no boyfriend in the picture, no rival to be afraid of, and that she [is] with him now in the same way he [is] with her" (ll. 45-50).

Amy is truly shaken by the events in Birmingham and determined to "[...] work for the cause, bleed for the cause, make the cause the central purpose of her life" (ll. 69-71). Her determination to actively support the civil rights movement portrays her as mature and well aware of what is going on around her. This stands in contrast to Archie's immature and naïve behaviour. For Archie, making Amy his girlfriend is his main concern (ll. 33-40). When Amy calls him, he listens to every word she says, but without really understanding their meaning or even making up his own mind about the church burning in Birmingham and the possible consequences one should draw from it. A stylistic device which highlights this is the use of just one extremely long, winding sentence that stretches over many lines (ll. 50-71) to relate what Amy tells Archie. He does not interrupt her or ask questions but merely listens to her, while his own thoughts revolve around her as a prospective girlfriend.

Aufgabe 3.1

In this extract from Paul Auster's novel "4321", the political situation in the USA is described as an "endless tangle of horror and hope that seemed to define the American landscape" (ll. 28-30). Three important events are mentioned that point to the fact that 1963 would go down in history as an important year for the civil rights movement in the USA.
Amy and Archie talk about two of these events on the day they first meet: the assassination of Medgar Evers and Martin Luther King's famous speech, in which he outlines his vision of the USA as a country where all human beings have equal rights. This speech underpinned King's position as figurehead of the American civil rights movement. Two weeks later, Amy rings Archie when she hears about the church bombing in Birmingham, Alabama.
I believe that the quote is an accurate description of the political and social situation in 1963, especially if looked at in retrospect.
Auster's novel was first published in 2017, but if one looks at the current situation in the USA, his depiction of events being an "endless tangle of horror and hope" looks like an uncanny prediction of today's situation, too.
With the election of Donald Trump in 2016, the man who promised to "make America great again", nationalist tendencies grew stronger. Whereas Barack Obama, as the first African-American president, initiated Obamacare (affordable healthcare for everyone), negociated transatlantic treaties, and attempted to tackle social injustice and climate change, the focus of Trump's foreign policy is on securing the country's borders, national security and immigration control.
For many American citizens, the USA is not the "land of the free" with equal rights for everyone regardless of their ethnic or social background. Martin Luther King's vision of America still seems no more than a dream. In the last few months several acts of police brutality against African Americans, e.g. the case of George Floyd, who suffocated in police custody after a policeman knelt on his neck to restrain him, have led to nationwide protests that often turned into riots.
The gap between rich and poor Americans is wider than ever, and low-income earners often have to take on more than one job in order to make ends meet.

Aufgabe 3.2

The New York Times (NYT): "Good morning, Ms Schneiderman. I'm more than delighted that you have agreed to talk with me about your life, which you have devoted to fighting for civil rights. Today we are not only looking back at your life, but also taking a look at what you regard as crucial causes young people should fight for in the 21st century."

Amy Schneiderman (AS): "Well, I have to thank you for allowing me to share my experiences as a civil rights activist and to pass on some advice to younger generations. I believe that this wonderful planet of ours still offers some crucial causes to fight for."

NYT: "Let's go back to where it all began – do you remember the event that caused you to devote your life to becoming a civil rights advocate?"

AS: "Oh, yes! I remember that day as if it was yesterday. I had just started my senior year at Hunter in September 1963, when the 16th Street Baptist Church bombing took place in Birmingham, Alabama. Thanks to Martin Luther King and Medgar Evers, who I both found very inspiring, I was already interested in civil rights when the Ku Klux Klan bombed the church in Alabama, but the sheer brutality of this act shook me to the core. The murder of the four little girls who were trapped inside and could not escape deeply moved me. I felt so shocked, furious and helpless that I came to the conclusion that the fight for civil rights does not belong in the hands of a small group of people only, but should be a cause everyone – regardless of skin colour, level of education or social standing – should fight for. I still believe that this is our country and we should not let racists steal it from us."

NYT: "And how exactly did you become the civil rights activist we know?"

AS: "That day I decided to devote my entire life to the cause, and right after graduating from high school I hitchhiked to Alabama. There I joined a group of civil rights activists, went to rallies, organized sit-ins and protests and fought the bigots. I finally went to college and studied law so that I could work as a lawyer for a non-profit organization that helped victims of discrimination and social injustice."

NYT: "I assume you also risked your personal safety raising your voice against members of the Ku Klux Klan as well as other racist groups. If you look back at those times – is there anything you would change?"

AS: "No, I would not change a single thing! I still believe that everyone has the moral obligation to fight for the causes that are crucial to his or her generation."

NYT: "Which causes to you regard as crucial for young people today?"

AS: "Well, tackling climate change is an issue of major importance. We only have one planet, and if you continue to exploit, pollute and destroy Planet Earth there is the great risk that one day Planet Earth will not be fit for human habitation any longer. The slash-and-burn-policy in Brazil, for example, or droughts in India and elsewhere, will lead to migration, as people no longer see any future for their families and themselves in their home countries. The ever-growing gap between the rich and the poor is also something we should pay close attention to, as social inequality causes frustration and anger that will erupt in protests. You see – there is still a lot to be done!"

NYT: "Well, that sounds like a rather pessimistic vision of the future ..."

AS: "But this vision does not have to become reality! If more people devote their energy, enthusiasm and knowledge to tackling these challenges, we can make the world a better place, but we all need to become active! I don't think it's too late."

NYT: "Ms Schneiderman, thank you very much for this interview and all the best for the future. I'm sure that your lifelong activism inspires many young adults to become politically active and to help make the world a better place."

Klausurteil B

Wie sinnvoll wäre ein Pflichtdienst für junge Leute? *Julia Emmrich und Theresa Martus*

Raus aus der Schule – rein ins richtige Leben: Für viele junge Deutsche ist der Schritt alles andere als leicht. Ausbildung? Studium? Auslandsjahr? Oder erstmal jobben? Die Politik diskutiert in diesen Tagen über die Einführung eines verpflichtenden Dienstjahrs für Schulabgänger. Aber ist das überhaupt sinnvoll? Rund 100.000 junge Leute leisten derzeit bereits Jahr für Jahr Freiwilligendienste. Und: Es gibt jetzt schon mehr Bewerbungen als freie Stellen. Wäre es nicht besser, den Freiwilligendienst zu stärken?

Die traditionsreichste Form des freiwilligen Engagements ist das Freiwillige Soziale Jahr, kurz FSJ. Seinen Ursprung hat das Konzept in Aufrufen der Kirchen, sich ein Jahr lang freiwillig in den Dienst der Gemeinschaft zu stellen. Seit 1964 regelt das Gesetz Rahmenbedingungen für die Dienste. 1993 kam das Freiwillige Ökologische Jahr (FÖJ) dazu, bei dem sich junge Leute für Natur- und Umweltschutz einsetzen können.

Die Einsätze, die meist zwölf Monate lang sind, aber auch kürzer oder länger sein können, sind nicht auf das Inland beschränkt: Viele Träger bieten auch im Ausland FSJ-Plätze an.

[...]

Rund 100.000 Männer und Frauen leisten derzeit einen der Freiwilligendienste. Etwa 55.000 arbeiten im Rahmen der Jugenddienste. Der Trend geht aber nach Angaben des Familienministeriums seit Jahren nach oben. Die meisten Freiwilligen im Sozialen Jahr seien 18 Jahre alt, sagt Jaana Eichhorn vom Bundesarbeitskreis FSJ, einem Zusammenschluss der Trägerorganisationen. In den letzten Jahren sei zudem die Zahl der Minderjährigen gestiegen. [...]

Vor allem Unionspolitiker hatten Sympathie für die Idee eines Dienstjahrs ausgedrückt. Verbände dagegen sind skeptisch und sprechen sich eher für eine Stärkung der bestehenden Angebote aus. „Wir haben mit den Freiwilligendiensten zeigen können, dass dort, wo Menschen sich freiwillig einbringen, die Zufriedenheit bei allen Beteiligten extrem hoch ist", sagt Jaana Eichhorn vom Bundesarbeitskreis FSJ dieser Redaktion, „bei den Freiwilligen selbst genauso wie bei den Einrichtungen." Es mache einen Unterschied, ob jemand sich freiwillig für einen Dienst entscheide oder gezwungen sei.

Sie plädiert deshalb dafür, die existierenden Dienste attraktiver zu machen, zum Beispiel mit besserer Bezahlung. Denn während Zivildienstleistende die gleichen Bezüge erhielten wie Wehrdienstleistende, bekommen Menschen in den freiwilligen Jugenddiensten und im BFD nur ein Taschengeld. „Unsere Freiwilligen können meist nicht von zu Hause ausziehen und sind auf ihre Eltern angewiesen", sagt Eichhorn. Außerdem wünscht sie sich mehr gesellschaftliche Anerkennung, zum Beispiel in Form bevorzugter Studienzulassung.

Das Deutsche Rote Kreuz, nach eigenen Angaben der größte Träger von Freiwilligendiensten in Deutschland, begrüßt die Debatte um die Dienstpflicht, weil sie dazu beitragen könne, das Engagement zu stärken. Doch auch das DRK will mehr Engagement aus der Politik für freiwillige Optionen. „Wir wünschen uns mehr Anerkennung sozialen Engagements", sagt DRK-Sprecher Dieter Schütz, „denn wir werden in den nächsten Jahrzehnten zunehmend mehr Einsatz brauchen."

Anmerkungen:
Alle die Sprachrichtigkeit betreffenden Fehler im Originaltext wurden berichtigt.
32, 33 Freiwilligendienste/Jugenddienste – Im Gegensatz zu Jugenddiensten sind Freiwilligendienste auch offen für Erwachsene über 27 Jahren.
60, 61 Zivildienstleistende/Wehrdienstleistende – Bis 2011 bestand für männliche Jugendliche die Pflicht, entweder Wehr- oder Zivildienst zu leisten.
63 BFD – Bundesfreiwilligendienst

Beispiellösung

Aufgabe 4

Dear Judy,

I'm glad you are well. Your project on young people's social commitment across Europe sounds interesting! As you asked me for some information on volunteering in Germany, I have done some research and found out the following:

Over the last couple of years the number of young adults interested in voluntary work has been growing steadily. About 100,000 young adults engage in voluntary work after graduating from school, and German politicians are currently discussing whether a compulsory service year should be introduced for this age group. While some politicians regard a service year as beneficial for both the young adults and the organizations they support, others wonder whether making it compulsory is necessary, as the number of applications sometimes exceeds the number of available places anyway.

Moreover, the organizations employing voluntary workers emphasize the difference between work done freely and work done as an imposed duty: the former, they say, is more satisfying and fulfilling for all concerned.

There are various forms of voluntary work young people can engage in on leaving school – the most traditional is the 'voluntary social year', but since the 1990s there has also been a 'voluntary ecological year'. There are opportunities to spend the year working abroad as well as in Germany itself.

One of the main issues today is making voluntary work more attractive, on the one hand by making it better paid – and the model here is that of the former 'alternative service' from the time when, for young men, military service was mandatory – and on the other by raising its profile in terms of social recognition and acceptance, and hence also its popularity.

I hope this answers some of your questions.

I look forward to hearing from you.

Tom

Die sprachliche Leistung im Abitur

Der Stellenwert der sprachlichen Leistung

Bei der Bewertung der Abiturprüfung können 150 Punkte vergeben werden. Davon fallen 90 Punkte für die sprachliche und 60 Punkte für die inhaltliche Leistung an. Über das Fachwissen zu den lehrplanrelevanten Inhalten hinaus ist also die sprachliche Leistung im Englischen für ein gutes Ergebnis in der Abiturprüfung von grundlegender Bedeutung. Natürlich bedingen sich die beiden Teilbereiche gegenseitig: Ohne stichhaltigen Inhalt kann nicht die volle Punktzahl im Bereich Sprache erreicht werden und umgekehrt.
Die Entwicklung der englischen Sprachkompetenz ist ein komplexer Prozess, der sich über viele Jahre hinweg bis zum Abitur hin entwickelt. Es ist an dieser Stelle nicht möglich, eine umfassende Revision der sprachlichen Grundlagen anzubieten, aber Sie finden hier Hinweise auf die wichtigsten Aspekte, die Sie zum Zeitpunkt des Abiturs beherrschen sollten. Bei Bedarf können Sie dann das eine oder andere Kapitel mit Hilfe eines grammatikorientierten Buches wiederholen.

TIPP zur individuellen Wiederholung der Grammatik

Wenn Sie das Gefühl haben, in wichtigen Bereichen der Grammatik noch Defizite zu haben, analysieren Sie gezielt Ihre persönlichen Schwachpunkte aus den Klausuren und wiederholen Sie selbstständig die entsprechenden Kapitel anhand einer Grammatik oder eines Übungsbuches auf Sprachniveau B2 des Gemeinsamen Europäischen Referenzrahmens.
Klassische Fehlerquellen sind zum Beispiel *if*-Sätze, Passivkonstruktionen, die Wahl der richtigen Zeitform oder Präpositionen nach bestimmten Verben.

Die Leistungskriterien

Eigene Fehlerschwerpunkte erkennen

Um eigene Fehlerschwerpunkte zu erkennen, ist es empfehlenswert, die Darstellungsleistung in eigenen Klausuren genau zu analysieren.

- Lesen Sie Ihre eigenen Klausuren inklusive der Randbemerkungen und Kommentare Ihres Englischlehrers erneut durch und halten Sie auf einem separaten Blatt fest, welche Teilbereiche besonders „fehleranfällig" sind.
- Wenn Ihre Klausuren mittels eines Korrekturrasters bewertet worden sind, studieren Sie dieses in Hinblick auf die Darstellungsleistung genau: In welchen Teilbereichen haben Sie besonders wenige Punkte erhalten? Lesen Sie nun Ihre Klausuren in Hinblick auf diese Teilbereiche erneut durch. Halten Sie schriftlich fest, wo Ihre individuellen Fehlerschwerpunkte liegen.

Wenn Sie die eigenen Fehlerschwerpunkte identifiziert haben, sollten Sie diese beim Anfertigen – und anschließendem Korrekturlesen – schriftlicher Hausaufgaben und Klausuren besonders im Blick haben.
Defizite im Bereich der Grundgrammatik können Sie mit entsprechenden Übungsbüchern aufarbeiten. Auch hier gilt: Üben Sie konsequent über einen längeren Zeitraum hinweg und trainieren Sie immer wieder das Verfassen schriftlicher Texte, indem Sie z. B. im Unterricht angefertigte Stichpunkte ausformulieren.
In den meisten Wörterbüchern finden Sie Zusammenstellungen der unregelmäßigen Verben und der wichtigsten ***phrasal verbs.*** Es empfiehlt sich, diese vor Klausuren zu wiederholen.

Die Vorgehensweise in Klausuren und in der schriftlichen Abiturprüfung

Um in Klausuren und in der schriftlichen Abiturprüfung ein möglichst gutes Ergebnis zu erzielen, ist es unerlässlich, eine sinnvolle und gut strukturierte Vorarbeit zu leisten.
Lassen Sie sich nicht von Mitschülern irritieren und aus der Ruhe bringen, die nach kürzester Bearbeitungszeit und ohne das Anfertigen von Notizen sofort anfangen zu schreiben!
Je intensiver Sie sich mit der Aufgabenstellung und dem Ausgangstext auseinandersetzen und entsprechende Notizen anfertigen, desto einfacher wird es Ihnen fallen, die Aufgabenstellungen in zusammenhängenden Texten zu bearbeiten.

Die Bearbeitung in folgenden Schritten hat sich bewährt:

1. Lesen Sie zunächst die Aufgabenstellung und den Ausgangstext ein erstes Mal durch. Achten Sie hierbei auch auf eventuelle Erläuterungen, die dem Ausgangstext vorangestellt sind. Diese sind meist kursiv gedruckt und enthalten wichtige Zusatzinformationen, die Ihnen die Bearbeitung der Aufgaben erleichtern. Beim ersten Lesen sollten Sie auch Wörter unterstreichen, deren Bedeutung Sie nicht kennen und auch nicht aus dem Kontext erschließen können.

2. Schlagen Sie nun die Wörter nach, die Sie beim ersten Lesen nicht verstehen bzw. erschließen konnten, und die für das Textverständnis von Bedeutung sind. Oft lassen sich unbekannte Wörter aus dem Zusammenhang bzw. mit Rückgriff auf andere Sprachen erschließen.

3. Bevor Sie den Text nun erneut lesen, sollten Sie die Aufgabenstellungen einer genauen Betrachtung unterziehen. Achten Sie auf die verwendeten Operatoren – diese „verraten“ Ihnen, was genau Ihre Aufgabe ist bzw. welche Aspekte sie untersuchen sollen. Auch im Abitur werden Sie die „Dreiteilung“ in „Comprehension“,

„Analysis“ und „Evaluation: Comment/re-creation of text“ vorfinden. Beachten Sie: Bei der Bearbeitung der „Comprehension“-Aufgabe sollen – im Gegensatz zur „Analysis“-Aufgabe – keine Zitate und Textverweise verwendet werden!

4. Lesen Sie nun den Ausgangstext erneut und nehmen Sie zunächst (farbige) Markierungen und Randbemerkungen für die Bearbeitung der ersten Aufgabe vor. Auf einem separaten Blatt sollten Sie darüber hinaus Stichpunkte anfertigen, die Ihnen die anschließende Bearbeitung der jeweiligen Aufgabenstellung erleichtern. Bevor Sie die Stichpunkte ausformulieren, empfiehlt es sich, diese in eine sinnvolle Reihenfolge zu bringen, etwa durch Nummerierung. Denken Sie daran, Ihre Ausführungen zur ersten Aufgabe mit einem entsprechenden Einleitungssatz (Nennung von Autor, Titel, Textsorte, Erscheinungsdatum, Quelle und Thema) zu beginnen. Anschließend wenden Sie diese Verfahrensweise auf die Aufgaben 2 und 3 an. Für die Aufgaben 2 und 3 ist es nicht notwendig, den Einleitungssatz der ersten Aufgabe zu wiederholen – Ihr Leser weiß ja nun, welcher Ausgangstext Ihren Ausführungen zugrunde liegt! Es ist allerdings notwendig, kurz darzulegen, welche Aspekte nachfolgend untersucht bzw. bearbeitet werden.

5. Nachdem Sie alle Aufgaben bearbeitet haben, sollten Sie ausreichend Zeit (ca. 20 Minuten) einplanen, um Ihre Klausur Korrektur zu lesen. Achten Sie auf Ihre individuellen Fehlerschwerpunkte!

In der schriftlichen Abiturprüfung haben Sie im Fach Englisch im Grund- und im Leistungskurs die Auswahl zwischen jeweils zwei Klausurvorschlägen.
Hierbei handelt es sich stets um einen literarischen Text und einen Sach- oder Gebrauchstext – möglicherweise in Kombination mit einem Cartoon, einer Grafik oder einer Statistik.

Sie haben 30 Minuten Zeit, sich mit beiden Themenvorschlägen zu befassen und einen der beiden zur Bearbeitung auswählen. Der nicht gewählte Vorschlag verbleibt bei Ihnen. Theoretisch könnten Sie sich nach zwei Stunden noch umentscheiden. TUN SIE DIES JA NICHT! Wenn Sie sich entschieden haben, legen Sie den Vorschlag weit weg, am besten auf den Boden, um Verwechslungen zu vermeiden!
Anschließend dürfen Sie sofort mit der Bearbeitung des von Ihnen gewählten Vorschlags beginnen, d.h. Sie müssen nicht das Ende der dreißigminütigen Auswahlzeit abwarten.

Nur ein- und zweisprachige Wörterbücher und der Duden (für die Sprachmittlung) sind in der Klausur als Hilfsmittel zugelassen.
Bislang bezieht sich dies jedoch ausschließlich auf Wörterbücher in Printform. Elektronische Wörterbücher sind also im Abitur nicht erlaubt.

Kommunikative Textgestaltung

Aufgabenbezug, Textformate, Textaufbau, Ökonomie, Belegtechnik

Aufgabenbezug

Hier wird bewertet, ob der von Ihnen verfasste Text konsequent an der jeweiligen Aufgabenstellung ausgerichtet ist.
Dies hört sich recht banal an, doch aufgrund des im Unterricht erworbenen Vorwissens zu einem bestimmten Themenbereich ist in Klausuren die Versuchung oft groß, eben dieses Wissen in seiner Gesamtheit abzubilden und sich damit zu verzetteln. Achten Sie also genau darauf, was von Ihnen verlangt wird. Auch hier hilft Ihnen das Anfertigen von Stichpunkten zu den verschiedenen Aufgaben dabei, Ihre Gedanken zu bündeln und nicht den Überblick zu verlieren.
Die im Abitur gestellten Aufgaben enthalten stets die vom Schulministerium aufgelisteten Operatoren, die Sie auch auf S. 14 in diesem Buch finden.
Den verschiedenen Anforderungsbereichen („Comprehension“, „Analysis“ und „Evaluation“) sind unterschiedliche Operatoren zugeordnet, deren Bedeutung klar definiert ist.
Vor Bearbeitung der konkreten Aufgaben empfiehlt es sich, die Aufgabenstellung genau in den Blick zu nehmen. Es ist hilfreich, wenn Sie die verwendeten Operatoren farbig markieren und dann für sich die folgenden Fragen beantworten:

- Welche Operatoren werden verwendet?
- Was wird konkret von mir erwartet?
- In Hinblick auf welche inhaltlichen Schwerpunkte soll ich bei der Aufgabe „Comprehension“ den Text wiedergeben? Welche Gestaltungsmerkmale/stilistischen Mittel innerhalb des Textes soll ich bei Bearbeitung der Aufgabe zur „Analysis“ näher untersuchen?
- Welches Zieltextformat wird bei der Aufgabe „Evaluation/re-creation of text“ verlangt?

Textformate

TIPP zum Punktesammeln

Beim Verfassen der Zieltexte sollten Sie stets darauf achten, welche Textsorte Sie produzieren sollen. Eine Übersicht über die verschiedenen Zieltextformate, die in Klausuren von Ihnen verlangt werden können, finden Sie ab Seite 104 in diesem Buch.
Denken Sie daran, bei den oben genannten Teilaufgaben keine ***short forms*** wie *don't, isn't* oder Ähnliches zu verwenden.

Nachfolgend finden Sie eine allgemeine **Übersicht** über die Konventionen der verschiedenen Zieltextformate innerhalb der Schreibaufgabe:

Comprehension:

Beginnen Sie Ihre Ausführungen mit einem **Einleitungssatz** (Autor, Titel, Textsorte, Publikation, Ort und Jahr der Erscheinung). Sollte es sich bei dem Ihnen vorliegenden Text um einen Textauszug handeln oder sollte der Text an eine ganz bestimmte Zielgruppe gerichtet sein, dann merken Sie dies ebenfalls im Einleitungssatz an.
Zitate und Textverweise sind bei Teilaufgabe 1 **nicht angebracht.**

Analysis:

Während bei Aufgabe 1 eine erste inhaltliche Annäherung an den Text erfolgen soll, wird bei der zweiten Aufgabe **eine detaillierte Analyse des Ausgangstextes** unter Beachtung der in der Aufgabenstellung genannten Gesichtspunkte und **mit Rückgriff auf Zitate** beziehungsweise **Textverweise** verlangt.
Die Bearbeitung der zweiten Teilaufgabe sollte in einem **sachlich-neutralen Stil** erfolgen. Eine Darstellung der eigenen Meinung beziehungsweise eine Wertung erfolgen also nicht.
Zu den verschiedenen Herangehensweisen an die Analyse von literarischen Texten sowie von Sach- und Gebrauchstexten sei auf das entsprechende Kapitel in diesem Buch verwiesen (S. 79).

Evaluation:

Bei der dritten Aufgabe („evaluation“) haben Sie die Wahl zwischen zwei unterschiedlichen Aufgabentypen: der Kommentierung eines entsprechenden Sachverhalts („comment“) und einer kreativen Schreibaufgabe („re-creation of text“).

Comment:

Hier sind Sie aufgefordert, Ihrer **eigene Meinung** zu einem beziehungsweise **Ihre subjektive Sicht auf einen bestimmten Sachverhalt** zu erörtern und begründen.

Achten Sie darauf, Ihre Argumentation **logisch** zu entwickeln und die einzelnen Argumente sinnvoll aneinander anzuschließen.
Ihre Ausführungen sollten mit einem **abschließenden Fazit** enden.

Re-creation of text:

Sollte es bei der kreativen Aufgabe durch die Vorgabe der anzufertigenden Textsorte (z. B. Dialog, Blog-Eintrag, E-Mail, innerer Monolog) nicht zwangsläufig gefordert sein, sollten Sie beim Verfassen Ihres Zieltextes auch bei Aufgabe 3.2 (bzw. 4.2) auf die Verwendung umgangssprachlicher Formulierungen, Slang und Kurzformen *(can't, wouldn't, doesn't* usw.) unbedingt verzichten.
Achten Sie auch stets darauf, an wen Ihr Zieltext gerichtet sein soll. Bei Verfassen eines *speech script* ist es zum Beispiel mit Blick auf das Vorwissen und den Erfahrungsschatz des Adressaten ein großer Unterschied, ob Sie sich an eine Gruppe von

High School-Absolventen oder eine Versammlung von Managern richten. Dies sollten Sie durch die Verwendung passender sprachlicher Mittel kennzeichnen.

Textaufbau

Der von Ihnen verfasste Text soll für die Leserinnen und Leser leicht lesbar sein – und das nicht nur mit Hinblick auf das Schriftbild und die formale Gestaltung.
Mit „Textaufbau" ist vielmehr gemeint, dass ein für die Leserinnen und Leser leicht erkennbarer „roter Faden" durch Ihren Text führt und der von Ihnen verfasste Text klar und sachgerecht strukturiert ist.
Damit ist gemeint, dass Sie Ihren Text in klar erkennbare Abschnitte gliedern, die auch inhaltliche Sinneinheiten ergeben. Leiten Sie neue Gedanken durch die Verwendung von ***signal words*** (etwa *First ..., Second ..., Third, ...)* ein. Diese ermöglichen Ihnen die sinnvolle Gliederung Ihres Textes und strukturieren diesen auch für die Leserinnen und Leser in klare Einheiten.
Denken Sie daran, Ihre Argumentation logisch aufzubauen und vermeiden Sie Gedankensprünge, die den Leserinnen und Lesern das Textverständnis erschweren.
Durch Verwendung geeigneter Konnektoren gelingt es Ihnen, Ihre Argumente und Beobachtungen sinnvoll verknüpfen, sodass Ihre Leserinnen und Leser Ihren Ausführungen leicht folgen können.

Nachfolgend eine Übersicht über die wichtigsten Konnektoren:

Reihung von Argumenten

and	und
first(ly), ... second(ly), ... third(ly),	erstens, zweitens, drittens
furthermore,	außerdem, darüber hinaus
in addition to	zusätzlich zu
moreover,	ferner, überdies
not only ... but also	nicht nur ... sondern auch
as well as	sowie
finally,	schließlich

Gegensatz

but	aber, sondern
although	obwohl
however,	jedoch
despite the fact that	trotz der Tatsache, dass
in spite of	trotz
nevertheless, nonetheless,	nichtsdestotrotz
even so,	selbst dann

on the contrary	im Gegensatz dazu
on the one hand, ... on the other hand,	einerseits ... andererseits
unlike	anders als
whereas	während/wogegen/indessen
while/whilst	während (dagegen)
yet	dennoch

Bedingung

if	falls, wenn
unless	wenn nicht
otherwise	ansonsten

Folge

because	weil
since	da
so	daher
consequently,	folglich
as a result,	demzufolge
therefore,	daher, deshalb
due to	infolge
accordingly,	daher
that is why	deshalb

Vergleich

like	wie
in comparison with	im Vergleich zu
similarly,	ähnlich
equally,	gleichermaßen

Autorenintention

An mehreren Stellen in Ihrer Abiturklausur werden Sie Ihre eigenen Aussagen in Relation zur Autorenmeinung setzen müssen. Dafür empfiehlt es sich, eine Reihe von sprachlichen Ausdrücken parat zu haben, z. B.:

He/She points out/argues that ...	Er weist darauf hin/argumentiert, dass ...
He implies/claims/states that ...	Er behauptet, dass ...
He/She believes/suggests ...	Er/Sie glaubt/schlägt vor ...

He/She emphasizes …	Er/Sie legt sein/ihr Hauptaugenmerk auf …
His/Her idea was to …	Er/Sie wollte …
He/She writes with the intention of (+ gerund) …	Er/Sie schreibt mit der Absicht …
His/Her aim is to …	Sein/Ihr Ziel ist es …
His/Her attitude towards …	Seine/Ihre Einstellung gegenüber …
When he/she says/writes … he/she means that …	Wenn er/sie sagt/schreibt …, meint er/sie …
According to the author …	Dem Autor/der Autorin zufolge …

Ökonomie

TIPP zum Punktesammeln

Vorweg: Der Umfang des von Ihnen verfassten Zieltextes ist nicht zwangsläufig ausschlaggebend für die Qualität Ihrer Klausur. Bearbeiten Sie die Ihnen gestellten Aufgaben zielgerichtet und hinreichend ausführlich, aber vermeiden Sie inhaltliche Doppelungen. Anstatt einen Sachverhalt zu wiederholen, sollten Sie auf bereits erfolgte Erläuterungen zurückverweisen.
Verwenden Sie konkrete Beispiele, um komplexe Sachverhalte zu illustrieren.

Belegetechnik

Um Ihre Aussagen zu belegen, fügen Sie geeignete Zitate aus dem Originaltext in Ihre Antworten ein. Setzen Sie diese in englische Anführungszeichen – diese beginnen oben und enden oben. Da es sich in der Abiturklausur um einen relativ kurzen Ausgangstext handelt, genügt als Quellenangabe die Angabe der Zeilennummer in Klammern direkt hinter dem Zitat.

Beispiel zu Shakespeare, *Romeo and Juliet:*

In his speech Prince Escalus speaks about the Montagues and the Capulets as "enemies to peace" (l. 1) and finishes by even menacing them with "pain of death" (l. 23).
Verwenden Sie nicht das ganze Zitat, können Sie die ausgelassenen Passagen mit eckigen Klammern kennzeichnen. Genauso können Sie ein Bezugswort in eckigen Klammern einfügen, wenn dies aufgrund der Satzkonstruktion notwendig ist.
Die wörtliche Übernahme von Formulierungen aus dem Ausgangstext bzw. einem anderen Text ohne entsprechende Kennzeichnung ist nicht zulässig und wird negativ bewertet.
Da mit Zitaten Aussagen belegt oder gefestigt werden, stehen sie normalerweise nach der entsprechenden Behauptung. Diese sollten Sie zunächst mit eigenen Worten paraphrasieren. Nehmen Sie dabei Ihr einsprachiges Wörterbuch zur Hilfe, um nach Synonymen zu suchen.

Ausdrucksvermögen/Verfügbarkeit sprachlicher Mittel

Eigenständigkeit, allgemeiner und thematischer Wortschatz, Textbesprechungs- und Textproduktionswortschatz, Satzbau

Eigenständigkeit

Es wird in Klausuren von Ihnen erwartet, dass Sie einen eigenständigen Text formulieren und sich vom Ausgangstext lösen. Sie sollen also nicht Formulierungen aus dem Ausgangstext in Ihren Text übernehmen, ohne diese kenntlich zu machen.
Selbstverständlich können und sollen Sie aus dem Ausgangstext zitieren, um eigene Gedanken zu stützen. Allerdings müssen Sie Zitate auch immer als solche kennzeichnen, damit die Eigenständigkeit Ihrer Leistung zu erkennen ist.
Die Vorgaben des Ministeriums weisen aber auch darauf hin, dass „ein punktuell das Sprachmaterial des Ausgangstextes kreativ verarbeitendes Vorgehen (...) durchaus erwünscht (ist).“ Dies ist insbesondere beim Aufgabentyp 3.2 (bzw. 4.2) der Fall.

Allgemeiner und thematischer Wortschatz

Es wird erwartet, dass Sie sich sachlich und stilistisch angemessen ausdrücken (Beachten Sie das jeweilige Zieltextformat!). In diesem Buch finden Sie eine Vielzahl von Wortlisten, die Ihnen dabei helfen können, Ihren thematischen Wortschatz zu den einzelnen Unterrichtsinhalten zu festigen und zu erweitern.
Auch Wortwiederholungen sollten Sie vermeiden. Nachfolgend finden Sie eine Übersicht über Synonyme für häufig verwendete Wörter und Begriffe. Diese ermöglichen Ihnen, sich variantenreich auszudrücken und einen abwechslungsreich formulierten Text zu verfassen.

to say (im Sinne von „sagen“/„ausdrücken“)

state, remark, announce, affirm, assert, maintain, declare, express, put into words, tell, phrase, communicate, make known, convey, reveal, disclose, indicate, suggest

to see (im Sinne von „erkennen“/„verstehen“)

grasp, get, comprehend, follow, take in, know, realize, discover, learn

to think (im Sinne von „denken“/„meinen")

believe, suppose, expect, imagine, surmise, conjecture, guess, consider

to understand

comprehend, apprehend, grasp, see, take in, recognize, think, believe, conclude

because/because of

<u>because:</u> since, as, in view of the fact that, owing to the fact that, seeing that <u>because of:</u> on account of, as a result of, owing to, by reason of, as a consequence of, thanks to, by virtue of

many

numerous, a large/great number of, great quantities, multiple, various, several, frequent

few

not many, a small number, one or two, a handful

in addition to (im Sinne von „zusätzlich")

additionally, besides, as well (as)

furthermore (im Sinne von „außerdem")

moreover, further, additionally, on top of that, also, as well

Vermeiden Sie auch sogenannte ***false friends.*** Als *false friends* werden Wörter und Begriffe bezeichnet, von denen man annimmt, dass sie in Mutter- und Fremdsprache die gleiche Bedeutung haben, weil sie sich im Schriftbild oder in der Aussprache ähneln beziehungsweise ein identisches Schriftbild oder eine identische Aussprache besitzen. Ein bekanntes Beispiel ist das im Deutschen für Mobiltelefone verwendete Wort „handy", welches im Englisch zwar existiert, aber im Englischen unter anderem „geschickt" und „praktisch" bedeutet.

Hier finden Sie eine Übersicht über häufig miteinander verwechselte *false friends:*

deutsch	**englisch**	***false friend***
bekommen	to get	nicht: become
die Kritik	criticism	nicht: critic – der Kritiker
die Politik	politics	nicht: policy – persönliche Strategie – außer in Begriffen wie „foreign policy" = Außenpolitik
sensibel	sensitive	nicht: sensible – vernünftig

meinen/ glauben	to think	nicht: mean – bedeuten (oder Adj. = gemein)
aktuell	current	nicht: actually – in der Tat
also	so	nicht: also – auch
brav	honest, good	nicht: brave – mutig, tapfer
Chef	boss	nicht chef – der Küchenchef
engagiert	committed	nicht: engaged – verlobt; besetzt
eventuell	possibly	nicht: eventually – schließlich
Handy	mobile phone (AE: cell phone)	nicht: handy – handlich, praktisch
Konfession	denomination	nicht: confession – die Beichte
Konkurrenz	competition	nicht concurrence – Zusammentreffen
konsequent	consistent	nicht: consequently – folglich
Lager	warehouse	nicht: department store – Warenhaus
mobben	to bully	nicht: mob – das gemeine Volk
Mörder	murderer	nicht: murder – der Mord
prägnant	concise	nicht: pregnant – schwanger
prinzipiell	fundamentally, basically, in/on principle	nicht: principally – hauptsächlich
Prospekt	brochure, leaflet	nicht: prospect(s) – die Zukunftsaussichten
Protokoll	minutes	nicht: protocol – die Etikette (außer bei EDV)
Publikum	audience	nicht: public – die Öffentlichkeit
rentabel	profitable	nicht: rentable – zu mieten
Rückseite	back	nicht: backside – Hinterteil
spenden	to donate	nicht: to spend – ausgeben

Textbesprechungs- und Textproduktionswortschatz

Selbstverständlich ist es von großer Bedeutung, dass Sie nicht nur die entsprechenden Zieltextformate erstellen, sondern dass Sie dabei auch die entsprechenden sprachlichen Mittel verwenden.
Nachfolgend erhalten Sie einen ersten Überblick darüber, welche Art von Vokabular bei den Teilaufgaben 1, 2 und 3 des Klausurenteils A von Ihnen erwartet wird.

Teilaufgabe 1: Um diese Aufgabe erfolgreich bearbeiten zu können, sollten Sie über Vokabular zur Wiedergabe und Zusammenfassung von Inhalten verfügen.

Teilaufgabe 2: Grundsätzlich ist die Analyse eines Ausgangstextes (dies können auch Filmausschnitte, Karikaturen, Grafiken usw. sein) Gegenstand der zweiten Teilaufgabe. Vokabellisten, die Ihnen die Analyse von Texten erleichtern können, finden Sie im Kapitel „Methoden der Textarbeit“ (S. 79) in diesem Buch.

Teilaufgabe 3.1: Zur Bearbeitung dieser Teilaufgabe ist vor allen Dingen Vokabelmaterial zur eigenen Meinungsäußerung und Bewertung von Sachverhalten erforderlich. Wichtige Redewendungen sind in der nachfolgenden Übersicht enthalten.

Teilaufgabe 3.2: Bei dieser Teilaufgabe müssen Sie darauf achten, welches Zieltextformat von Ihnen verlangt wird, und das von Ihnen verwendete Vokabular entsprechend anpassen. Die verschiedenen Zieltextformate werden Ihnen auf den Seiten 104–113 genauer vorgestellt.

Eine Sicherheit ausdrücken

The fact is that ...	Es ist eine Tatsache, dass ...
It cannot be denied that ...	Man kann nicht leugnen, dass ...
It goes without saying that ...	Selbstredend ...
Undoubtedly, ...	Zweifellos (am Satzanfang) ...
I am convinced that ...	Ich bin überzeugt davon, dass ...
It is indisputable/obvious that ... There is no doubt that ...	Es ist unbestreitbar/offensichtlich/ kein Zweifel, dass ...
It is inevitable that ...	Es ist unvermeidbar, dass ...

Eine Vermutung ausdrücken

Apparently, ...	Anscheinend (am Satzanfang) ...
They will probably ...	Sie werden wahrscheinlich ...
It seems highly likely that ...	Es scheint äußerst wahrscheinlich, dass ...

It may be the case that …	Es kann sein, dass …

Einen Zweifel ausdrücken

It is doubtful whether …	Es ist zweifelhaft, ob …
I wonder if …	Ich frage mich, ob …
There is no proof/evidence that …	Es gibt keine Beweise, dass …

Einen Sachverhalt betonen

In order to stress that …	Um hervorzuheben, dass …
to emphasize	betonen
I would like to make it clear that …	Ich möchte klarstellen, dass …

Eine Meinung ausdrücken

In my opinion/To my mind/From my point of view	Meiner Meinung nach
My thoughts on the subject are …	Meine Meinung zu diesem Thema ist …
Personally, I think/My personal view is that …	Ich persönlich denke, dass …
As far as I am concerned …	Was mich angeht …
From my point of view	Aus meiner Sicht
I assume	Ich vermute
I am (not) convinced that …	Ich bin (nicht) überzeugt davon, dass …
I can't help thinking that …	Ich kann nicht umhin zu denken, dass …
I get the impression that …	Ich habe den Eindruck, dass …
I am afraid that …	Ich fürchte, dass (abschwächend) …
Honestly, … To be honest, …	Ehrlich gesagt …
I can't judge …	Ich kann … nicht beurteilen
I am in no position to say …	Es steht mir nicht zu, mich zu … zu äußern.

Einen Widerspruch einräumen

in contrast to	im Gegensatz zu
On the contrary, …	Ganz im Gegenteil (am Satzanfang)
whereas	während (dagegen)
I strongly object to …	Ich spreche mich deutlich gegen … aus

One could argue that ... but ...	Man könnte argumentieren, dass ... , aber ...
Although it is true that ... it would be wrong to claim that ...	Obwohl es wahr ist, dass ..., wäre es falsch zu behaupten, dass ...

Zustimmung ausdrücken

Fortunately, ...	Glücklicherweise (am Satzanfang)
I entirely agree with/I share the opinion that ...	Ich stimme vollkommen mit ... überein
I support his view.	Ich unterstütze seine Meinung.
I share her views.	Ich teile ihre Meinung.
I am of the same opinion (as) ...	Ich bin der gleichen Meinung (wie) ...
I approve of his/her opinion.	Ich bin mit seiner/ihrer Meinung einverstanden.
I take your point about ...	Ich akzeptiere Ihre Meinung über ...
I am in favour of ...	Ich bin für ...
He rightly mentions that ...	Zu Recht betont er, dass ...
I won't object to ...	Ich widerspreche ... nicht.
It cannot be justified that ...	Es gibt keine Rechtfertigung für ...
Nobody would disagree with that statement.	Niemand würde dieser Behauptung widersprechen.
This statement is very convincing.	Diese Aussage ist sehr überzeugend.
I have to admit that the author ...	Ich muss zugeben, dass der Autor/die Autorin ...

Ablehnung ausdrücken

It is only partly true that ...	Es entspricht nur teilweise der Wahrheit, dass ...
I disagree completely with ...	Ich muss widersprechen ...
I see things differently.	Ich sehe den Sachverhalt anders.
I (must) have to disagree on this matter.	Ich bin in dieser Angelegenheit anderer Meinung.
One cannot possibly accept that ...	Man kann unmöglich akzeptieren, dass ...
I must object to	Ich muss ... widersprechen.
I have to criticize strongly that	Ich muss scharf kritisieren, dass ...
I doubt whether	Ich bezweifle, dass ...
This statement entirely contradicts ...	Diese Behauptung widerspricht ganz und gar ...

However, ...	jedoch (am Satzanfang)
It is not as simple as it seems.	Es ist nicht so einfach wie es scheint.
Unlike the author, I think ...	Abweichend vom Autor/der Autorin glaube ich ...
I cannot share the author's view on ...	Ich kann die Meinung des Autors/der Autorin über ... nicht teilen.

Einen Grund angeben

As/Since	Da/Weil (am Satzanfang)
In view of the fact that ...	Angesichts der Tatsache, dass ...
The reason for this development lies in ...	Der Grund für diese Entwicklung liegt bei ...
This causes confusion.	Das sorgt für Verwirrung.
That is why	Aus diesem Grund
Given that ...	In Anbetracht der Tatsache, dass ...
therefore	deshalb
That was caused by ...	Das wurde verursacht durch ...
For this reason/purpose	Aus diesem Grund

Eine Folge darstellen

Consequently, ... /As a consequence,	Folglich (am Satzanfang)
In view of this statement	In Anbetracht dieser Behauptung
in order to	um zu
as a result of	als Folge von

Vergleiche anstellen

to be comparable	vergleichbar sein
compared to/in comparison with	im Vergleich zu
to be different from	sich unterscheiden von
differentiate between (A and B)	(A von B) unterscheiden
to be considerably better than	wesentlich besser sein als
get more and more difficult	immer schwieriger werden
Nowadays, it is less and less common	Heutzutage ist es immer weniger üblich
superior/inferior to	überlegen/unterlegen
The former ... the latter	Der erstere ... der letztere
They have little in common.	Sie haben wenig gemeinsam.
They are equal in price.	Sie haben den gleichen Preis.

Beispiele anführen

For example/For instance	Zum Beispiel
Let me give you an example.	Lassen Sie mich ein Beispiel anführen.
such as	wie (zum Beispiel)
Look at ...	Sehen wir uns einmal ... an.

Conclusion

To sum up, ...	Zusammenfassend kann man sagen ...
I come to the conclusion that ...	Ich komme zu der Schlussfolgerung, dass ...
In short, ...	Kurz gesagt
To put it all in a nutshell ...	Um es auf einen Nenner zu bringen
I can support the author's view on ...	Ich kann die Ansicht des Autors/der Autorin über ... unterstützen
To summarize, ...	Um das zusammenzufassen ...
All in all, I believe that ...	Insgesamt glaube ich ...

Satzbau

Ein abwechslungsreicher und klarer Satzbau erleichtert Ihren Leserinnen und Lesern die Lesbarkeit Ihres Textes.

TIPP zum Punktesammeln

Versuchen Sie nicht krampfhaft, mehrere Gedanken in einen Satz zu packen. Bedenken Sie: Überlange Sätze sind fehleranfälliger als mehrere kurze, prägnante und sinnvoll miteinander verbundene Sätze.

Machen Sie sich gegebenenfalls noch einmal mit den grammatischen Eigenschaften von z. B. Aktiv- und Passivkonstruktionen sowie Gerundial-, Partizipial und Infinitivkonstruktionen vertraut.

Sprachliche Richtigkeit

Wortschatz und Grammatik

Zu den Bereichen Wortschatz und Grammatik ist an anderer Stelle in diesem Buch schon einiges gesagt worden. Der Übersicht des Ministeriums auf der nächsten Seite können Sie entnehmen, wie die für diese Kriterien maximal erreichbaren Punkte aufgeteilt sind.

Orthografie

Beim Verfassen eines Klausurtextes passiert es schnell, dass sich Rechtschreibfehler einschleichen.
Daher ist es wichtig, dass Sie zum Korrekturlesen Ihres Textes genug Zeit einplanen. Achten Sie insbesondere auf Wörter, deren Aussprache oder Schreibweise zwar ähnlich oder sogar identisch ist, deren Bedeutung aber eine vollkommen andere ist, beispielsweise„sale“ (Verkauf) und „sail“ (das Segel, segeln).

Orientierungsangaben des Ministeriums für den Bereich Sprachrichtigkeit

Punkte	Wortschatz	Grammatik	Orthographie
volle Punktzahl keine Punkte	• Der Wortgebrauch (Struktur – und Inhaltswörter) ist fast über den gesamten Text hinweg korrekt. • Vereinzelt ist eine falsche Wortwahl feststellbar. Abschnitte bzw. Textpassagen sind weitgehend frei von lexikalischen Verstößen. • Einzelne Sätze sind frei von lexikalischen Verstößen. Fehler beim Wortgebrauch beeinträchtigen z. T. das Lesen und Verstehen. • In nahezu jedem Satz sind Schwächen im korrekten Gebrauch der Wörter feststellbar. Die Mängel im Wortgebrauch erschweren das Lesen und Textverständnis erheblich und verursachen Missverständnisse.	• Der Text ist weitgehend frei von Verstößen gegen Regeln der Grammatik. Wenn Grammatikfehler auftreten, betreffen sie den komplexen Satz und sind ein Zeichen dafür, dass die Schülerin/der Schüler Risiken beim Verfassen des Textes eingeht, um sich dem Leser differenziert mitzuteilen. • Es sind vereinzelt Verstöße gegen die Regeln der Grammatik feststellbar. Jedoch sind Abschnitte bzw. Textpassagen weitgehend frei von Grammatikfehlern. Das Lesen des Textes wird durch die auftretenden Grammatikfehler nicht erschwert. • Einzelne Sätze sind frei von Verstößen gegen grundlegende Regeln der Grammatik. Grammatikfehler beeinträchtigen z. T. das Lesen und Verstehen. • In nahezu jedem Satz ist wenigstens ein Verstoß gegen die grundlegenden Regeln der Grammatik feststellbar. Diese erschweren das Lesen erheblich und verursachen Missverständnisse.	• Der Text ist weitgehend frei von Verstößen gegen orthographische Normen. Wenn vereinzelt Orthographiefehler auftreten, haben sie den Charakter von Flüchtigkeitsfehlern, d. h. sie deuten nicht auf Unkenntnis von Regeln hin. • Es sind zwar durchaus Orthographiefehler feststellbar, jedoch sind Abschnitte bzw. Textpassagen weitgehend ohne Verstoß gegen orthographische Normen. Das Lesen des Textes wird durch die auftretenden Orthographiefehler nicht wesentlich beeinträchtigt. • Einzelne Sätze sind frei von Verstößen gegen orthographische Normen, Orthographiefehler beeinträchtigen z. T. das Lesen und Verstehen. • In nahezu jedem Satz ist wenigstens ein Verstoß gegen die Regeln der Orthographie feststellbar. Die Orthographiefehler erschweren das Lesen erheblich und verursachen Missverständnisse.

Quelle: https://www.standardsicherung.schulministerium.nrw.de/cms/zentralabitur-gost/faecher/getfile.php?file=4307)

Stichwortverzeichnis